Everyday numbers /
510 EVE

BEN

D1035998

Everyday
Numbers

BENBROOK PUBLIC LIBRARY

Everyday Numbers

General Editor

Patrick McSharry

Contributing Editor

Debbie Robinson

Random House Reference
New York

Everyday Numbers: Tips and Shortcuts for ...
Copyright © 2002 by Helicon Publishing Ltd.
Copyright © 2002 for North American edition by Random House Inc.

All rights reserved under International and Pan-American Copyright Conventions. No part of this book may be reproduced in any form or by any means, electronic or mechanical, including photocopying, without the written permission of the publisher. All inquiries should be addressed to Random House Reference, Random House, Inc., New York, NY. Published in the United States by Random House, Inc., New York and simultaneously in Canada by Random House of Canada Limited.

This work was originally published in Great Britain as *Hutchinson Everyday Numbers* by Helicon Publishing Ltd.

This book is available for special purchases in bulk by organizations and institutions, not for resale, at special discounts. Please direct your inquiries to the Random House Special Sales Department, toll-free 888-591-1200 or fax 212-572-4961.

Please address inquiries about electronic licensing of reference products, for use on a network or in software or on CD-ROM, to the Subsidiary Rights Department, Random House Reference, fax 212-940-7352.

Library of Congress Cataloging-in-Publication Data is available

Visit the Random House Reference Web site at
www.randomwords.com

Typeset by Saxon Graphics Ltd, Derby, UK
Printed and bound in the USA

0 9 8 7 6 5 4 3 2 1
February 2002

ISBN: 0-375-71983-0

New York Toronto London Sydney Auckland

Contents

Introduction

Why We Count

Numbers, numbers everywhere... but just mention the word mathematics and watch for the stampede exiting the room. Despite the majority's claims of incompetency, we all use mathematics every day without giving it a thought, from balancing our checkbooks to decorating our houses, cooking our meals to planning a trip. Most of it we take for granted. Some of it blinds us (financial planning and mortgage buying, for instance). Much of it we learned in grade school. Lots of it we have simply forgotten.

Before we can speak, we already have some intuitive understanding of numbers. As we develop, we are taught how to count by holding up our fingers and calling out "how many." We learn which numerals we associate with our fingers and toes, "1,2,3, 4 . . ." and in what order they come.

By the time we enter grade school, we are already familiar with concepts such as counting, time (clocks, calendars), rules, patterns, shapes (geometry), measurement, and money. In subsequent years, we learn to differentiate between different sorts of numbers – whole numbers, integers, fractions, and decimals, and begin to appreciate the whole spectrum of ways in which our lives are dependent on numbers.

As adults, however, we often fail to appreciate just how much we already know about numbers and their usefulness. In the course of our daily lives, we call on our number skills repeatedly and without conscious effort. While it would be nice to believe that we mastered all of the basic skills we were taught in school, this is often not the case.

So for everyone with hectic lives to organize, a business to run, or children to teach, here's a book that will take the pain out of practical, everyday number juggling.

At its simplest this book will assist you with calculations, evaluations, and manipulations of numbers you come across on a regular basis. At its most ambitious, it will provide you with the skills you need to problem-solve with renewed confidence. At its most inspirational, it will allow you to see the world of numbers as a magical land of opportunity, a place that will intrigue and delight you, a place from which you will no longer hide.

Mathematics is a universal language. The relationships and meanings we assign to numbers is one of the most creative, most unifying forces known to humanity. Its fundamental principles and evolving applications are understood and accepted throughout the world, without which our lives would shudder to a stop. Through its symbols and logic, it gives us the tools we need to successfully navigate our surroundings and communicate with each other. Its magic is a world awaiting your exploration.

Numbers are the highest degree of knowledge. It is knowledge itself.

Plato

Section One

Brushing Up

Mathematics is more than just numbers. It is actually a powerful way of thinking, a useful method of expressing relationships between objects and concepts in our world. Take for instance, the Richter scale (see *Appendix*). When we say an earthquake registered a 5.8 on the Richter scale, we are really giving our audience the tools to comprehend the earthquake's impact on its environment. Instead of saying that San Francisco was hit by a hugely destructive and devastating earthquake, a description that could canvas a wide range of interpretations by different people, we use the Richter scale to quickly and meaningfully communicate the severity of a tremor. We may not know exactly how big an earthquake with a magnitude of 5.8 is, but we all agree that it is of greater concern than a 2.4 and of less concern than a 7.2. We all now have approximately the same impression of the earthquake's severity.

However, in order to understand the comparison made, we first need to understand exactly what a number is and how it is used. For some of you this may seem obvious. Others will benefit from a refresher course on basic math skills and that's what this section is designed to provide. If you think that you've mastered all the basics, skim through the next few pages, then proceed to the *Figure it Out* section (page 42) where you will find practical examples of numbers in our everyday lives. For the rest, here's a quick overview to wipe the mathematical cobwebs from your brain.

Numbers

Almost every culture has had the need to develop some sort of numerical representation, a means of representing a multitude of things using a small number of symbols. Accomplishing this has been one of the most important feats of the human intellect. Without it, the development of language and arithmetic would have never advanced as it has.

Underlying each number system are the same basic principles and definitions. We begin here by defining the concept of a number and proceed by describing it in terms of its properties and practical uses.

A **number** is an expression of quantity or order. We use symbols, or digits, to represent those expressions. A **numeral** is the name given to that symbol. So, the quantity known as 2 in the Arabic, or decimal, system can be represented as II in the Roman numeral system, and 10 in the binary numeral system. All three represent the same quantity but their symbols and names are distinctly different.

Arabic	Egyptian	Ionic (Greek)	Hebrew	Chinese	Mayan	Babylonian	Roman
1	I	α	א	一	•	𒁹	I
2	II	β	ב	二	• •	𒐀	II
3	III	γ	ג	三	•••	𒐁	III
4	II II	δ	ד	四	••••	𒐂	IV
5	III II	ε	ה	五	—	𒐃	V
6	III III	Γ	ו	六	╍	𒐄	VI
7	IIII III	ζ	ז	七	╍╍	𒐅	VII
8	IIII IIII	η	ח	八	•••	𒐆	VIII
9	III III III	θ	ט	九	••••	𒐇	IX
10	∩	I	'	十	=	𒌋	X

The **decimal** or **base ten number system** is our modern system of counting. The system is dependent on counting in groups of ten (remember fingers and toes), using the Hindu–Arabic symbols 0, 1, 2, 3, 4, 5, 6, 7, 8, 9.

In order to be able to compare two numbers, we use the **place value system**. The position of a digit determines its value in a number. Each place has a value ten times that of the place to its right and one-tenth the value of the place to its left. Three places in a place value system make up a **period**. A comma separates each period. Periods are always counted from the left of any decimal point, beginning with the "ones" or "units" column, followed by the "tens" column, and the "hundreds" column.

The value of any position in a normal decimal, or base ten, number increases by powers of 10 with each move from right to left (1, 10, 100, 1,000, 10,000, and so on). For example, the whole number 2,567 stands for: $(2 \times 1,000) + (5 \times 100) + (6 \times 10) + (7 \times 1)$.

In decimal notation, numbers to the right of the decimal point represent tenths, hundredths, thousandths, and so on. So the number below would be read as one million, two hundred, thirty-four thousand, five hundred, sixty, AND 789 thousandths.

1,234,560.789

In the place value system, the number 0 is considered a **placeholder**. It represents the quantity, zero, in the column it appears and its importance cannot be underestimated. Without it, our whole number system would fail to make sense.

Zero

*The word **zero** came originally from the Hindi sunya, meaning 'empty', and traveled through Arabic (sifr), Latin (zephirum), to become eventually the English **zero**. The Greeks would distinguish between 109 and 190 by using completely different symbols for 9 and 90. The Babylonians found a partial use for zero in their sexagesimal system, namely in medial positions (1O9) but not in final positions (19O). The need for zero arose, however, when the place value decimal system was created by the Hindu–Arabic mathematicians in the 8th century. No longer could all numbers be expressed by simply using the nine figures 1 to 9 because a sign 19 could mean 109, 190, or simply 19. Without the zero all were as likely.*

Numbers as sets

Within the decimal system, numbers are grouped according to various properties. The easiest way of thinking about these groups is to think of them as sets. A **set** is any well-defined collection of objects – elements that are considered a single thing.

> *For number is units, and the unit is precisely a certain kind of one.*
>
> **Aristotle**

The **counting numbers**, or **natural numbers**, are the numbers you normally use for counting: 1, 2, 3, 4, ...

The three dots to the right mean that the numbers go on towards infinity. **Infinity** is a subtle, but important concept in mathematics. Though often thought of as the largest possible number, it is not a number at all. It is best thought of as a numerical concept that allows us to think in terms of endless numbers. Most people have an intuitive understanding of infinity based on the assumption that it is always possible to add 1 to any whole number, no matter how large. Infinity is represented by the symbol ∞.

Whole numbers are the set of counting (natural) numbers, plus the number zero: 0, 1, 2, 3, ...

Why the distinction between whole numbers and natural numbers? Because interestingly, 0 is NOT considered a natural number, probably because we don't begin counting at zero. When a school teacher takes a head count, he or she does not call out, "Matthew 0, Hannah 1, Max 2." Yet, if someone asks you how many children you have and you don't have any, you tell them zero to represent a quantity.

An **integer** is any whole number, positive or negative, plus the number zero. The set of integers is best represented by the number line below:

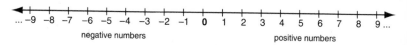

... −9 −8 −7 −6 −5 −4 −3 −2 −1 **0** 1 2 3 4 5 6 7 8 9 ...

negative numbers   positive numbers

Rational numbers include all integers, fractions, and repeating decimals. Fractions and decimals will be discussed in greater detail later in this chapter. The set of rational numbers includes numbers such as $\frac{1}{2}, \frac{3}{4}, -\frac{2}{3}$, and −5.

Irrational numbers are numbers that can be expressed as decimals but not as exact fractions, in other words the decimal continues forever without falling into a pattern that repeats endlessly. Pi and $\sqrt{2}$ are examples of irrational numbers.

Real numbers are all of the rational and all of the irrational numbers put together. Taken together, the real numbers form what is known as a **continuum**. The most familiar and useful picture we use is called **the real number line**:

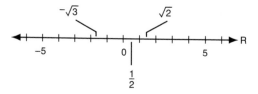

Every point on the real number line (R) corresponds to a unique real number, and every real number corresponds to a unique point on the line. Using this visualization, we see that the real numbers are totally ordered, and include every kind of number we might need.

Complex numbers include real numbers plus other kinds of numbers called imaginary numbers. Complex numbers are written in the form $a + ib$, where a and b are real numbers and i is the imaginary number equal to the square root of -1, or $\sqrt{-1}$. Some equations in algebra, such as $x^2 + 2 = 0$, cannot be solved without using complex numbers, because the set of real numbers does not include square roots of negative numbers (remember that a negative times a negative equals a positive using real numbers). Although imaginary numbers do have their uses (when investigating fractals, for instance), we don't generally consider them on a day-to-day basis.

Number shapes, primes, and factors

Numbers can also be described, or classified, in several other ways, such as odd, even, square, rectangular, or prime. Visualizing these concepts provides instant insight:

Even numbers include the numbers 0 and 2 and all numbers that can be divided evenly by 2. Even numbers can be visualized as pairs, for example:

Odd numbers are all numbers that cannot be divided evenly by 2. Presumably they get their name from the fact that there is always an odd one left out:

A **square number** is any number that can be shaped into a square. The numbers 4 and 9 are examples of square numbers. (This is a particularly useful visualization when thinking in terms of exponents to the power of 2 to be discussed later in this chapter.)

A **triangular number** is any number that can be shaped into a triangle. The number 6 is an example of a triangular number:

A **rectangular number** is any number that can be shaped into a rectangle. The number 8 is an example of a rectangular number:

Any number that cannot be shaped into a rectangle or a square is a **prime number**.

A **prime number** is a whole number greater than 1 that can only be divided by 1 and itself. A prime number can also be described as a whole number that has exactly two factors, again 1 and itself. Below is the set of prime numbers between 1 and 1,000. See also pages 183–84 in *Magical Math*.

All the prime numbers between 1 and 1,000

2	3	5	7	11	13	17	19	23	29
31	37	41	43	47	53	59	61	67	71
73	79	83	89	97	101	103	107	109	113
127	131	137	139	149	151	157	163	167	173
179	181	191	193	197	199	211	223	227	229
233	239	241	251	257	263	269	271	277	281
283	293	307	311	313	317	331	337	347	349
353	359	367	373	379	383	389	397	401	409
419	421	431	433	439	443	449	457	461	463
467	479	487	491	499	503	509	521	523	541
547	557	563	569	571	577	587	593	599	601
607	613	617	619	631	641	643	647	653	659
661	673	677	683	691	701	709	719	727	733
739	743	751	757	761	769	773	787	797	809
811	821	823	827	829	839	853	857	859	863
877	881	883	887	907	911	919	929	937	941
947	953	967	971	977	983	991	997		

A **factor** is a number that when multiplied by another number (factor) forms a new number called a **product**. For example, 2, 3, 4, and 6 are all factors of the number 12. Another way of saying this is that the number 12 is divisible by the factors 1, 2, 3, 4, 6, and itself.

Composite numbers are whole numbers that have more than two factors. For example, the number 9 is a composite number because it has three factors: 1, 3, and 9. Composite numbers are divisible by at least three whole numbers.

The **highest common factor** (HCF), or greatest common divisor, is the largest of all the factors that will divide two or more numbers without leaving a remainder. For example, 12 is the highest common factor of 36, 48, and 72.

We will be taking a closer look at prime numbers, perfect numbers, and numbers with special properties, such as the Fibonacci sequence in the *Magical Math* section (page 185).

Operations

If we took anything away from grade school math class, it was a basic understanding of the four rules, or operations, of arithmetic – addition, subtraction, multiplication, and division. Most of what we accomplish numerically each day touches, in some form or another, upon one of these four operations.

Basic math symbols

+	plus, add	∅	empty set
−	minus, subtract	≥	is greater than or equal to
±	plus or minus, add or subtract	≤	is less than or equal to
×, *, •	multiply, multiplied by	:	is compared to, ratio
÷	divide, divided by	∞	infinity
/	divide, divided by	∠	angle
=	equal to	⊥	perpendicular
≠	not equal to	‖	parallel to
>	is greater than	√	square root
<	is less than	%	percent

Addition

Combining two or more numbers to form a new sum is called **addition**. The symbol for addition is the "plus" sign (+). The order in which you add is not important. This is known as the **commutative** property of addition where:

$$a + b = b + a \qquad 3 + 4 = 7 \qquad 4 + 3 = 7$$

When adding more than two numbers, it does not matter which two you add together first. This is known as the **associative** property of addition where:

$$(a + b) + c = a + (b + c) \qquad (3 + 4) + 5 = 12 \qquad 3 + (4 + 5) = 12$$

$$7 + 5 = 12 \qquad 3 + 9 = 12$$

The "plus" sign can also indicate a positive value or direction, for example, when you read stock quotations, $+ 1\frac{1}{2}$ means a net gain of $1.50 on the stock's value.

Subtraction

When we want to find the difference between numbers, we "take away" one from the other. Taking one or more numbers from another number is called **subtraction**. The symbol for subtraction is the "minus" sign (–). The order in which you subtract one number from the other *is* important. Subtraction is neither commutative nor associative: $a - b$ does not equal $b - a$!

$$a - b \neq b - a \qquad 4 - 3 = 1 \qquad 3 - 4 = -1$$

The symbol (–) can also indicate a negative value or direction.

Adding and subtracting negatives

When you add a negative number to a positive number, you are actually subtracting the value of the negative number from the positive one, for example:

$$5 + -3 = 5 - 3 = 2$$

When you add a negative number to a negative number, you add together the value of the numbers and place the negative sign in front of your sum, for example:

$$-5 + -3 = -(5 + 3) = -8$$

When you subtract a negative number from a negative number, you are actually adding a positive number to the negative number, for example:

$$-2 - (-4) = -2 + 4 = 2$$

When you subtract a positive number of greater value from another positive number of less value, your answer will be a negative number, for example:

$$4 - 8 = -4$$

Multiplication

Multiplication is really just a quick version of addition. When you multiply two numbers together, usually written in the form $a \times b$ or ab, you are simply adding a to itself b times.

Like addition, multiplication has both commutative and associative properties. In other words, the product of two or more numbers will always be the same no matter in what order you multiply them or how you group them. According to the commutative property of multiplication:

$$a \times b = b \times a \qquad 2 \times 3 = 6 \qquad 3 \times 2 = 6$$

Using the associative property of multiplication:

$$(a \times b) \times c = a \times (b \times c)$$

$$\begin{array}{ll} (2 \times 3) \times 4 = 24 & 2 \times (3 \times 4) = 24 \\ 6 \times 4 = 24 & 2 \times 12 = 24 \end{array}$$

There is one more property called the **distributive property,** which says that multiplication and addition can be linked together by "distributing" the multiplier over the numbers being added in an equation. For example:

$$a \times (b + c) = (a \times b) + (a \times c)$$
$$2 \times (3 + 4) = (2 \times 3) + (2 \times 4)$$
$$2 \times 7 = 6 + 8$$
$$14 = 14$$

Division

Division is simply the process of finding out how many times one number, the **divisor**, will fit into another number, the **dividend**. The result of that process is the **quotient**. There are three signs associated with division: $\div$, $\overline{\smash{\big)}\,}$, and / all mean divided by.

Division, like subtraction, is not commutative or associative; therefore the order in which numbers appear in an equation is important.

$$a \div b \neq b \div a \qquad 4 \div 2 = 2 \qquad 2 \div 4 = \tfrac{1}{2} \qquad 8 \div 2 = 4$$

Multiplication table in the range 2 to 25

×	2	3	4	5	6	7	8	9	10	11	12	13	14	15	16	17	18	19	20	21	22	23	24	25
2	4	6	8	10	12	14	16	18	20	22	24	26	28	30	32	34	36	38	40	42	44	46	48	50
3	6	9	12	15	18	21	24	27	30	33	36	39	42	45	48	51	54	57	60	63	66	69	72	75
4	8	12	16	20	24	28	32	36	40	44	48	52	56	60	64	68	72	76	80	84	88	92	96	100
5	10	15	20	25	30	35	40	45	50	55	60	65	70	75	80	85	90	95	100	105	110	115	120	125
6	12	18	24	30	36	42	48	54	60	66	72	78	84	90	96	102	108	114	120	126	132	138	144	150
7	14	21	28	35	42	49	56	63	70	77	84	91	98	105	112	119	126	133	140	147	154	161	168	175
8	16	24	32	40	48	56	64	72	80	88	96	104	112	120	128	136	144	152	160	168	176	184	192	200
9	18	27	36	45	54	63	72	81	90	99	108	117	126	135	144	153	162	171	180	189	198	207	216	225
10	20	30	40	50	60	70	80	90	100	110	120	130	140	150	160	170	180	190	200	210	220	230	240	250
11	22	33	44	55	66	77	88	99	110	121	132	143	154	165	176	187	198	209	220	231	242	253	264	275
12	24	36	48	60	72	84	96	108	120	132	144	156	168	180	192	204	216	228	240	252	264	276	288	300
13	26	39	52	65	78	91	104	117	130	143	156	169	182	195	208	221	234	247	260	273	286	299	312	325
14	28	42	56	70	84	98	112	126	140	154	168	182	196	210	224	238	252	266	280	294	308	322	336	350
15	30	45	60	75	90	105	120	135	150	165	180	195	210	225	240	255	270	285	300	315	330	345	360	375
16	32	48	64	80	96	112	128	144	160	176	192	208	224	240	256	272	288	304	320	336	352	368	384	400
17	34	51	68	85	102	119	136	153	170	187	204	221	238	255	272	289	306	323	340	357	374	391	408	425
18	36	54	72	90	108	126	144	162	180	198	216	234	252	270	288	306	324	342	360	378	396	414	432	450
19	38	57	76	95	114	133	152	171	190	209	228	247	266	285	304	323	342	361	380	399	418	437	456	475
20	40	60	80	100	120	140	160	180	200	220	240	260	280	300	320	340	360	380	400	420	440	460	480	500
21	42	63	84	105	126	147	168	189	210	231	252	273	294	315	336	357	378	399	420	441	462	483	504	525
22	44	66	88	110	132	154	176	198	220	242	264	286	308	330	352	374	396	418	440	462	484	506	528	550
23	46	69	92	115	138	161	184	207	230	253	276	299	322	345	368	391	414	437	460	483	506	529	552	575
24	48	72	96	120	144	168	192	216	240	264	288	312	336	360	384	408	432	456	480	504	528	552	576	600
25	50	75	100	125	150	175	200	225	250	275	300	325	350	375	400	425	450	475	500	525	550	575	600	625

Many numbers do not fit evenly into other numbers. If one number is not evenly divisible by another, the number that is left over is called the **remainder**.

$$3\overline{)10}^{\,3}$$

$\frac{1}{3}$ remainder

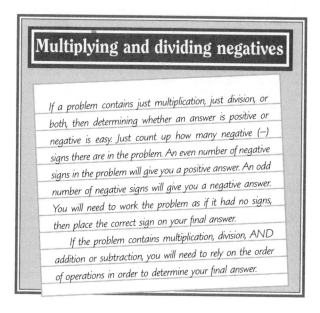

Multiplying and dividing negatives

If a problem contains just multiplication, just division, or both, then determining whether an answer is positive or negative is easy. Just count up how many negative (−) signs there are in the problem. An even number of negative signs in the problem will give you a positive answer. An odd number of negative signs will give you a negative answer. You will need to work the problem as if it had no signs, then place the correct sign on your final answer.

If the problem contains multiplication, division, AND addition or subtraction, you will need to rely on the order of operations in order to determine your final answer.

Order of operations

When you are faced with calculations involving several operations, the order in which you do the calculation is important. Use the phrase "**Please excuse my dear Aunt Sally**" (or the initials PEMDAS) to remember the conventional order of operations:

• parentheses or brackets first – perform whatever operation is required within them to get partial answer

• exponents

- multiplication and division; from left to right

- addition and subtraction; from left to right.

Example

Find $(18 - 9) \times 7 \div 3$

Solution

- Calculate what is inside the parenthesis first, so $18 - 9 = 9$
- Next, multiply (because it comes first in the equation) the answer by 7, so $9 \times 7 = 63$
- Finally, divide by 3, so $63 \div 3 = 21$
Your answer is 21.

Fractions

A fraction is a number that indicates one or more equal parts of a whole. The word comes from the Latin word *fractio*, meaning 'to break into pieces'. A fraction has two parts, a **numerator** and a **denominator**. The denominator is the number of equal parts into which the whole is divided and is written below a horizontal line. The numerator is the number of parts of the whole being counted and is written above; thus $\frac{2}{3}$ or $\frac{3}{4}$. Such fractions are called **simple fractions**. The denominator can never be zero.

A **proper fraction** is one in which the numerator is less than the denominator. An **improper fraction** has a numerator that is larger than the denominator, for example $\frac{3}{2}$. The value of an improper fraction is always greater than or equal to one. It can therefore be expressed as a **mixed number**, for example, $1\frac{1}{2}$. A combination such as $\frac{5}{0}$ is not regarded as a fraction (an object cannot be divided into zero equal parts). Mathematically, any number divided by 0 is equal to infinity.

Fractions are also known as rational numbers; that is, numbers formed by a ratio. An integer may be expressed as a fraction with a denominator of 1, for example 6 is $\frac{6}{1}$.

Adding and subtracting fractions

To add or subtract with fractions, follow these steps:

- Find the **smallest common denominator** (SMC). A **common denominator** is a number divisible by both the bottom numbers. The smallest common denominator is the smallest number into which both the bottom numbers divide evenly. The SMC of $\frac{3}{4} + \frac{5}{6}$ is 12.

- Convert to equivalent fractions using the smallest common denominator:

$\frac{3}{4} = \frac{9}{12}$ and $\frac{5}{6} = \frac{10}{12}$

- Add or subtract the numbers:

$\frac{9}{12} + \frac{10}{12} = \frac{19}{12} = 1\frac{7}{12}$

Note that if whole numbers appear in the calculation they can be added/subtracted separately first.

Multiplying and dividing fractions

All whole numbers in a division or multiplication calculation must be first converted into improper fractions. For multiplication, the numerators are then multiplied together and the denominators are then multiplied to provide the solution. For example:

$\frac{3}{7} \times \frac{2}{5} = \frac{3 \times 2}{7 \times 5} = \frac{6}{35}$

In division, the procedure is similar, but the second fraction must be inverted (turned upside down) before multiplying across. For example:

$\frac{3}{7} \div \frac{2}{5} = \frac{3 \times 5}{7 \times 2} = \frac{15}{14} = 1\frac{1}{14}$

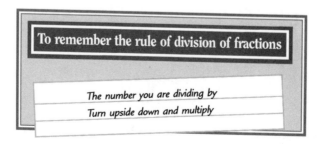

To remember the rule of division of fractions

The number you are dividing by
Turn upside down and multiply

Decimals

A decimal fraction has as its denominator any higher power of 10. Thus $\frac{3}{10}$, $\frac{51}{100}$, and $\frac{23}{1000}$ are decimal fractions and are normally expressed as 0.3, 0.51, and 0.023. In any number, the digits to the right of the decimal point indicate the numerators of common fractions whose denominators are 10, 100, 1,000, and so on. The use of decimals greatly simplifies addition and multiplication of fractions. Though not all fractions can be expressed exactly as decimal fractions ($\frac{1}{3} = 0.333\ldots$), most can.

John Napier (1550–1617)

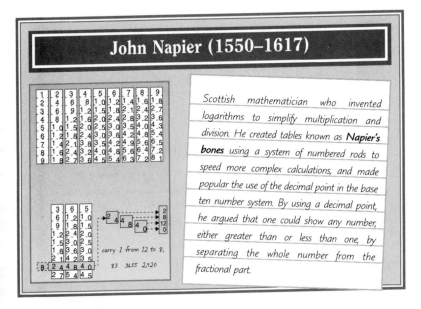

Scottish mathematician who invented logarithms to simplify multiplication and division. He created tables known as **Napier's bones** using a system of numbered rods to speed more complex calculations, and made popular the use of the decimal point in the base ten number system. By using a decimal point, he argued that one could show any number, either greater than or less than one, by separating the whole number from the fractional part.

Percentages

A percentage is a way of representing a number as a fraction of 100. Thus 45 percent (45%) equals $\frac{45}{100}$ and 45% of 20 is $\frac{45}{100} \times 20 = 9$. The use of percentages often makes it easier to compare fractions that do not have a common denominator.

To express a fraction as a percentage, multiply by 100. For example, to convert $\frac{3}{5}$ to a percentage, multiply the numerator, 3, by 100, and divide by the denominator, 5: $(3 \times 100) \div 5 = 60\%$.

To convert a fraction to a percentage on a calculator, divide the numerator by the denominator. The percentage will correspond to the first figures of the decimal, for example $\frac{7}{8} = 0.875 = 87.5\%$ correct to three decimal places.

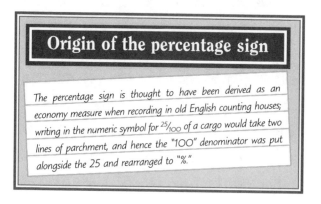

Origin of the percentage sign

The percentage sign is thought to have been derived as an economy measure when recording in old English counting houses; writing in the numeric symbol for $^{25}/_{100}$ of a cargo would take two lines of parchment, and hence the "100" denominator was put alongside the 25 and rearranged to "%."

Calculating percentage increase/decrease

In general, if a quantity x changes to y, the percentage change is $100(y - x) \div x$, where x is the initial value and y is the final value. Thus, if the number of people in a room changes from 40 to 50, the percentage increase is $(100 \times 10) \div 40 = 25\%$.

The following table expresses a list of percentages as both decimals and fractions.

Percentages as fractions or decimals (1 – 39%)

%	Decimal	Fraction
1	0.01	$^1/_{100}$
2	0.02	$^1/_{50}$
3	0.03	$^3/_{100}$
4	0.04	$^1/_{25}$
5	0.05	$^1/_{20}$
6	0.06	$^3/_{50}$
7	0.07	$^7/_{100}$
8	0.08	$^2/_{25}$
$8^1/_3$	0.083	$^1/_{12}$
9	0.09	$^9/_{100}$
10	0.10	$^1/_{10}$
11	0.11	$^{11}/_{100}$
12	0.12	$^3/_{25}$
$12^1/_2$	0.125	$^1/_8$
13	0.13	$^{13}/_{100}$
14	0.14	$^7/_{50}$
15	0.15	$^3/_{20}$
16	0.16	$^4/_{25}$
$16^2/_3$	0.167	$^1/_6$
17	0.17	$^{17}/_{100}$
18	0.18	$^9/_{50}$
19	0.19	$^{19}/_{100}$
20	0.20	$^1/_5$
21	0.21	$^{21}/_{100}$
22	0.22	$^{11}/_{50}$
23	0.23	$^{23}/_{100}$
24	0.24	$^6/_{25}$
25	0.25	$^1/_4$
26	0.26	$^{13}/_{50}$
27	0.27	$^{27}/_{100}$
28	0.28	$^7/_{25}$
29	0.29	$^{29}/_{100}$
30	0.30	$^3/_{10}$
31	0.31	$^{31}/_{100}$
32	0.32	$^8/_{25}$
33	0.33	$^{33}/_{100}$
$33^1/_3$	0.333	$^1/_3$
34	0.34	$^{17}/_{50}$
35	0.35	$^7/_{20}$
36	0.36	$^9/_{25}$
37	0.37	$^{37}/_{100}$
38	0.38	$^{19}/_{50}$
39	0.39	$^{39}/_{100}$

continued

Percentages as fractions or decimals (40 – 100%)

%	Decimal	Fraction
40	0.40	$2/5$
41	0.41	$41/100$
42	0.42	$21/50$
43	0.43	$43/100$
44	0.44	$11/25$
45	0.45	$9/20$
46	0.46	$23/50$
47	0.47	$47/100$
48	0.48	$12/25$
49	0.49	$49/100$
50	0.50	$1/2$
55	0.55	$11/20$
60	0.60	$3/5$
65	0.65	$13/20$
$66\frac{2}{3}$	0.667	$2/3$
70	0.70	$7/10$
75	0.75	$3/4$
80	0.80	$4/5$
85	0.85	$17/20$
90	0.90	$9/10$
95	0.95	$19/20$
100	1.00	1

Ratios and Proportions

A ratio is the measure of the relative size of two quantities or of two measurements (in similar units), expressed as a proportion. For example, the ratio of vowels to consonants in the alphabet is 5:21; the ratio of 500 m to 2 km is 500:2,000, or 1:4. Ratios are normally expressed as whole numbers, so 2:3.5 would become 4:7 (the ratio remains the same provided both numbers are multiplied or divided by the same number).

Examples:

• international standards in color chart
• octaves in music.

Exponents

Just as multiplication was created as a shortcut to addition, exponents were invented as a shortcut for multiplication. Rather than writing $2 \times 2 \times 2 \times 2 \times 2$, we can simply write 2^5. This expression means "2 multiplied 5 times." Here, 5 is the **exponent** and 2 is the **base**. Notice that the exponent is written as a superscript (meaning it is higher than the other numbers) and is set to the right of the base. When reading the expression aloud, you say "2 to the power 5," "2 to the 5th power," or just "2 to the 5th."

Exponents are the basis of **scientific notation**. Scientific notation was developed for computations involving very large or very small numbers. Using scientific notation, any number can be expressed as a number between 1 and 10 multiplied by a power of 10. For example:

$259 = 2.59 \times 10^2$

$15,800 = 1.58 \times 10^4$

$0.095 = 9.5 \times 10^{-2}$

Large numbers

Nomenclature for large numbers varies in different countries: in the UK and Germany, numbers have traditionally advanced by increments of a million, whereas in the USA and France numbers advance by increments of a thousand. The US usage is becoming prevalent worldwide and is now universally used by economists and statisticians.

Nomenclature for large numbers

UK and Germany		
million	1,000,000	1×10^6
billion	1,000,000,000,000	1×10^{12}
trillion	1,000,000,000,000,000,000	1×10^{18}
quadrillion	1,000,000,000,000,000,000,000,000	1×10^{24}
USA and France		
million	1,000,000	1×10^6
billion	1,000,0 00,000	1×10^9
trillion	1,000,000,000,000	1×10^{12}
quadrillion	1,000,000,000,000,000	1×10^{15}

Higher numbers		
	UK	**USA**
quintillion	1×10^{30}	1×10^{18}
sextillion	1×10^{36}	1×10^{21}
septillion	1×10^{42}	1×10^{24}
octillion	1×10^{48}	1×10^{27}
nonillion	1×10^{54}	1×10^{30}
decillion	1×10^{60}	1×10^{33}
vigintillion	1×10^{120}	1×10^{63}
centillion	1×10^{600}	1×10^{303}

Squares, cubes, and roots

Any quantity multiplied by itself is called a **square** and is noted using an exponent of power 2. For example:

$4 \times 4 = 4^2 = 16$

$6.8 \times 6.8 = 6.8^2 = 46.24$

A number that has a whole number as its square root is known as a **perfect square**; for example, 25, 144, and 54,756 are perfect squares (with roots of 5, 12, and 234, respectively).

The **cube** of a number is calculated by multiplying a number by itself and then by itself again. For example:

$5 \text{ cubed} = 5^3 = 5 \times 5 \times 5 = 125$

The term **cube** also refers to the number formed by cubing. For example, 1, 8, 27, and 64 are the first four cubes.

Examples of a number of squares, cubes, and roots

Number	Square	Cube	Square root	Cube root
1	1	1	1.000	1.000
2	4	8	1.414	1.260
3	9	27	1.732	1.442
4	16	64	2.000	1.587
5	25	125	2.236	1.710
6	36	216	2.449	1.817
7	49	343	2.646	1.913
8	64	512	2.828	2.000
9	81	729	3.000	2.080
10	100	1,000	3.162	2.154
11	121	1,331	3.317	2.224
12	144	1,728	3.464	2.289
13	169	2,197	3.606	2.351
14	196	2,744	3.742	2.410
15	225	3,375	3.873	2.466
16	256	4,096	4.000	2.520
17	289	4,913	4.123	2.571
18	324	5,832	4.243	2.621
19	361	6,859	4.359	2.668
20	400	8,000	4.472	2.714
25	625	15,625	5.000	2.924
30	900	27,000	5.477	3.107
40	1,600	64,000	6.325	3.420
50	2,500	125,000	7.071	3.684

A **square root** is a number that multiplied by itself equals a given number. For example, the square root of 25 (written $\sqrt{25}$) is ± 5 (plus or minus 5), because:

$5 \times 5 = 25$, and $(-5) \times (-5) = 25$

As an exponent, a square root is represented by 1/2, for example, $16^{\frac{1}{2}} = 4$.

A **cube root** is a number which, multiplied into itself, and then into the product, produces the cube, thus $3 \times 3 \times 3 = 27$, 3 being the cube root of 27, which is the cube of 3.

Graphs and Charts

When we pick up the newspaper each day, we are inundated with data and statistics that we need to interpret quickly and efficiently. Replacing boring type with eye-catching graphs is the easiest way to translate large amounts of information to your reader. A graph is a pictorial illustration of numerical data. It is a useful tool for interpreting data and is often used to spot trends or approximate a solution. Here are a few examples of the most common charts and graphs you may find:

Pie charts

Pie charts are most useful when you are breaking down the components of a whole.

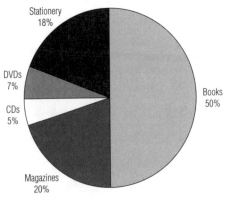

Total Online Sales $3.5 million. Major US Retailer

Diagrams

Diagrams, like the scattergraphs below, show different kinds of correlation. The "x" represents various responses. Following the line (or trend) created, a causal relationship between two variables may be proved or disproved, provided there are no hidden factors.

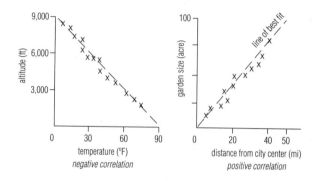

negative correlation

positive correlation

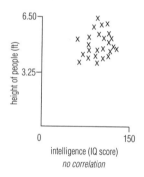

no correlation

Measurements and Conversions

Measuring is a way of describing and giving meaning to various things in our world. Every day we measure quality and quantity without being aware of it. How accurately we describe something is dependent on what we are measuring and why we are measuring it.

There are three standard systems of measurement: US, imperial (British), and metric. With global trade a requisite, the USA is increasingly relying on the metric system as its primary system of measurement. Over 95% of the people of the world use the metric system, better known as the Système International d'Unités, or SI system. There are seven basic units of measurement: length, area, volume, mass, time, force, and pressure.

SI (metric) prefixes

The following table gives a list of prefixes and their symbols, used for specifying multiples of units for measuring different quantities. Everyday examples include the **milligram** (mg), **centimeter** (cm), **kilowatt** (kW), **megahertz** (MHz), and **gigabyte** (Gb). See also *Appendix*.

SI prefixes and their symbols

Multiple	Prefix	Symbol	Example
1,000,000,000,000,000,000 (10^{18})	exa-	E	Eg (exagram)
1,000,000,000,000,000 (10^{15})	peta-	P	PJ (petajoule)
1,000,000,000,000 (10^{12})	tera-	T	TV (teravolt)
1,000,000,000 (10^{9})	giga-	G	GW (gigawatt)
1,000,000 (10^{6})	mega-	M	MHz (megahertz)
1,000 (10^{3})	kilo-	k	kg (kilogram)
100 (10^{2})	hecto-	h	hm (hectometer)
10 (10^{1})	deca-	da	daN (decanewton)
1/10 (10^{-1})	deci-	d	dC (decicoulomb)
1/100 (10^{-2})	centi-	c	cm (centimeter)
1/1,000 (10^{-3})	milli-	m	mm (millimeter)
1/1,000,000 (10^{-6})	micro-	µ	µF (microfarad)
1/1,000,000,000 (10^{-9})	nano-	n	nm (nanometer)
1/1,000,000,000,000 (10^{-12})	pico-	p	ps (picosecond)
1/1,000,000,000,000,000 (10^{-15})	femto-	f	frad (femtoradian)

Length

We usually refer to length as being one-dimensional because it involves measuring in only one direction. Tools such as rulers help us to measure length.

inches

Length conversions

Units of Length – US	
12 inches (in.)	= 1 foot (ft)
3 feet	= 1 yard (yd)
16½ feet	= 1 rod (rd), pole, or perch
40 rods	= 1 furlong (fur) = 660 feet
8 furlongs	= 1 US statute mile (mi) = 5,280 feet
1,852 meters	= 6,076.115 49 feet (approximately) = 1 international nautical mile

The SI unit for length is the **meter**, which is the length of the path traveled by light in a vacuum during a time interval of 1/299,792,458 of a second.

Length conversions

To convert	Multiply by
US to metric	
Inches to millimeters	25.4
Inches to centimeters	2.54
Feet to meters	0.3048
Yards to meters	0.9144
Furlongs to kilometers	0.201168
Miles to kilometers	1.61
Metric to US	
Millimeters to inches	0.03937
Centimeters to inches	0.3937
Meters to feet	3.28
Meters to yards	1.0936
Kilometers to furlongs	4.97097
Kilometers to miles	0.621

Area

Area refers to the size of a surface. It is measured in square units, usually square inches (in.^{2}), square yards (yd^2), or square miles (mi^2). **Surface area** is the area of the outer surface of a solid.

Formulas for calculating area

Surface	Description	Area
Circle	r = radius	πr^2
Ellipse	a,b = lengths of the semi–major and semi–minor axes	πab
Triangle	b = base, h = height	$\frac{1}{2} bh$
Trapezium	h = height, $l = \frac{1}{2}$ sum of parallel sides	hl

Rectangles and squares

Problems involving surfaces (i.e. paper, carpet) are considered two-dimensional because we measure the length and width (or breadth). If you wish to put new carpets in your house, you measure the surface of your floor space by measuring its length and its width to find its area (A).

A = length × width

Example: A small bathroom measures 5 feet long and 5 feet wide. How much is the total area of floor space in the room?

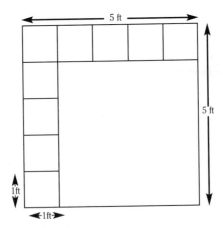

Solution: If area = length × width, then room area = $5 \times 5 = 25$ ft^2. Looking at the given diagram, you can see how we derive the concept of square units. In effect what you are showing is that it would take 25 squares of a single foot size to fill in the entire room area.

Area of a rectangle given its length and breadth

Length	Breadth									
	0.5	1.0	1.5	2.0	2.5	3.0	3.5	4.0	4.5	5.0
0.5	0.25	0.50	0.75	1.00	1.25	1.50	1.75	2.00	2.25	2.50
1.0	0.50	1.00	1.50	2.00	2.50	3.00	3.50	4.00	4.50	5.00
1.5	0.75	1.50	2.25	3.00	3.75	4.50	5.25	6.00	6.75	7.50
2.0	1.00	2.00	3.00	4.00	5.00	6.00	7.00	8.00	9.00	10.00
2.5	1.25	2.50	3.75	5.00	6.25	7.50	8.75	10.00	11.25	12.50
3.0	1.50	3.00	4.50	6.00	7.50	9.00	10.50	12.00	13.50	15.00
3.5	1.75	3.50	5.25	7.00	8.75	10.50	12.25	14.00	15.75	17.50
4.0	2.00	4.00	6.00	8.00	10.00	12.00	14.00	16.00	18.00	20.00
4.5	2.25	4.50	6.75	9.00	11.25	13.50	15.75	18.00	20.25	22.50
5.0	2.50	5.00	7.50	10.00	12.50	15.00	17.50	20.00	22.50	25.00
5.5	2.75	5.50	8.25	11.00	13.75	16.50	19.25	22.00	24.75	27.50
6.0	3.00	6.00	9.00	12.00	15.00	18.00	21.00	24.00	27.00	30.00
6.5	3.25	6.50	9.75	13.00	16.25	19.50	22.75	26.00	29.25	32.50
7.0	3.50	7.00	10.50	14.00	17.50	21.00	24.50	28.00	31.50	35.00
7.5	3.70	7.50	11.25	15.00	18.75	22.50	26.25	30.00	33.75	37.50
8.0	4.00	8.00	12.00	16.00	20.00	24.00	28.00	32.00	36.00	40.00
8.5	4.25	8.50	12.75	17.00	21.25	25.50	29.75	34.00	38.25	42.50
9.0	4.50	9.00	13.50	18.00	22.50	27.00	31.50	36.00	40.50	45.00
9.5	4.75	9.50	14.25	19.00	23.75	28.50	33.25	38.00	42.75	47.50
10.0	5.00	10.00	15.00	20.00	25.00	30.00	35.00	40.00	45.00	50.00

continued

Area of a rectangle given its length and breadth– *continued*

Length	Breadth									
	5.5	6.0	6.5	7.0	7.5	8.0	8.5	9.0	9.5	10.0
0.5	2.75	3.00	3.25	3.50	3.75	4.00	4.25	4.50	4.75	5.00
1.0	5.50	6.00	6.50	7.00	7.50	8.00	8.50	9.00	9.50	10.00
1.5	8.25	9.00	9.75	10.50	11.25	12.00	12.75	13.50	14.25	15.00
2.0	11.00	12.00	13.00	14.00	15.00	16.00	17.00	18.00	19.00	20.00
2.5	13.75	15.00	16.25	17.50	18.75	20.00	21.25	22.50	23.75	25.00
3.0	16.50	18.00	19.50	21.00	22.50	24.00	25.50	27.00	28.50	30.00
3.5	19.25	21.00	22.75	24.50	26.25	28.00	29.75	31.50	33.25	35.00
4.0	22.00	24.00	26.00	28.00	30.00	32.00	34.00	36.00	38.00	40.00
4.5	24.75	27.00	29.25	31.50	33.75	36.00	38.25	40.50	42.75	45.00
5.0	27.50	30.00	32.50	35.00	37.50	40.00	42.50	45.00	47.50	50.00
5.5	30.25	33.00	35.75	38.50	41.25	44.00	46.75	49.50	52.25	55.00
6.0	33.00	36.00	39.00	42.00	45.00	48.00	51.00	54.00	57.00	60.00
6.5	35.75	39.00	42.25	45.50	48.75	52.00	55.25	58.50	61.75	65.00
7.0	38.50	42.00	45.50	49.00	52.50	56.00	59.50	63.00	66.50	70.00
7.5	41.25	45.00	48.75	52.50	56.25	60.00	63.75	67.50	71.25	75.00
8.0	44.00	48.00	52.00	56.00	60.00	64.00	68.00	72.00	76.00	80.00
8.5	46.75	51.00	55.25	59.50	63.75	68.00	72.25	76.50	80.75	85.00
9.0	49.50	54.00	58.50	63.00	67.50	72.00	76.50	81.00	85.50	90.00
9.5	52.25	57.00	61.75	66.50	71.25	76.00	80.75	85.50	90.25	95.00
10.0	55.00	60.00	65.00	70.00	75.00	80.00	85.00	90.00	95.00	100.00

Circles

To find the area of a circle, we rely on the formula:

$$\text{area} = \pi \times r^2$$

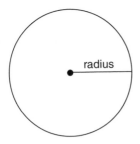

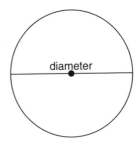

Where r = radius of the circle being measured and $\pi \cong 3.14$. The radius is half of the diameter of a circle. The diameter is the straight line dividing a circle in half.

You can calculate the area of a circle using the tables below. First, measure the radius. If the radius is a whole or half number, find it in the far left column and read your answer from the column to the immediate right. If the radius is, for example, 4.8 you can find the area by finding 4.5 in the far left column and then reading across for the value lying under the column headed 0.3 (4.5 plus 0.3 equals 4.8). In this example the area is 72.38.

Area of a circle given its radius

	0.00	0.05	0.10	0.15	0.20	0.25	0.30	0.35	0.40	0.45
0.0	0.00	0.01	0.03	0.07	0.13	0.20	0.28	0.38	0.50	0.64
0.5	0.79	0.95	1.13	1.33	1.54	1.77	2.01	2.27	2.54	2.84
1.0	3.14	3.46	3.80	4.15	4.52	4.91	5.31	5.73	6.16	6.61
1.5	7.07	7.55	8.04	8.55	9.08	9.62	10.18	10.75	11.34	11.95
2.0	12.57	13.20	13.85	14.52	15.21	15.90	16.62	17.35	18.10	18.86
2.5	19.63	20.43	21.24	22.06	22.90	23.76	24.63	25.52	26.42	27.34
3.0	28.27	29.22	30.19	31.17	32.17	33.18	34.21	35.26	36.32	37.39
3.5	38.48	39.59	40.72	41.85	43.01	44.18	45.36	46.57	47.78	49.02
4.0	50.27	51.53	52.81	54.11	55.42	56.75	58.09	59.45	60.82	62.21
4.5	63.62	65.04	66.48	67.93	69.40	70.88	72.38	73.90	75.43	76.98
5.0	78.54	80.12	81.71	83.32	84.95	86.59	88.25	89.92	91.61	93.31
5.5	95.03	96.77	98.52	100.29	102.07	103.87	105.68	107.51	109.36	111.22
6.0	113.10	114.99	116.90	118.82	120.76	122.72	124.69	126.68	128.68	130.70
6.5	132.73	134.78	136.85	138.93	141.03	143.14	145.27	147.41	149.57	151.75
7.0	153.94	156.15	158.37	160.61	162.86	165.13	167.42	169.72	172.03	174.37
7.5	176.71	179.08	181.46	183.85	186.27	188.69	191.13	193.59	196.07	198.56
8.0	201.06	203.58	206.12	208.67	211.24	213.82	216.42	219.04	221.67	224.32
8.5	226.98	229.66	232.35	235.06	237.79	240.53	243.28	246.06	248.85	251.65
9.0	254.47	257.30	260.16	263.02	265.90	268.80	271.72	274.65	277.59	280.55
9.5	283.53	286.52	289.53	292.55	295.59	298.65	301.72	304.81	307.91	311.03

	0.50	0.55	0.60	0.65	0.70	0.75	0.80	0.85	0.90	0.95
0.0	0.79	0.95	1.13	1.33	1.54	1.77	2.01	2.27	2.54	2.84
0.5	3.14	3.46	3.80	4.15	4.52	4.91	5.31	5.73	6.16	6.61
1.0	7.07	7.55	8.04	8.55	9.08	9.62	10.18	10.75	11.34	11.95
1.5	12.57	13.20	13.85	14.52	15.21	15.90	16.62	17.35	18.10	18.86
2.0	19.63	20.43	21.24	22.06	22.90	23.76	24.63	25.52	26.42	27.34
2.5	28.27	29.22	30.19	31.17	32.17	33.18	34.21	35.26	36.32	37.39
3.0	38.48	39.59	40.72	41.85	43.01	44.18	45.36	46.57	47.78	49.02
3.5	50.27	51.53	52.81	54.11	55.42	56.75	58.09	59.45	60.82	62.21
4.0	63.62	65.04	66.48	67.93	69.40	70.88	72.38	73.90	75.43	76.98
4.5	78.54	80.12	81.71	83.32	84.95	86.59	88.25	89.92	91.61	93.31
5.0	95.03	96.77	98.52	100.29	102.07	103.87	105.68	107.51	109.36	111.22
5.5	113.10	114.99	116.90	118.82	120.76	122.72	124.69	126.68	128.68	130.70
6.0	132.73	134.78	136.85	138.93	141.03	143.14	145.27	147.41	149.57	151.75
6.5	153.94	156.15	158.37	160.61	162.86	165.13	167.42	169.72	172.03	174.37
7.0	176.71	179.08	181.46	183.85	186.27	188.69	191.13	193.59	196.07	198.56
7.5	201.06	203.58	206.12	208.67	211.24	213.82	216.42	219.04	221.67	224.32
8.0	226.98	229.66	232.35	235.06	237.79	240.53	243.28	246.06	248.85	251.65
8.5	254.47	257.30	260.16	263.02	265.90	268.80	271.72	274.65	277.59	280.55
9.0	283.53	286.52	289.53	292.55	295.59	298.65	301.72	304.81	307.91	311.03
9.5	314.16	317.31	320.47	323.65	326.85	330.06	333.29	336.54	339.79	343.07

Triangles

To find the area of a triangle, we use the formula:

$$A = \tfrac{1}{2}b \times h$$

The following table gives the area of a triangle whose base is specified in the far left column and height in the top row. For example, $b = 3.5$, $h = 4.0$, implies $A = 7$.

Area of a triangle given its base and height

Base	Height									
	0.5	1.0	1.5	2.0	2.5	3.0	3.5	4.0	4.5	5.0
0.5	0.12	0.25	0.38	0.50	0.62	0.75	0.88	1.00	1.12	1.25
1.0	0.25	0.50	0.75	1.00	1.25	1.50	1.75	2.00	2.25	2.50
1.5	0.38	0.75	1.12	1.50	1.88	2.25	2.62	3.00	3.38	3.75
2.0	0.50	1.00	1.50	2.00	2.50	3.00	3.50	4.00	4.50	5.00
2.5	0.62	1.25	1.88	2.50	3.12	3.75	4.38	5.00	5.62	6.25
3.0	0.75	1.50	2.25	3.00	3.75	4.50	5.25	6.00	6.75	7.50
3.5	0.88	1.75	2.62	3.50	4.38	5.25	6.12	7.00	7.88	8.75
4.0	1.00	2.00	3.00	4.00	5.00	6.00	7.00	8.00	9.00	10.00
4.5	1.12	2.25	3.38	4.50	5.62	6.75	7.88	9.00	10.12	11.25
5.0	1.25	2.50	3.75	5.00	6.25	7.50	8.75	10.00	11.25	12.50
5.5	1.38	2.75	4.12	5.50	6.88	8.25	9.62	11.00	12.38	13.75
6.0	1.50	3.00	4.50	6.00	7.50	9.00	10.50	12.00	13.50	15.00
6.5	1.62	3.25	4.88	6.50	8.12	9.75	11.38	13.00	14.62	16.25
7.0	1.75	3.50	5.25	7.00	8.75	10.50	12.25	14.00	15.75	17.50
7.5	1.88	3.75	5.62	7.50	9.38	11.25	13.12	15.00	16.88	18.75
8.0	2.00	4.00	6.00	8.00	10.00	12.00	14.00	16.00	18.00	20.00
8.5	2.12	4.25	6.38	8.50	10.62	12.75	14.88	17.00	19.12	21.25
9.0	2.25	4.50	6.75	9.00	11.25	13.50	15.75	18.00	20.25	22.50
9.5	2.38	4.75	7.12	9.50	11.88	14.25	16.62	19.00	21.38	23.75
10.0	2.50	5.00	7.50	10.00	12.50	15.00	17.50	20.00	22.50	25.00

Base	Height									
	5.5	6.0	6.5	7.0	7.5	8.0	8.5	9.0	9.5	10.0
0.5	1.38	1.50	1.62	1.75	1.88	2.00	2.12	2.25	2.38	2.50
1.0	2.75	3.00	3.25	3.50	3.75	4.00	4.25	4.50	4.75	5.00
1.5	4.12	4.50	4.88	5.25	5.62	6.00	6.38	6.75	7.12	7.50
2.0	5.50	6.00	6.50	7.00	7.50	8.00	8.50	9.00	9.50	10.00
2.5	6.88	7.50	8.12	8.75	9.38	10.00	10.62	11.25	11.88	12.50
3.0	8.25	9.00	9.75	10.50	11.25	12.00	12.75	13.50	14.25	15.00
3.5	9.62	10.50	11.38	12.25	13.12	14.00	14.88	15.75	16.62	17.50
4.0	11.00	12.00	13.00	14.00	15.00	16.00	17.00	18.00	19.00	20.00
4.5	12.38	13.50	14.62	15.75	16.88	18.00	19.12	20.25	21.38	22.50
5.0	13.75	15.00	16.25	17.50	18.75	20.00	21.25	22.50	23.75	25.00
5.5	15.12	16.50	17.88	19.25	20.62	22.00	23.38	24.75	26.12	27.50
6.0	16.50	18.00	19.50	21.00	22.50	24.00	25.50	27.00	28.50	30.00
6.5	17.88	19.50	21.12	22.75	24.38	26.00	27.62	29.25	30.88	32.50
7.0	19.25	21.00	22.75	24.50	26.25	28.00	29.75	31.50	33.25	35.00
7.5	20.62	22.50	24.38	26.25	28.12	30.00	31.88	33.75	35.62	37.50
8.0	22.00	24.00	26.00	28.00	30.00	32.00	34.00	36.00	38.00	40.00
8.5	23.38	25.50	27.62	29.75	31.88	34.00	36.12	38.25	40.38	42.50
9.0	24.75	27.00	29.25	31.50	33.75	36.00	38.25	40.50	42.75	45.00
9.5	26.12	28.50	30.88	33.25	35.62	38.00	40.38	42.75	45.12	47.50
10.0	27.50	30.00	32.50	35.00	37.50	40.00	42.50	45.00	47.50	50.00

Area conversions

Area	
144 square inches (in²)	= 1 square foot (ft²)
9 square feet	= 1 square yard (yd²)
272¼ square feet	= 1 square rod (sq rd)
160 square rods	= 1 acre = 43,560 square feet
640 acre	= 1 square mile (mi²)
1 mile square	= 1 section of land
6 miles square	= 1 township = 36 sections = 36 square miles

To convert	Multiply by
US to metric	
square inches to square centimeters	6.4516
square feet to square meters	0.092903
square yards to square meters	0.836127
square miles to square kilometers	2.589988
acres to square meters	4046.856422
acres to hectares	0.404866
Metric to US	
square centimeters to square inches	0.1550
square meters to square feet	10.7639
square meters to square yards	1.19599
square kilometers to square miles	0.386102
square meters to acres	0.000247
hectares to acres	2.469955

Volume and Capacity

Volume (V) is the amount of space an object takes up and has the property of three-dimensionality. It is usually measured in cubic units. We say that a 1 cm cube has a volume of 1 cubic centimeter, and is written as 1 cm³.

To find the volume of a rectangular box, or cuboid, we use the following formula:

$$V = \text{length} \times \text{breadth} \times \text{height}$$

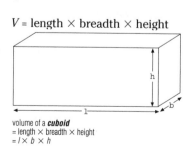

volume of a ***cuboid***
= length × breadth × height
= $l \times b \times h$

To find the volume of a cylinder, we rely on the formula:

$V = \pi r^2 \times$ height

volume = $\pi r^2 h$
area of curved
surface = $2 \pi r h$

Formulas for calculating volumes

Solid object	Parameters	Surface area	Volume
sphere	r = radius	$4\pi r^2$	$\dfrac{4\pi r^3}{3}$
cube	a = side of cube	$6a^2$	a^3
cylinder	r = radius, h = height	$2\pi r\,(r + h)$	$\pi r^2 h$
cone	r = radius, h = height, l = slant height	$\pi r(l + r)$	$\dfrac{\pi r^2 h}{3}$

Volume and capacity conversions

Units of Volume – US and Imperial

1,728 cubic inches (in.³)	= 1 cubic foot (ft³)
27 cubic feet	= 1 cubic yard (yd³)
1 cubic meter	= 1,000 cubic decimeters

Units of Weight – US and Imperial

1 dram	= 27.344 grains
1 ounce	= 16 drams
1 pound	= 16 ounces
1 stone (imperial)	= 14 pounds
1 quarter (imperial)	= 28 pounds = 2 stone

Units of Liquid Volume – US and Imperial

1 tablespoon	= 3 teaspoons = 0.5 fluid ounce
1 cup	= 8 fluid ounces
1 pint (US)	= 2 cups = 16 fluid ounces
1 pint (imperial)	= 19.2 ounces
1 quart	= 2 pints = 4 cups = 32 fluid ounces
1 gallon (US)	= 4 quarts = 16 cups = 128 fluid ounces
1 gallon (imperial)	= 153.6 (US)/160 (UK) fluid ounces

Volume/capacity conversions

To convert	Multiply by
US and Imperial to metric	
cubic inches to cubic centimeters	16.387162
cubic feet to cubic meters	0.028317
cubic yards to cubic meters	0.764553
cubic miles to cubic kilometers	4.1682
fluid ounces to milliliters	29.5729
pints (US) to liters	0.473167
quarts (US) to liters	0.946333
gallons (US) to liters	3.7853
Metric to US and Imperial	
cubic centimeters to cubic inches	0.061023
cubic meters to cubic feet	35.314445
cubic meters to cubic yards	1.3079428
cubic kilometers to cubic miles	0.239912
milliliters to fluid ounces	0.0338147
liters to pints (US)	2.1134
liters to quarts (US)	1.056710
liters to gallons (US)	0.26417762

Mass

In the SI system, the base unit of mass is the **kilogram**. The standard unit of mass to which all other masses are compared is a platinum–iridium cylinder of 1 kg, which is kept at the International Bureau of Weights and Measures in Sèvres, France.

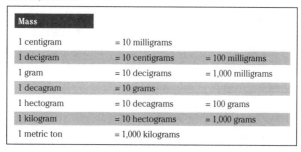

Mass		
1 centigram	= 10 milligrams	
1 decigram	= 10 centigrams	= 100 milligrams
1 gram	= 10 decigrams	= 1,000 milligrams
1 decagram	= 10 grams	
1 hectogram	= 10 decagrams	= 100 grams
1 kilogram	= 10 hectograms	= 1,000 grams
1 metric ton	= 1,000 kilograms	

Mass conversions

To convert	Multiply by
US and Imperial to metric	
ounces to grams	28.349523
pounds to kilograms	0.453592
stone (14 lb) to kilograms	6.350293
tons (imperial) to kilograms	1016.046909
tons (US) to metric tons	0.907185
tons (imperial) to metric tons	1.016047
Metric to US and Imperial	
grams to ounces	0.035274
kilograms to pounds	2.20462
kilograms to stone (14 lb)	0.157473
kilograms to tons (imperial)	0.000984
metric tons to tons (US)	1.10231
metric tons to tons (imperial)	0.984207

Time

Time refers to the continuous passage of existence, recorded by division into hours, minutes, and seconds. Formerly the measurement of time was based on the earth's rotation on its axis, but this was found to be irregular. Therefore the **second**, the standard SI unit of time, was redefined in 1956 in terms of the earth's annual orbit of the sun, and in 1967 in terms of a radiation pattern of the element cesium. The following table lists the conversion factors for changing between various units of time.

Time conversions

Time	
1,000,000 nanoseconds	= 1 millisecond
1,000 milliseconds	= 1 second
60 seconds	= 1 minute
86,400 seconds	= 1 day
1,440 minutes	= 1 day
24 hours	= 1 day
168 hours	= 1 week
7 days	= 1 week
365 days	= 1 year
12 months	= 1 year
10 years	= 1 decade
100 years	= 1 century
1,000 years	= 1 millennium

Force

Force is defined as any influence that tends to change the state of rest, or the uniform motion in a straight line, of a body. The action of an unbalanced or resultant force results in the acceleration of a body in the direction of action of the force, or it may, if the body is unable to move freely, result in its deformation. Force is a vector quantity, possessing both magnitude and direction; its SI unit is the **newton**.

Force conversions

To convert	Multiply by
pound force to newton	4.44822
kilogram force to newton	9.80665
newton to pound force	0.224809
newton to kilogram force	0.101972

Pressure

In a fluid, pressure is the force that would act normally (at right angles) per unit surface area of a body immersed in the fluid. The SI unit of pressure is the **pascal** (Pa), equal to a pressure of one newton per square meter. In the atmosphere, the pressure declines with height from about 100 kPa at sea level to zero where the atmosphere fades into space. Pressure is commonly measured with a barometer, manometer, or Bourdon gauge.

Pressure conversions

To convert	Multiply by
pound force per square inch to kilopascals	6.89476
tons force per square inch (US) to megapascals	17.2948
atmospheres to newtons per square centimeter	10.1325
atmospheres to pounds force per square inch	14.695942
kilopascals to pound force per square inch	0.145038
megapascals to tons force per square inch (US)	0.057848
newtons per square centimeter to atmospheres	0.098692
pounds force per square inch to atmospheres	0.068948

Angles

Measurement of an angle is the degree of turning between two straight lines. We use angles to measure turn or change in direction as in a compass or a weathervane. Angles are measured using protractors and are given in **degrees**. The length of a line does not affect the size of the angle.

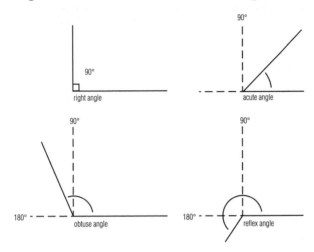

Angle terminology

Right angle	90° or a quarter turn
Acute angle	an angle less than 90°
Obtuse angle	an angle greater than 90°
Straight angle	180° or a half turn
Reflex angle	an angle greater than 180°
Complete turn	360°
Complementary angles	two angles with a sum of 90°
Supplementary angles	two angles with a sum of 180°

Mean, Median, and Mode

Every day, we are confronted by discussions or statistics referring to the "average," whether it is height, income, family size, or anything that can be quantified and examined. In statistics, the term average usually refers to what is known as the mean.

To find the **mean** of a set or group of terms or quantities, you simply add all of the measurements taken and then divide by the number of items in the group.

The **median** is the value directly in the middle of a set or group. If there is no one middle number, the average of the two middle numbers is taken.

The **mode** is the measurement that occurs most often.

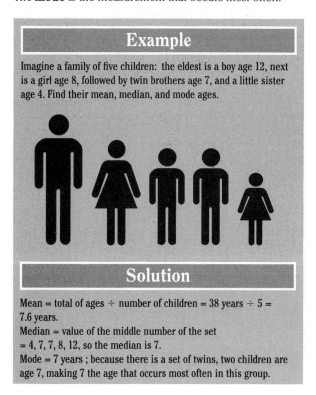

Example

Imagine a family of five children: the eldest is a boy age 12, next is a girl age 8, followed by twin brothers age 7, and a little sister age 4. Find their mean, median, and mode ages.

Solution

Mean = total of ages ÷ number of children = 38 years ÷ 5 = 7.6 years.
Median = value of the middle number of the set = 4, 7, 7, 8, 12, so the median is 7.
Mode = 7 years ; because there is a set of twins, two children are age 7, making 7 the age that occurs most often in this group.

How to Use a Calculator

Simple calculators

Most basic calculators will look similar to the one above. Some may not have memory keys or the % key; others may have a combined on/off key with a separate key for clearing everything (C or AC) or just the last entry (CE). Some, like the above, may have a combined C/CE button, which when pressed once will clear the last entry only, and if pressed twice will clear everything. Some may have an enter key instead of an equals (=) key. Some may not even have an on/off button.

Calculator keys

Key	Meaning
On/Off	Turns calculator on and off
C or AC	Clears calculator of all previous calculations
CE	Clears calculator of last entry only and allows you to continue with your current calculation
.	Decimal point
√	Calculates square root of a number
%	Calculates percentage
M+	Adds calculation to number in memory
M–	Subtracts calculation from number in memory
MC	Clears calculation from memory
MR	Memory recall – recalls calculation from memory

When using a calculator, always press your C/AC button first to ensure you are starting fresh. To find the sum of 17 + 34, press the following keys:

| C | 1 | 7 | + | 3 | 4 | = |

As you input, be sure to check your screen to ensure the correct number or sign has been input. When you press the equals (=) key, your final answer will appear on your display. In this case, the correct answer is 51.

If you have input a number incorrectly, you can press the CE key to erase your last entry, then reinput the correct entry. Taking the above example, imagine that you entered an 8 rather than a 7 for the number 17. Rather than erase the entire calculation, simply hit your CE button after you have hit the 8, and then press the 7 button and carry on with the rest of the operation:

| C | 1 | 8 | CE | 7 | + | 3 | 4 | = |

Order of operations

Calculators operate in different ways. You need to be aware of what type of calculator you are using, so before attempting any important calculations, you should test your calculator by pressing the keys in this order:

| AC | 1 | + | 2 | x | 3 | = |

If your answer appears as a 9, you have a simple "four-rule" or standard calculator. If the answer is 7, then you are working with a scientific calculator. The "four-rule" calculator performs operations based on the order in which you entered them, using what is known as **arithmetic logic**. Scientific calculators follow the PEMDAS (see page 13) rule and use what is known as **algebraic logic**. They perform multiplication and division first, then any additions and subtractions in the order they come in the equation.

If you work on a computer that includes a calculator as one of your desktop accessories, you may have the option to use it in standard or scientific mode.

Knowing how your calculator "thinks" will ensure you are getting the answer you need. If you want to know the cost of a skirt and two tops, a scientific calculator will do the work for you automatically If you are using a standard calculator however, you must manipulate the entry to get the right answer.

You wish to purchase a $25 skirt and two $10 blouses. How much will you have to pay in total?

Using the standard calculator, you would need to do the following:

1) Multiply the cost of the blouse by 2 ($2 \times 10 = 20$)

| AC | 2 | x | 1 | 0 | = |

2) Then add the cost of the skirt ($20 + 25$) to get your final answer of $45.

| AC | 2 | 0 | + | 2 | 5 | = |

Using a scientific calculator you only need to key:

| AC | 2 | 5 | + | 2 | x | 1 | 0 | = |

Rounding Numbers

Multiplying whole numbers will always result in another whole number. However, dividing whole numbers by whole numbers does not necessarily produce another whole number.

For example, to find the quotient of $42 \div 5$, press your calculator keys as shown below. Your answer should be displayed as 8.4.

| AC | 4 | 2 | ÷ | 5 | = |

If you are asked to find your answer to the nearest whole number, the answer would be 8 because the digit after the decimal point is less than 5. When rounding numbers, digits 5 and above are rounded up. So 8.5 would become 9. Figures 4 and below round down, so 8.1 would become 8.

When rounding to the nearest whole number, always refer to the digit to the right of the decimal point. It does not matter what any other digits to the right of it are. It is only the tenths placement that tells you whether to round up or round down.

Likewise, if you are asked to round to the nearest 10, look to the digit in the units/ones place to tell you whether to round up or down.

Significant Digits

The number 1,264 contains four digits. The most significant digit is the number 1 because it is the highest place value digit. The least significant is the number 4 because it is in the lowest place value position. If you are asked for a number to a specific significant digit, count in from the highest place value to that position (so 1 significant digit is the highest place value, 2 significant digits is the next highest place value, and so on). Check the digit in the next place value to determine whether you should round up or down, and then you have your answer. Here is a table to illustrate significant digits for the number 1,264.

Correct to	Number (1,264)
1 significant digit	1,000
2 significant digits	1,300
3 significant digits	1,260
4 significant digits	1,264

Section Two – Figure it Out

Personal Finance

Organizing your finances is one of the most challenging, but necessary, applications of everyday numbers. You may be the type who prefers to play it safe and avoid any sort of risky financial investment, but you may not be playing it smart if the money you save is earning less than the money you owe. A classic example of this is the person who earns 3% on their savings account but pays as much as 24% on his or her credit card balances. Learning the basics of borrowing and lending can help you manage the way your money grows and allow you to create a financial plan that works for you.

Income Tax and Liabilities

Basic individual income tax is calculated as follows:

 Taxable income = adjusted gross income
        – deductions
        – exemptions
        – credits

The Internal Revenue Service (IRS) supplies taxpayers with a number of tax return forms to suit their individual needs, the most common being the 1040, 1040A, or the 1040EZ. Each form has the same basic format designed to help you arrive at a final figure for taxable income. The tax return is broken down into sub-sections for easy computation based on the above formula.

Section	Description
Adjusted gross income	Covers all sources of income less any non-taxable income (i.e. welfare payments, municipal bond interest).
Deductions	Includes standard deduction applicable to everyone plus individual deductions, such as state and local property taxes, mortgage interest payments, charitable contributions, moving expenses from job relocation, medical expenses in excess of 7.5% of adjusted income, and casualty losses.
Exemptions	Includes personal exemption plus one for spouse and for each dependent not claimed on anyone else's tax returns.
Credits	Available to the poor and elderly, dependent on individual circumstance.

Once you find your final taxable income, the amount of tax you will be expected to pay can be found in Tax Tables published by the IRS for each tax year. As an example, below is the 2001 Tax Table for single individuals:

Unmarried Individuals (other than surviving spouses and heads of household) Tax Year 2001

Taxable Income	Tax
Up to $27,050	15% of the taxable income
$27,051–65,550	$4,057.50 plus 28% of the excess over $27,050
$65,551–136,750	$14,837.50 plus 31% of the excess over $65,550
$136,751–297,350	$36,909.50 plus 36% of the excess over $136,750
Over $297,350	$94,725.50 plus 39.6% of the excess over $297,350

Note: The new 10% rate bracket created by the Tax Relief Act of 2001 is not included in this schedule.

Payroll deductions

By law, all businesses are obliged to deduct state and federal taxes from their employees' paychecks. These are paid directly to the government. Other deductions can also be made such as contributions to health care programs, unemployment compensation, social security, Medicare, any elective tax-deferred options, day care, insurance or prepaid taxes.

Your payroll statement will list your **gross income** (full earnings) less any deductions to arrive at your **net income**, the amount of income you actually have at your disposal to spend. At the end of the fiscal year, employers must provide each employee with a W-2 form, which lists total wages/salary earned within that year, total state, federal and local taxes withheld, plus any other deduction that might be tax-deferred.

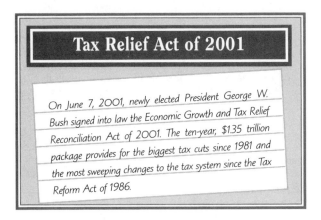

Tax Relief Act of 2001

On June 7, 2001, newly elected President George W. Bush signed into law the Economic Growth and Tax Relief Reconciliation Act of 2001. The ten-year, $1.35 trillion package provides for the biggest tax cuts since 1981 and the most sweeping changes to the tax system since the Tax Reform Act of 1986.

Budgeting

Once you have established your annual net income after taxes, social security, and any other deductions taken directly from your paycheck, you can set up a monthly budget to help clarify your current financial position. To create a monthly budget, first identify your fixed expenses – those bills or obligations that you must pay monthly – and then estimate your semi-fixed costs and variable expenses. With these figures to hand, you can create a monthly budget that will tell you how much you can spend and how much you might save if you stick with your plan.

Example

Here is an example of a monthly budget for a family of four, receiving a net income of $3,000 per month. The fixed costs are subtracted from the net monthly income. Semi-fixed costs are then subtracted. Keep in mind that these can potentially change over longer periods of time depending on your usage. Variable spending is usually an estimate based on what you know to be your average spending per month. These costs tend to be more difficult to track and can sneak up on you if you don't make it your goal to stick to the amount allocated. Keeping within the budget you set allows you to save money each month and will give you future financial freedom if you invest it wisely.

Monthly budget

	($)	($)
Net monthly income:		
Husband and wife (combined salaries)	3,000	
Total	3,000	**3,000**
Fixed spending		
Rent or mortgage (incl. property tax)	1,650	
Content insurance	20	
Total	1,670	− 1,670
		1,330
Semi-fixed/annual or quarterly payments		
Car/maintenance	100	
Car insurance	50	
Telephone	100	
Electricity/gas	225	
Sewage/water	50	
Cable connection	15	
Total	540	− 540
		790
Variable spending		
Food	400	
Vacation	50	
Entertainment	100	
Clothes	50	
Miscellaneous	50	
Total	650	− 650
Estimated monthly savings		**140**

Banking - Getting the Most Out of Your Accounts

There are two main types of bank accounts: checking accounts and savings accounts. **Checking accounts** allow account holders the option of paying bills by check, by standing order, or by direct debit. Most banks now offer an ATM card that you can use like cash: simply hand it over, sign the transaction slip, and the money is automatically debited from your account.

Checking accounts sometimes come with an overdraft option. An overdraft allows the account holder to overdraw on his or her account up to a certain limit for a specified time. Interest is then payable on the amount borrowed. An overdraft is roughly equivalent to the credit terms offered by major credit-card companies. Since the penalties for bouncing a check – writing one for more money than you have in your account – are high, it is worth asking if your bank will set up an overdraft facility for you.

A **savings account** is an account in which money is left to attract interest, often for a fixed term. Popular savings accounts include passbook, statement, IRAs, and certificate savings plans. There are sometimes restrictions on how many times per year you can access the money in your deposit account. In effect the bank borrows your money to lend to other borrowers. For the privilege of reinvesting your money elsewhere, the bank rewards you with a sum of money (interest) on your investment.

There are two types of interest: **simple interest** – interest that is calculated as a straight percentage of the amount loaned or invested, and **compound interest** – interest earned over a period of time (for example, yearly) which is added to the investment, so that at the end of the next period interest is paid on that total.

Simple interest

This is the interest calculated on the principal, which is the amount invested or borrowed. The formula for simple interest I is:

$I = \dfrac{Prn}{100}$

where P is the principal, r is the annual interest rate expressed as a percentage, and n is the total number of years the principal is invested. The final amount F may be calculated using:

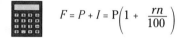 $F = P + I = P\left(1 + \dfrac{rn}{100}\right)$

To find the final amount you can expect to receive on a simple interest-bearing account, use the reference chart below. Find your interest rate in the left-hand column. Scroll across until you find the relevant rate for the number of years (top row) you expect to invest it. Multiply your initial investment by that number to get the value of your investment at the end of your agreed term.

Simple interest rates

Interest rates (%)	Number of years									
	1	2	3	4	5	10	15	20	25	30
0.5	1.005	1.010	1.015	1.020	1.025	1.050	1.075	1.100	1.125	1.150
1.0	1.010	1.020	1.030	1.040	1.050	1.100	1.150	1.200	1.250	1.300
1.5	1.015	1.030	1.045	1.060	1.075	1.150	1.225	1.300	1.375	1.450
2.0	1.020	1.040	1.060	1.080	1.100	1.200	1.300	1.400	1.500	1.600
2.5	1.025	1.050	1.075	1.100	1.125	1.250	1.375	1.500	1.625	1.750
3.0	1.030	1.060	1.090	1.120	1.150	1.300	1.450	1.600	1.750	1.900
3.5	1.035	1.070	1.105	1.140	1.175	1.350	1.525	1.700	1.875	2.050
4.0	1.040	1.080	1.120	1.160	1.200	1.400	1.600	1.800	2.000	2.200
4.5	1.045	1.090	1.135	1.180	1.225	1.450	1.675	1.900	2.125	2.350
5.0	1.050	1.100	1.150	1.200	1.250	1.500	1.750	2.000	2.250	2.500
5.5	1.055	1.110	1.165	1.220	1.275	1.550	1.825	2.100	2.375	2.650
6.0	1.060	1.120	1.180	1.240	1.300	1.600	1.900	2.200	2.500	2.800
6.5	1.065	1.130	1.195	1.260	1.325	1.650	1.975	2.300	2.625	2.950
7.0	1.070	1.140	1.210	1.280	1.350	1.700	2.050	2.400	2.750	3.100
7.5	1.075	1.150	1.225	1.300	1.375	1.750	2.125	2.500	2.875	3.250
8.0	1.080	1.160	1.240	1.320	1.400	1.800	2.200	2.600	3.000	3.400
8.5	1.085	1.170	1.255	1.340	1.425	1.850	2.275	2.700	3.125	3.550
9.0	1.090	1.180	1.270	1.360	1.450	1.900	2.350	2.800	3.250	3.700
9.5	1.095	1.190	1.285	1.380	1.475	1.950	2.425	2.900	3.375	3.850
10	1.100	1.200	1.300	1.400	1.500	2.000	2.500	3.000	3.500	4.000

Example

Find the final amount you can expect on a $2,000 investment at 3% simple interest per annum for five years.

Solution

Using the chart, the rate for 3% per annum for five years is 1.150.
1.150 x $2,000 = $2,300

Compound interest

Compound interest is calculated by applying the interest rate to the original principal plus any interest earned and reinvested at agreed conversion periods. The formula for compound interest I is:

 $$I = P\left[(1 + \frac{r}{100})^n - 1\right]$$

where P is the principal, r is the interest rate for each conversion period expressed as a percentage, and n is the total number of conversion periods the principal is invested.

Example

Find the final amount you can expect on $1,000 invested for two years at 6% per annum, where it is agreed that the interest is compounded half-yearly.

Solution

Conversion period	Bank balance	Interest earned	New balance
After 6 months	3% of $1,000.00 =	$30.00	$1,030.00
After 12 months	3% of $1,030.00 =	$30.90	$1,060.90
After 18 months	3% of $1,060.90 =	$31.83	$1,092.73
After 24 months	3% of $1,092.73 =	$32.78	$1,125.51
Total interest earned		$125.51	

This can be confirmed using the above formula for compound interest, noting that there are $n = 4$ half-yearly periods at $r = 3\%$ for each half-year, giving:

 $I = \$1,000 \times \left[\left(1 + \frac{3}{100} \right)^4 - 1 \right] = \$125.51$

Note that the corresponding interest earned at 6% simple interest over the same period would be only $120.00.

If r is the annual compound interest rate and n is the number of years for which the interest is compounded, then the amount accumulated from 1 unit is given by the expression:

 $F = 1 \times \left(\frac{1 + r}{100} \right)^n$

To find the final amount you can expect to receive on an annually compounded interest-bearing account, use the reference chart on page 50. Find your interest rate in the left-hand column. Scroll across until you find the relevant rate for the number of years (top row) you expect to invest it. Multiply your initial investment by that number to get the value of your investment at the end of your agreed term.

Example

Find the final amount you can expect on a $1,000 investment at 4.5% compound interest per annum for five years.

Solution

Using the chart following, the rate for 4.5% per annum for five years is 1.2462.
$1.2462 \times \$1,000 = \$1,246.20$
You will have earned $246.20 on your initial investment of $1,000.

BENBROOK PUBLIC LIBRARY

Compound interest rates

Interest rates (%)	Number of years									
	1	2	3	4	5	10	15	20	25	50
0.25	1.0025	1.0050	1.0075	1.0100	1.0126	1.0253	1.0382	1.0512	1.0644	1.1330
0.50	1.0050	1.0100	1.0151	1.0202	1.0253	1.0511	1.0777	1.1049	1.1328	1.2832
0.75	1.0075	1.0151	1.0227	1.0303	1.0381	1.0776	1.1186	1.1612	1.2054	1.4530
1.00	1.0100	1.0201	1.0303	1.0406	1.0510	1.1046	1.1610	1.2202	1.2824	1.6446
1.25	1.0125	1.0252	1.0380	1.0509	1.0641	1.1323	1.2048	1.2820	1.3642	1.8610
1.50	1.0150	1.0302	1.0457	1.0614	1.0773	1.1605	1.2502	1.3469	1.4509	2.1052
1.75	1.0175	1.0353	1.0534	1.0719	1.0906	1.1894	1.2972	1.4148	1.5430	2.3808
2.00	1.0200	1.0404	1.0612	1.0824	1.1041	1.2190	1.3459	1.4859	1.6406	2.6916
2.25	1.0225	1.0455	1.0690	1.0931	1.1177	1.2492	1.3962	1.5605	1.7441	3.0420
2.50	1.0250	1.0506	1.0769	1.1038	1.1314	1.2801	1.4483	1.6386	1.8539	3.4371
3.00	1.0300	1.0609	1.0927	1.1255	1.1593	1.3439	1.5580	1.8061	2.0938	4.3839
3.50	1.0350	1.0712	1.1087	1.1475	1.1877	1.4106	1.6753	1.9898	2.3632	5.5849
4.00	1.0400	1.0816	1.1249	1.1699	1.2167	1.4802	1.8009	2.1911	2.6658	7.1067
4.50	1.0450	1.0920	1.1412	1.1925	1.2462	1.5530	1.9353	2.4117	3.0054	9.0326
5.00	1.0500	1.1025	1.1576	1.2155	1.2763	1.6289	2.0789	2.6533	3.3864	11.4674
5.50	1.0550	1.1130	1.1742	1.2388	1.3070	1.7081	2.2325	2.9178	3.8134	14.5420
6.00	1.0600	1.1236	1.1910	1.2625	1.3382	1.7908	2.3966	3.2071	4.2919	18.4202
6.50	10.650	1.1342	1.2079	1.2865	1.3701	1.8771	2.5718	3.5236	4.8277	23.3067
7.00	1.0700	1.1449	1.2250	1.3108	1.4026	1.9672	2.7590	3.8697	5.4274	29.4570
7.50	1.0750	1.1556	1.2423	1.3355	1.4356	2.0610	2.9589	4.2479	6.0983	37.1897
8.00	1.080	1.166	1.260	1.360	1.469	2.159	3.172	4.661	6.848	46.902
8.50	1.085	1.177	1.277	1.386	1.504	2.261	3.400	5.112	7.687	59.086
9.00	1.090	1.188	1.295	1.412	1.539	2.367	3.642	5.604	8.623	74.358
9.50	1.095	1.199	1.313	1.438	1.574	2.478	3.901	6.142	9.668	93.477
10.00	1.100	1.210	1.331	1.464	1.611	2.594	4.177	6.727	10.835	117.391
10.50	1.105	1.221	1.349	1.491	1.647	2.714	4.471	7.366	12.135	147.270
11.00	1.110	1.232	1.368	1.518	1.685	2.839	4.785	8.062	13.585	184.565
11.50	1.115	1.243	1.386	1.546	1.723	2.970	5.118	8.821	15.201	231.070
12.00	1.120	1.254	1.405	1.574	1.762	3.106	5.474	9.646	17.000	289.002
12.50	1.125	1.266	1.424	1.602	1.802	3.247	5.852	10.545	19.003	361.099
13.00	1.130	1.277	1.443	1.630	1.842	3.395	6.254	11.523	21.231	450.736
14.00	1.140	1.300	1.482	1.689	1.925	3.707	7.138	13.743	26.462	700.233
15.00	1.150	1.323	1.521	1.749	2.011	4.046	8.137	16.367	32.919	1083.66
16.00	1.160	1.346	1.561	1.811	2.100	4.411	9.266	19.461	40.874	1670.70
17.00	1.170	1.369	1.602	1.874	2.192	4.807	10.539	23.106	50.658	2566.22
18.00	1.180	1.392	1.643	1.939	2.288	5.234	11.974	27.393	62.669	3927.36
19.00	1.190	1.416	1.685	2.005	2.386	5.695	13.590	32.429	77.388	5998.91
20.00	1.200	1.440	1.728	2.074	2.488	6.192	15.407	38.338	95.396	9110.44
21.00	1.210	1.464	1.772	2.144	2.594	6.727	17.449	45.259	117.391	13780.6
22.00	1.220	1.488	1.816	2.215	2.703	7.305	19.742	53.358	144.210	20796.6

Compound growth

The following table gives the number of years required for a sum of money invested at a variety of interest rates to double, triple, and quadruple. For example, at a compound interest rate of 0.25%, it will take 555.2 years for the sum invested to quadruple.

Number of years required for a sum of money invested at a variety of compound interest rates to double, triple, and quadruple

Interest rates (%)	Double	Triple	Quadruple	Quintuple	Sextuple
0.25	277.6	440.0	555.2	644.6	717.6
0.50	139.0	220.3	278.0	322.7	359.2
0.75	92.8	147.0	185.5	215.4	239.8
1.00	69.7	110.4	139.3	161.7	180.1
1.25	55.8	88.4	111.6	129.6	144.2
1.50	46.6	73.8	93.1	108.1	120.3
1.75	40.0	63.3	79.9	92.8	103.3
2.00	35.0	55.5	70.0	81.3	90.5
2.25	31.2	49.4	62.3	72.3	80.5
2.50	28.1	44.5	56.1	65.2	72.6
2.75	25.6	40.5	51.1	59.3	66.0
3.00	23.4	37.2	46.9	54.4	60.6
3.25	21.7	34.3	43.3	50.3	56.0
3.50	20.1	31.9	40.3	46.8	52.1
3.75	18.8	29.8	37.7	43.7	48.7
4.00	17.7	28.0	35.3	41.0	45.7
4.25	16.7	26.4	33.3	38.7	43.0
4.50	15.7	25.0	31.5	36.6	40.7
4.75	14.9	23.7	29.9	34.7	38.6
5.00	14.2	22.5	28.4	33.0	36.7
5.25	13.5	21.5	27.1	31.5	35.0
5.50	12.9	20.5	25.9	30.1	33.5
5.75	12.4	19.7	24.8	28.8	32.0
6.00	11.9	18.9	23.8	27.6	30.7
6.25	11.4	18.1	22.9	26.5	29.6
6.50	11.0	17.4	22.0	25.6	28.5
6.75	10.6	16.8	21.2	24.6	27.4
7.00	10.2	16.2	20.5	23.8	26.5
7.25	9.9	15.7	19.8	23.0	25.6
7.50	9.6	15.2	19.2	22.3	24.8
7.75	9.3	14.7	18.6	21.6	24.0
8.00	9.0	14.3	18.0	20.9	23.3
8.25	8.7	13.9	17.5	20.3	22.6
8.50	8.5	13.5	17.0	19.7	22.0
8.75	8.3	13.1	16.5	19.2	21.4
9.00	8.0	12.7	16.1	18.7	20.8
9.25	7.8	12.4	15.7	18.2	20.3
9.50	7.6	12.1	15.3	17.7	19.7
9.75	7.5	11.8	14.9	17.3	19.3
10.00	7.3	11.5	14.5	16.9	18.8
10.25	7.1	11.3	14.2	16.5	18.4
10.50	6.9	11.0	13.9	16.1	17.9
10.75	6.8	10.8	13.6	15.8	17.5
11.00	6.6	10.5	13.3	15.4	17.2

continued

Number of years required for a sum of money invested at a variety of compound interest rates to double, triple, and quadruple – *continued*

Interest rates (%)	Double	Triple	Quadruple	Quintuple	Sextuple
11.25	6.5	10.3	13.0	15.1	16.8
11.50	6.4	10.1	12.7	14.8	16.5
11.75	6.2	9.9	12.5	14.5	16.1
12.00	6.1	9.7	12.2	14.2	15.8
12.25	6.0	9.5	12.0	13.9	15.5
12.50	5.9	9.3	11.8	13.7	15.2
12.75	5.8	9.2	11.6	13.4	14.9
13.00	5.7	9.0	11.3	13.2	14.7
13.25	5.6	8.8	11.1	12.9	14.4
13.50	5.5	8.7	10.9	12.7	14.1
13.75	5.4	8.5	10.8	12.5	13.9
14.00	5.3	8.4	10.6	12.3	13.7
14.25	5.2	8.2	10.4	12.1	13.4
14.50	5.1	8.1	10.2	11.9	13.2
14.75	5.0	8.0	10.1	11.7	13.0
15.00	5.0	7.9	9.9	11.5	12.8
15.25	4.9	7.7	9.8	11.3	12.6
15.50	4.8	7.6	9.6	11.2	12.4
15.75	4.7	7.5	9.5	11.0	12.3
16.00	4.7	7.4	9.3	10.8	12.1
16.25	4.6	7.3	9.2	10.7	11.9
16.50	4.5	7.2	9.1	10.5	11.7
16.75	4.5	7.1	9.0	10.4	11.6
17.00	4.4	7.0	8.8	10.3	11.4
17.25	4.4	6.9	8.7	10.1	11.3
17.50	4.3	6.8	8.6	10.0	11.1
17.75	4.2	6.7	8.5	9.9	11.0
18.00	4.2	6.6	8.4	9.7	10.8
18.25	4.1	6.6	8.3	9.6	10.7
18.50	4.1	6.5	8.2	9.5	10.6
18.75	4.0	6.4	8.1	9.4	10.4
19.00	4.0	6.3	8.0	9.3	10.3
19.25	3.9	6.2	7.9	9.1	10.2
19.50	3.9	6.2	7.8	9.0	10.1
19.75	3.8	6.1	7.7	8.9	9.9
20.00	3.8	6.0	7.6	8.8	9.8

Doubling up – the rule of 72

The rule of 72 is a simple formula for estimating the number of years (n) required for a sum of money to double if the interest is compounded annually at a rate of r %. This rule may be expressed as:

$$n = \frac{72}{r}$$

For example, with an interest rate of 7% the investment would double in value in approximately ($\approx$) ten years.

$$n = \frac{72}{7}$$

$$n \approx 10$$

Borrowing

During your life, you will have reason to borrow money as well as to save it. Most loans are charged at a specific rate of interest, with the rate and timing of repayments influencing how much the loan eventually costs you. In order to compare the cost of borrowing money, it is important to know both the actual rate of interest and to understand the different repayment systems.

Fixed-rate repayment

In paying back any loan, there are usually two parts to the repayment:

- repaying the initial sum borrowed

- paying interest for having borrowed it.

A fixed-rate repayment loan is one in which you agree to borrow a set amount and to repay it at an interest rate r per annum for a period of n years.

Example

How much interest will be due each year on a three-year loan of $2,000 with an interest rate of 7%?

Solution

Assuming that the initial amount borrowed is repaid in full at the end of the three-year period, the annual rate of interest is figured as:

$$\frac{7}{100} \times 2{,}000 = \$140$$

As the loan is for three years, the total cost of the loan will be:

$$\$140 \times 3 = \$420$$

Annual percentage rate

When loans are repaid in installments, rather than a lump sum at the end of a loan period, then the flat rate of interest is not the true rate of interest because you are paying a portion of your initial sum borrowed along with any current interest due. The flat rate of interest then only applies to the first repayment period. After that the true rate of interest increases because you will have begun paying off the initial amount borrowed on the loan.

The true rate of interest on a loan is often referred to as the annual percentage rate (APR). A loan's APR is the average percentage rate for a 12-month period. Information about the rates of interest charged for loans and customer credit is typically accompanied by the equivalent APR, so that the consumer can make a realistic assessment of the cost of the loan. The APR can be calculated using:

$$\text{APR} = 100 \times \left[\left(1 + \frac{r}{100} \right)^n - 1 \right]$$

where r is the interest rate for a period less than one year, and n is the total number of such periods in one year.

For example, monthly repayments at an interest rate of $r = 2.5$ has an APR given by:

$$\text{APR} = 100 \times \left[\left(1 + \frac{2.5}{100}\right)^{12} - 1\right] = 34.49\%.$$

The table below lists the APR corresponding to a monthly repayment ($n = 12$) at an interest rate r given by adding a value, corresponding to the whole number part of the interest rate, in the far left column to a value, corresponding to the decimal part of the interest rate, in the top row. The APR in the example above, where $r = 2.5 = 2.0 + 0.5$, may be found from the intersection of the row containing 2.0 in the far left column with the column containing 0.5 in the top row, that is 34.5%.

Monthly interest rates and corresponding APRs

	0.0	0.1	0.2	0.3	0.4	0.5	0.6	0.7	0.8	0.9
0	0.0	1.2	2.4	3.7	4.9	6.2	7.4	8.7	10.0	11.4
1	12.7	14.0	15.4	16.8	18.2	19.6	21.0	22.4	23.9	25.3
2	26.8	28.3	29.8	31.4	32.9	34.5	36.1	37.7	39.3	40.9
3	42.6	44.2	45.9	47.6	49.4	51.1	52.9	54.6	56.4	58.3
4	60.1	62.0	63.8	65.7	67.7	69.6	71.5	73.5	75.5	77.5
5	79.6	81.6	83.7	85.8	88.0	90.1	92.3	94.5	96.7	99.0
6	101.2	103.5	105.8	108.2	110.5	112.9	115.3	117.8	120.2	122.7
7	125.2	127.8	130.3	132.9	135.5	138.2	140.9	143.6	146.3	149.0
8	151.8	154.6	157.5	160.3	163.2	166.2	169.1	172.1	175.1	178.2
9	181.3	184.4	187.5	190.7	193.9	197.1	200.4	203.7	207.1	210.4
10	213.8	217.3	220.8	224.3	227.8	231.4	235.0	238.7	242.4	246.1
11	249.8	253.6	257.5	261.4	265.3	269.2	273.2	277.3	281.3	285.4
12	289.6	293.8	298.0	302.3	306.6	311.0	315.4	319.8	324.3	328.9
13	333.5	338.1	342.7	347.5	352.2	357.0	361.9	366.8	371.7	376.7
14	381.8	386.9	392.0	397.2	402.5	407.8	413.1	418.5	424.0	429.5
15	435.0	440.6	446.3	452.0	457.8	463.6	469.5	475.4	481.4	487.5
16	493.6	499.8	506.0	512.3	518.6	525.0	531.5	538.0	544.6	551.3
17	558.0	564.8	571.6	578.5	585.5	592.6	599.7	606.8	614.1	621.4
18	628.8	636.2	643.7	651.3	659.0	666.7	674.5	682.4	690.3	698.3
19	706.4	714.6	722.8	731.2	739.6	748.0	756.6	765.2	773.9	782.7
20	791.6	800.6	809.6	818.7	827.9	837.2	846.6	856.1	865.6	875.2
21	885.0	894.8	904.7	914.7	924.8	934.9	945.2	955.6	966.0	976.6
22	987.2	998.0	1008.8	1019.7	1030.8	1041.9	1053.1	1064.5	1075.9	1087.5
23	1099.1	1110.9	1122.7	1134.7	1146.8	1158.9	1171.2	1183.6	1196.1	1208.7
24	1221.5	1234.3	1247.3	1260.4	1273.6	1286.9	1300.3	1313.8	1327.5	1341.3
25	1355.2	1369.2	1383.4	1397.7	1412.1	1426.6	1441.3	1456.0	1471.0	1486.0

If a sum of money P is borrowed and repaid as a lump sum I after a time n years has elapsed, then the APR can be calculated using:

$$APR = 100 \times \left[\left(1 + \frac{I - P}{P} \right)^{1/n} - 1 \right]$$

The table on page 57 can be used to help you practice the calculation above. Imagine you borrowed $100 and repaid a lump sum of $150 after 6 months (only a loan shark would expect this!), your calculation should look like this:

$$APR = 100 \times \left[\left(1 + \frac{150 - 100}{100} \right)^{1/0.5} - 1 \right]$$

$$= 125\%.$$

Now refer to the table to see if you are correct by locating the amount you paid ($150) in the far left column, scroll across the top column to find the number of months elapsed (6). The corresponding APR is indeed 125%.

Period and amount of loan and corresponding APRs

Amount	Number of months											
	1	2	3	4	5	6	7	8	9	10	11	12
100	0.0	0.0	0.0	0.0	0.0	0.0	0.0	0.0	0.0	0.0	0.0	0.0
101	12.7	6.2	4.1	3.0	2.4	2.0	1.7	1.5	1.3	1.2	1.1	1.0
102	26.8	12.6	8.2	6.1	4.9	4.0	3.5	3.0	2.7	2.4	2.2	2.0
103	42.6	19.4	12.6	9.3	7.4	6.1	5.2	4.5	4.0	3.6	3.3	3.0
104	60.1	26.5	17.0	12.5	9.9	8.2	7.0	6.1	5.4	4.8	4.4	4.0
105	79.6	34.0	21.6	15.8	12.4	10.3	8.7	7.6	6.7	6.0	5.5	5.0
106	101.2	41.9	26.2	19.1	15.0	12.4	10.5	9.1	8.1	7.2	6.6	6.0
107	125.2	50.1	31.1	22.5	17.6	14.5	12.3	10.7	9.4	8.5	7.7	7.0
108	151.8	58.7	36.0	26.0	20.3	16.6	14.1	12.2	10.8	9.7	8.8	8.0
109	181.3	67.7	41.2	29.5	23.0	18.8	15.9	13.8	12.2	10.9	9.9	9.0
110	213.8	77.2	46.4	33.1	25.7	21.0	17.7	15.4	13.6	12.1	11.0	10.0
111	249.8	87.0	51.8	36.8	28.5	23.2	19.6	16.9	14.9	13.3	12.1	11.0
112	289.6	97.4	57.4	40.5	31.3	25.4	21.4	18.5	16.3	14.6	13.2	12.0
113	333.5	108.2	63.0	44.3	34.1	27.7	23.3	20.1	17.7	15.8	14.3	13.0
114	381.8	119.5	68.9	48.2	37.0	30.0	25.2	21.7	19.1	17.0	15.4	14.0
115	435.0	131.3	74.9	52.1	39.9	32.2	27.1	23.3	20.5	18.3	16.5	15.0
116	493.6	143.6	81.1	56.1	42.8	34.6	29.0	24.9	21.9	19.5	17.6	16.0
117	558.0	156.5	87.4	60.2	45.8	36.9	30.9	26.6	23.3	20.7	18.7	17.0
118	628.8	170.0	93.9	64.3	48.8	39.2	32.8	28.2	24.7	22.0	19.8	18.0
119	706.4	184.0	100.5	68.5	51.8	41.6	34.7	29.8	26.1	23.2	20.9	19.0
120	791.6	198.6	107.4	72.8	54.9	44.0	36.7	31.5	27.5	24.5	22.0	20.0
121	885.0	213.8	114.4	77.2	58.0	46.4	38.6	33.1	28.9	25.7	23.1	21.0
122	987.2	229.7	121.5	81.6	61.2	48.8	40.6	34.8	30.4	26.9	24.2	22.0
123	1099.1	246.3	128.9	86.1	64.4	51.3	42.6	36.4	31.8	28.2	25.3	23.0
124	1221.5	263.5	136.4	90.7	67.6	53.8	44.6	38.1	33.2	29.5	26.4	24.0
125	1355.2	281.5	144.1	95.3	70.8	56.2	46.6	39.8	34.7	30.7	27.6	25.0
126	1501.2	300.2	152.0	100.0	74.1	58.8	48.6	41.4	36.1	32.0	28.7	26.0
127	1660.5	319.6	160.1	104.8	77.5	61.3	50.6	43.1	37.5	33.2	29.8	27.0
128	1834.3	339.8	168.4	109.7	80.8	63.8	52.7	44.8	39.0	34.5	30.9	28.0
129	2023.6	360.8	176.9	114.7	84.3	66.4	54.7	46.5	40.4	35.7	32.0	29.0
130	2229.8	382.7	185.6	119.7	87.7	69.0	56.8	48.2	41.9	37.0	33.1	30.0
131	2454.2	405.4	194.5	124.8	91.2	71.6	58.9	49.9	43.3	38.3	34.3	31.0
132	2698.3	429.0	203.6	130.0	94.7	74.2	61.0	51.7	44.8	39.5	35.4	32.0
133	2963.5	453.5	212.9	135.3	98.3	76.9	63.0	53.4	46.3	40.8	36.5	33.0
134	3251.6	478.9	222.4	140.6	101.9	79.6	65.2	55.1	47.7	42.1	37.6	34.0
135	3564.4	505.3	232.2	146.0	105.5	82.2	67.3	56.9	49.2	43.4	38.7	35.0
136	3903.7	532.8	242.1	151.5	109.2	85.0	69.4	58.6	50.7	44.6	39.9	36.0
137	4271.7	561.2	252.3	157.1	112.9	87.7	71.5	60.4	52.2	45.9	41.0	37.0
138	4670.3	590.7	262.7	162.8	116.6	90.4	73.7	62.1	53.6	47.2	42.1	38.0
139	5102.1	621.3	273.3	168.6	120.4	93.2	75.9	63.9	55.1	48.5	43.2	39.0
140	5569.4	653.0	284.2	174.4	124.2	96.0	78.0	65.7	56.6	49.7	44.3	40.0
141	6074.9	685.8	295.3	180.3	128.1	98.8	80.2	67.4	58.1	51.0	45.5	41.0
142	6621.4	719.8	306.6	186.3	132.0	101.6	82.4	69.2	59.6	52.3	46.6	42.0
143	7211.9	755.1	318.2	192.4	135.9	104.5	84.6	71.0	61.1	53.6	47.7	43.0
144	7849.7	791.6	330.0	198.6	139.9	107.4	86.8	72.8	62.6	54.9	48.9	44.0
145	8538.1	829.4	342.1	204.9	143.9	110.2	89.1	74.6	64.1	56.2	50.0	45.0
146	9280.7	868.5	354.4	211.2	148.0	113.2	91.3	76.4	65.6	57.5	51.1	46.0
147	10081.4	909.0	366.9	217.7	152.1	116.1	93.6	78.2	67.1	58.8	52.2	47.0
148	10944.4	950.9	379.8	224.2	156.2	119.0	95.8	80.0	68.7	60.1	53.4	48.0
149	11873.9	994.3	392.9	230.8	160.4	122.0	98.1	81.9	70.2	61.4	54.5	49.0
150	12874.6	1039.1	406.2	237.5	164.6	125.0	100.4	83.7	71.7	62.7	55.6	50.0

Mortgages

A mortgage refers to a transfer of property, usually a house, as a security for repayment of a loan. The loan is normally repaid to a bank or credit union over a period of years.

If r is the annual compound interest rate and n is the number of years for which the payment is made, then the equal annual payment p required to pay off a loan of one unit is given by:

$$p = \frac{r/100}{1 - [1 + r/100]^{-n}}$$

For example, if the interest rate is $r = 5\%$, one dollar is paid off after $n = 25$ years by an equal annual payment of $p = 0.0710$. What this is saying is that you are effectively paying 7 cents for every dollar borrowed given the terms of your loan. The tables below show how many cents per dollar you borrowed (p in the equation) that you must pay annually to repay a mortgage for n years if the annual compound interest rate is r.

To calculate the monthly payment on a mortgage of $60,000 over 15 years at $r = 6\%$, the table states that the yearly payment on one dollar with $n = 15$ and $r = 6$ is $p = 0.1030$. This means that the yearly payment on $60,000 is $60,000 \times 0.1030 = \$6,180$. The monthly payment is given by $\$6,180 \div 12 = \$515$.

Debt check

How can you tell if you are getting too far into debt? Here's a quick check to size up just how deep you're in:

- add up your monthly payments excluding housing
- multiply by 100
- divide this figure by your monthly take-home pay.

This figure will tell you the percentage going into monthly payments. Resource management specialists advise not to exceed 15–20% of your monthly take-home income. If you pay a high monthly rent or mortgage you will want to stick closer to the 15%; if you own your home or have a low mortgage, then 20% may be comfortable for you, provided you are investing in durable goods with long-term value.

Annual payments required to repay a mortgage

Years	Interest rates (%)							
	1.00	**2.50**	**5.00**	**5.50**	**6.00**	**6.50**	**7.00**	**7.50**
1	1.0100	1.0250	1.0500	1.0550	1.0600	1.0650	1.0700	1.0750
2	0.5075	0.5188	0.5378	0.5416	0.5454	0.5493	0.5531	0.5569
3	0.3400	0.3501	0.3672	0.3707	0.3741	0.3776	0.3811	0.3845
4	0.2563	0.2658	0.2820	0.2853	0.2886	0.2919	0.2952	0.2986
5	0.2060	0.2152	0.2310	0.2342	0.2374	0.2406	0.2439	0.2472
10	0.1056	0.1143	0.1295	0.1327	0.1359	0.1391	0.1424	0.1457
15	0.0721	0.0808	0.0963	0.0996	0.1030	0.1064	0.1098	0.1133
20	0.0554	0.0641	0.0802	0.0837	0.0872	0.0908	0.0944	0.0981
25	0.0454	0.0543	0.0710	0.0745	0.0782	0.0820	0.0858	0.0897
30	0.0387	0.0478	0.0651	0.0688	0.0726	0.0766	0.0806	0.0847

Years	Interest rates (%)									
	8.00	**8.50**	**9.00**	**9.50**	**10.00**	**10.50**	**11.00**	**11.50**	**12.00**	**12.50**
1	1.0800	1.0850	1.0900	1.0950	1.1000	1.1050	1.1100	1.1150	1.1200	1.1250
2	0.5608	0.5646	0.5685	0.5723	0.5762	0.5801	0.5839	0.5878	0.5917	0.5956
3	0.3880	0.3915	0.3951	0.3986	0.4021	0.4057	0.4092	0.4128	0.4163	0.4199
4	0.3019	0.3053	0.3087	0.3121	0.3155	0.3189	0.3223	0.3258	0.3292	0.3327
5	0.2505	0.2538	0.2571	0.2604	0.2638	0.2672	0.2706	0.2740	0.2774	0.2809
10	0.1490	0.1524	0.1558	0.1593	0.1627	0.1663	0.1698	0.1734	0.1770	0.1806
15	0.1168	0.1204	0.1241	0.1277	0.1315	0.1352	0.1391	0.1429	0.1468	0.1508
20	0.1019	0.1057	0.1095	0.1135	0.1175	0.1215	0.1256	0.1297	0.1339	0.1381
25	0.0937	0.0977	0.1018	0.1060	0.1102	0.1144	0.1187	0.1231	0.1275	0.1319
30	0.0888	0.0931	0.0973	0.1017	0.1061	0.1105	0.1150	0.1196	0.1241	0.1288

Years	Interest rates (%)									
	13.00	**14.00**	**15.00**	**16.00**	**17.00**	**18.00**	**19.00**	**20.00**	**21.00**	**22.00**
1	1.1300	1.1400	1.1500	1.1600	1.1700	1.1800	1.1900	1.2000	1.2100	1.2200
2	0.5995	0.6073	0.6151	0.6230	0.6308	0.6387	0.6466	0.6545	0.6625	0.6705
3	0.4235	0.4307	0.4380	0.4453	0.4526	0.4599	0.4673	0.4747	0.4822	0.4897
4	0.3362	0.3432	0.3503	0.3574	0.3645	0.3717	0.3790	0.3863	0.3936	0.4010
5	0.2843	0.2913	0.2983	0.3054	0.3126	0.3198	0.3271	0.3344	0.3418	0.3492
10	0.1843	0.1917	0.1993	0.2069	0.2147	0.2225	0.2305	0.2385	0.2467	0.2549
15	0.1547	0.1628	0.1710	0.1794	0.1878	0.1964	0.2051	0.2139	0.2228	0.2317
20	0.1424	0.1510	0.1598	0.1687	0.1777	0.1868	0.1960	0.2054	0.2147	0.2242
25	0.1364	0.1455	0.1547	0.1640	0.1734	0.1829	0.1925	0.2021	0.2118	0.2215
30	0.1334	0.1428	0.1523	0.1619	0.1715	0.1813	0.1910	0.2008	0.2107	0.2206

Inflation

Inflation describes a persistent increase in prices and corresponding fall in the purchasing value of money. The factor F by which the purchasing value of money will decrease may be calculated using the formula:

$$F = \frac{1}{(1 + r/100)^n}$$

where r is the annual rate of inflation and n is the number of years.

The table on page 61 gives a list of the decrease factors associated with a given number of years for particular inflation rates. For example, over ten years at 7% inflation, the purchasing value of a dollar will approximately halve:

$$F = \frac{1}{(1 + 7/100)^{10}} = 0.51$$

Consumer price index

Inflation is measured in the USA by the consumer price index (CPI). This official measurement is calculated on a monthly basis by taking a sample of goods and services that the typical household might buy, such as food, heating, housing, household goods, transportation, and medical expenses. The value of the index for a particular month measures the ratio of the overall level of prices in that month to the overall level of prices on a date at which the index was fixed at a starting value of 100. That date is called the base date, and has no other significance other than that it has been chosen as an agreed reference point.

Decrease factors associated with a number of years for particular inflation rates

Years	Inflation rate (%)									
	0.5	1.0	1.5	2.0	2.5	3.0	3.5	4.0	4.5	5.0
1	0.995	0.990	0.985	0.980	0.976	0.971	0.966	0.962	0.957	0.952
2	0.990	0.980	0.971	0.961	0.952	0.943	0.934	0.925	0.916	0.907
3	0.985	0.971	0.956	0.942	0.929	0.915	0.902	0.889	0.876	0.864
4	0.980	0.961	0.942	0.924	0.906	0.888	0.871	0.855	0.839	0.823
5	0.975	0.951	0.928	0.906	0.884	0.863	0.842	0.822	0.802	0.784
6	0.971	0.942	0.915	0.888	0.862	0.837	0.814	0.790	0.768	0.746
7	0.966	0.933	0.901	0.871	0.841	0.813	0.786	0.760	0.735	0.711
8	0.961	0.923	0.888	0.853	0.821	0.789	0.759	0.731	0.703	0.677
9	0.956	0.914	0.875	0.837	0.801	0.766	0.734	0.703	0.673	0.645
10	0.951	0.905	0.862	0.820	0.781	0.744	0.709	0.676	0.644	0.614
15	0.928	0.861	0.800	0.743	0.690	0.642	0.597	0.555	0.517	0.481
20	0.905	0.820	0.742	0.673	0.610	0.554	0.503	0.456	0.415	0.377
25	0.883	0.780	0.689	0.610	0.539	0.478	0.423	0.375	0.333	0.295
30	0.861	0.742	0.640	0.552	0.477	0.412	0.356	0.308	0.267	0.231
35	0.840	0.706	0.594	0.500	0.421	0.355	0.300	0.253	0.214	0.181
40	0.819	0.672	0.551	0.453	0.372	0.307	0.253	0.208	0.172	0.142
45	0.799	0.639	0.512	0.410	0.329	0.264	0.213	0.171	0.138	0.111
50	0.779	0.608	0.475	0.372	0.291	0.228	0.179	0.141	0.111	0.087
55	0.760	0.579	0.441	0.337	0.257	0.197	0.151	0.116	0.089	0.068
60	0.741	0.550	0.409	0.305	0.227	0.170	0.127	0.095	0.071	0.054

Years	Inflation rate (%)									
	5.5	6.0	6.5	7.0	7.5	8.0	8.5	9.0	9.5	10.0
1	0.948	0.943	0.939	0.935	0.930	0.926	0.922	0.917	0.913	0.909
2	0.898	0.890	0.882	0.873	0.865	0.857	0.849	0.842	0.834	0.826
3	0.852	0.840	0.828	0.816	0.805	0.794	0.783	0.772	0.762	0.751
4	0.807	0.792	0.777	0.763	0.749	0.735	0.722	0.708	0.696	0.683
5	0.765	0.747	0.730	0.713	0.697	0.681	0.665	0.650	0.635	0.621
6	0.725	0.705	0.685	0.666	0.648	0.630	0.613	0.596	0.580	0.564
7	0.687	0.665	0.644	0.623	0.603	0.583	0.565	0.547	0.530	0.513
8	0.652	0.627	0.604	0.582	0.561	0.540	0.521	0.502	0.484	0.467
9	0.618	0.592	0.567	0.544	0.522	0.500	0.480	0.460	0.442	0.424
10	0.585	0.558	0.533	0.508	0.485	0.463	0.442	0.422	0.404	0.386
15	0.448	0.417	0.389	0.362	0.338	0.315	0.294	0.275	0.256	0.239
20	0.343	0.312	0.284	0.258	0.235	0.215	0.196	0.178	0.163	0.149
25	0.262	0.233	0.207	0.184	0.164	0.146	0.130	0.116	0.103	0.092
30	0.201	0.174	0.151	0.131	0.114	0.099	0.087	0.075	0.066	0.057
35	0.154	0.130	0.110	0.094	0.080	0.068	0.058	0.049	0.042	0.036
40	0.117	0.097	0.081	0.067	0.055	0.046	0.038	0.032	0.027	0.022
45	0.090	0.073	0.059	0.048	0.039	0.031	0.025	0.021	0.017	0.014
50	0.069	0.054	0.043	0.034	0.027	0.021	0.017	0.013	0.011	0.009
55	0.053	0.041	0.031	0.024	0.019	0.015	0.011	0.009	0.007	0.005
60	0.040	0.030	0.023	0.017	0.013	0.010	0.007	0.006	0.004	0.003

CPI Market Basket

To measure price increases, the Bureau of Labor Statistics (BLS) constructs an imaginary "market basket" of goods that includes what they estimate the average family needs on a regular basis. Specific items relating to housing, food, transportation, medical care, clothing, entertainment, education, and communication are selected for inclusion. There are approximately 80,000 items currently in the basket.

The BLS collects price data for these items on a monthly basis from 22,500 specific outlets and 7,300 specific housing units in 44 urban areas. Prices for identical goods are averaged, and individual price indices are calculated for each item and geographic area. The individual price indices are then added to get the price of the entire market basket.

The final price is a weighted sum to reflect the amount of money spent on different categories and differences in geographic buying preferences. The table below shows recent weightings for the broadest item categories:

Category	Weighting (%)
Housing	39.6
Transportation	17.6
Food	16.3
Entertainment	6.1
Medical care	5.6
Education and communication	5.5
Apparel and upkeep	4.9
Other	4.3

Monthly Consumer Price Index – US since 1991

Not Seasonally Adjusted

Area: US city average

Item: All items

Base Period: 1982–84 = 100

Year	Jan	Feb	Mar	Apr	May	Jun	Jul	Aug	Sep	Oct	Nov	Dec	Annual average	Half 1	Half 2
1991	134.6	134.8	135.0	135.2	135.6	136.0	136.2	136.6	137.2	137.4	137.8	137.9	136.2	135.2	137.2
1992	138.1	138.6	139.3	139.5	139.7	140.2	140.5	140.9	141.3	141.8	142.0	141.9	140.3	139.2	141.4
1993	142.6	143.1	143.6	144.0	144.2	144.4	144.4	144.8	145.1	145.7	145.8	145.8	144.5	143.7	145.3
1994	146.2	146.7	147.2	147.4	147.5	148.0	148.4	149.0	149.4	149.5	149.7	149.7	148.2	147.2	149.3
1995	150.3	150.9	151.4	151.9	152.2	152.5	152.5	152.9	153.2	153.7	153.6	153.5	152.4	151.5	153.2
1996	154.4	154.9	155.7	156.3	156.6	156.7	157.0	157.3	157.8	158.3	158.6	158.6	156.9	155.8	157.9
1997	159.1	159.6	160.0	160.2	160.1	160.3	160.5	160.8	161.2	161.6	161.5	161.3	160.5	159.9	161.2
1998	161.6	161.9	162.2	162.5	162.8	163.0	163.2	163.4	163.6	164.0	164.0	163.9	163.0	162.3	163.7
1999	164.3	164.5	165.0	166.2	166.2	166.2	166.7	167.1	167.9	168.2	168.3	168.3	166.6	165.4	167.8
2000	168.8	169.8	171.2	171.3	171.5	172.4	172.8	172.8	173.7	174.0	174.1	174.0	172.2	170.8	173.6
2001	175.1	175.8	176.2	176.9	177.7	178.0	177.5							176.6	

Calculating Index Changes

Index fluctuations from one month to another are generally expressed as percent changes rather than changes in index points, because index point changes are affected by the level of the index in relation to its base period while percent changes are not.

The example below illustrates the computation of index point and percent changes.

Index Point Change	
CPI	152.4
Less previous index	148.2
Equals index point change	4.2

Percent Change	
Index point difference	4.2
Divided by the previous index	148.2
Equals	0.028
Results multiplied by one hundred	0.028×100
Equals percent change	2.8%

US Annual Consumer Price Index 1950–95

Year	CPI
1950	24.1
1951	26.0
1952	26.5
1953	26.7
1954	26.9
1955	26.8
1956	27.2
1957	28.1
1958	28.9
1959	29.1
1960	29.6
1961	29.9
1962	30.2
1963	30.6
1964	31.0
1965	31.5
1966	32.4
1967	33.4
1968	34.8
1969	36.7
1970	38.9
1971	40.5
1972	41.8
1973	44.4
1974	49.3
1975	53.8
1976	56.9
1977	60.6
1978	65.3
1979	72.5
1980	82.4
1981	90.9
1982	96.5
1983	99.6
1984	103.9
1985	107.6
1986	109.6
1987	113.6
1988	118.3
1989	124.0
1990	130.7
1991	136.2
1992	140.3
1993	144.5
1994	148.2
1995	152.4

The effects of inflation on savings

One of the first things to understand about your money is that left untouched, it will actually decrease in value over time. Imagine putting $10,000 cash in a safe in your house for ten years. If inflation is running at an annual rate of 2%, then in ten years time, your savings will only have the purchasing power of $8,200.

Likewise, investing in a standard savings account may appear a safe bet in terms of knowing how much you will have at the end of the deposit period. It is certainly safe in that you will not be exposed to some of the financial risks of, say, stock-market investments. However, if you placed your investment in a 3% simple interest-bearing account for a five-year period, but the average rate of inflation was running at 5%, then you could be losing as much as 2% of the value of your investment every year.

So to protect the real value of your capital, you need to allow for inflation and consider investments that will give you **capital growth** as well.

A sustainable savings account

Given a large sum of money invested at a fixed rate of interest that keeps pace with inflationary growth, it is useful to know how long it would last if a fixed percentage of the initial sum were withdrawn each year. The following table illustrates how many years such a savings account can be sustained. Note that blank entries occur where the withdrawal rate is smaller than the interest rate implying that the account could be sustained indefinitely.

The number of years a savings account can be sustained when a fixed percentage of the initial sum is withdrawn each year

Withdrawal rate (%)	Interest rate (%)						
	3	4	5	6	7	8	9
4	46						
5	30	41					
6	23	28	36				
7	18	21	25	33			
8	15	17	20	23	30		
9	13	14	16	18	22	28	
10	12	13	14	15	17	20	26

Saving for Retirement

Investing a portion of your salary on a regular basis to ensure that you will have a nest egg when you retire is one of the most important things a sound financial planner can do. The following table helps to decide what proportion of a salary must be set aside in order to accumulate a nest egg equal to a final year's income. For example, to fund a retirement 25 years from now that is equal to a final year's salary, given that the yearly earnings have risen 5.75% per year, the table states that 4.2% of the salary must be set aside each year.

Retirement funding

Years to retirement	Level* salary (%)	Salary increased by 5.75% per year (%)
5	18.1	19.8
10	8.0	10.1
15	4.6	6.8
20	3.0	5.2
25	2.1	4.2
30	1.5	3.6

*i.e., a salary that does not change; can also be used to mean in line with inflation if the final amount of the nest egg is to reflect the future cost of living

Stocks and Shares

One of the most controversial ways to earn on your investments is to play the stock market. The image of a high-rolling, cigar-smoking gambler immediately springs to mind for many who fear high risks attached to stock market investments. The reality, however, could not be further from the truth. Investing in the stock market may prove over time to be the wisest way of managing your money.

The Dow-Jones Industrial Average is a weighted average of the equity prices (prices of stocks and shares) of thirty industrial stocks quoted on the New York Stock Exchange. **The FTSE 100 Share Index** is a weighted average of the equity prices of the 100 largest companies quoted on the London Stock Exchange. The following table shows the levels of both these indices along with their yearly percentage change. This table becomes all the more interesting from an investment perspective when you compare the % change per year of the Dow-Jones with the annual rate of inflation using the Consumer Price Index chart (on page 64).

Stocks and shares – basic terms

Rate of return ratio that expresses the profits generated as a percentage of the capital employed in a company.

Earnings profits available for shareholders after payment of interest and dividends.

Earnings per share total earnings divided by the number of ordinary shares.

Dividends amount of a company's profits that are distributed to the ordinary shareholders; usually expressed either as a percentage of the nominal value of the ordinary share capital or as an absolute amount per share.

Price per earnings ratio (P/E ratio) quoted price of an ordinary share divided by the year's earnings per share.

Earnings yield ratio of earnings per share divided by price per share expressed as a percentage.

Dividends yield ratio of gross dividend per share divided by price per share expressed as a percentage.

Nominal value the face value of a share – expressed in current money prices without adjustment for changes in prices over time.

Dow-Jones and FTSE Industrial Average indices and their yearly percentage changes

Year end	FTSE 100 Index (£)	% change per year	Dow Jones Industrial Average ($)	% change per year
1981	684.3	5.7	875.0	–9.2
1982	834.3	21.9	1046.6	19.6
1983	1000	19.9	1258.6	20.3
1984	1232.2	23.2	1211.6	–3.7
1985	1412.6	14.6	1546.7	27.7
1986	1679	18.9	1896.0	22.6
1987	1712.7	2.0	1938.8	2.3
1988	1793.1	4.7	2168.6	11.8
1989	2422.7	35.1	2735.2	27.0
1990	2143.5	-11.5	2633.7	–4.3
1991	2493.1	16.3	3168.8	20.3
1992	2846.5	14.2	3301.1	4.2
1993	3418.4	20.1	3754.1	13.7
1994	3065.5	-10.3	3834.4	2.1
1995	3689.3	20.3	5117.1	33.5
1996	4118.5	11.6	6448.3	26.0
1997	5135.5	24.7	7908.3	22.6

Long-term investment strategies

The following chart makes it easy to see that earning 5% interest on a typical interest-bearing account pales to the amount one could hope to earn at rates of 10% to 20% over a long period of time. It is over time that the stock market has historically been the best place to put your money.

$100 invested at various growth rates

Year	5%	10%	15%	20%
2000	$100	$100	$100	$100
2005	$128	$161	$201	$249
2010	$163	$259	$405	$619
2015	$208	$418	$814	$1,541
2025	$339	$1,083	$3,292	$9,540
2035	$552	$2,810	$13,318	$59,067
2045	$899	$7,289	$53,877	$365,726
2050	$1,147	$11,739	$108,366	$910,044

Why is this? Because if you're getting, say, a guaranteed 5% a year, then you might be missing out on the average 12.2% (over the past 80 years) that a stock market index fund could have been gaining for you, perhaps even larger gains if you prefer riskier strategies. While it is true that you are protected from losing your initial investment if you take the conservative bank account route, you could also be kept from more lucrative rewards.

Saving for Children

Investing in your child's future is an incredibly gratifying experience if you are fortunate enough to be in a position to save any money at all. Taking every opportunity you get to save and invest for your child now will reap generous rewards when they reach adulthood.

- Resist the urge to buy superfluous things when family and friends give children cash presents.

- Place a small sum per month in a separate interest-bearing account in the child's name.

Opening your child's account

You can open a bank or credit union account for each of your children, into which all of their savings should go. The account can be opened in the child's name with you as the custodian. This means that while you have control of the account, the money is treated as theirs, and they will be able to take control of it when they reach legal age.

Take advantage of educational savings accounts for your children if you can. These are designed to help families save for their children's college, although it is hoped that the accounts will eventually extend to elementary and secondary education. Parents receive tax breaks via educational savings accounts that they would not receive under normal savings accounts.

Encouraging your child to save their allowance and to put some in their account is a smart way of introducing them to the wild world of personal finance. They will enjoy watching their bank balance grow as they get older.

Stock market investments for children

Once you have built up a reasonable sum of money in your child's bank account, you might consider buying shares in **blue chip companies**, companies you can rely on for long-term dividends and basically forget about, until your children come of age. Again, think long-term. You need to be able to tuck the money away for a minimum of five years – preferably longer. Remember too that you should always monitor the performance of the companies in which you have invested and stick with them unless you can find somewhere better to invest the money.

Buying shares in your child's name

If you are buying shares for your child, you are likely to do so in a custodial account. You are the custodian for the child, looking after the investment until the child reaches the legal age in their states, typically 18 or 21.

The advantage of investing for your child is that children have time on their side and you can keep adding to their investments over the years. Just as you would on your own investments, beware of initial charges or exit fees, plus annual management charges and taxes on earnings. All of these can add up and take away from your, and their, hard-earned money.

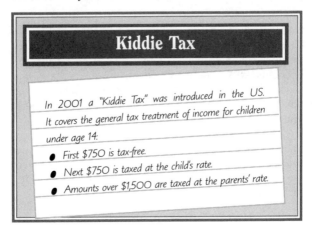

Kiddie Tax

In 2001 a "Kiddie Tax" was introduced in the US. It covers the general tax treatment of income for children under age 14:
- First $750 is tax-free.
- Next $750 is taxed at the child's rate.
- Amounts over $1,500 are taxed at the parents' rate.

Tax-Free Savings

Very little in the world of finance comes for free. While there are such things as tax-free investments, you need to read the fine print very carefully to understand the terms and possible drawbacks to such investments.

Comparison between tax-free investments and taxable investments is often required when making a decision about the most appropriate savings plan. One way to approach such a financial decision is to calculate the effective yield y % that would be earned from an equivalent taxable investment. Suppose that your income tax bracket is t % and that the tax-free investment yields r %, then the effective taxable yield is:

$$y = \frac{100 \times r}{100 - t}$$

The following table gives some further examples of the conversions between tax-free and taxable investments at the 30% income-tax bracket. For example, an 8% tax-free investment corresponds to an 11.43% taxable investment.

Conversions between tax-free and taxable investments at a 30% income-tax bracket

Tax-free yield	Taxable yield	Tax-free yield	Taxable yield
0.25	0.36	10.25	14.64
0.50	0.71	10.50	15.00
0.75	1.07	10.75	15.36
1.00	1.43	11.00	15.91
1.25	1.77	11.25	16.07
1.50	2.14	11.50	16.43
1.75	2.50	11.75	16.79
2.00	2.86	12.00	17.14
2.25	3.21	12.25	17.50
2.50	3.57	12.50	17.86
2.75	3.93	12.75	18.21
3.00	4.29	13.00	18.59
3.25	4.64	13.25	18.93
3.50	5.00	13.50	19.29
3.75	5.36	13.75	19.64
4.00	5.71	14.00	20.00
4.25	6.07	14.25	20.36
4.50	6.43	14.50	20.79
4.75	6.79	14.75	21.07
5.00	7.14	15.00	21.43
5.25	7.50	15.25	21.79
5.50	7.86	15.50	22.14
5.75	8.21	15.75	22.50
6.00	8.59	16.00	22.86
6.25	8.93	16.25	23.21
6.50	9.29	16.50	23.57
6.75	9.64	16.75	23.93
7.00	10.00	17.00	24.29
7.25	10.36	17.25	24.64
7.50	10.71	17.50	25.00
7.75	11.07	17.75	25.36
8.00	11.43	18.00	25.71
8.25	11.76	18.25	26.07
8.50	12.04	18.50	26.43
8.75	12.50	18.75	26.79
9.00	12.86	19.00	27.14
9.25	13.21	19.25	27.50
9.50	13.57	19.50	27.86
9.75	13.93	19.75	28.21
10.00	14.29	20.00	28.57

Checking accounts with Benford's law

Lists of numbers generated by a variety of natural processes follow a similar pattern, which is called Benford's law. This law states that the digit d appears as the first digit with a frequency proportional to $\log10(1 + 1/d)$, meaning that 1 is expected to appear as the first digit in about 30% of cases, 2 in 18% of cases, 3 in 12%, 4 in 9%, 5 in 8%. The second digit is most likely to be 0, appearing in 12% of cases, whereas 9 is the most unlikely, appearing in 8.5% of cases. This law has been shown to describe the frequency of digits occurring in many sources of data including logarithm tables, census data, stock market prices, and population figures. Benford's law has recently been applied to sales figures to detect tax evasion and fraud. A frequency analysis of accounts is used to help auditors decide whether or not books have been modified.

Home

From taps to tables, gardening to gadgets, there is no end to the numbers you will meet around the house. In this section we take a look at how numbers make your everyday life easier and much more comfortable!

Power Sources

Electricity is one of the basic physical forces of the universe, generated by the motion of tiny charged atomic particles (electrons and protons). Electrical power is the rate at which an electrical machine uses electrical energy or converts it into other forms of energy – for example, light, heat, and mechanical energy. Power is usually measured in **watts**. It is equal to the product of the voltage and the current flowing.

An electric bulb that passes a current of 0.4 amperes (units that measure the flow of current through a system) at 250 volts uses 100 watts of electrical power and converts it into light and heat – in ordinary terms it is a 100-watt bulb. An electric motor that requires 6 amperes at the same voltage consumes 1,500 watts (1.5 kilowatts), equivalent to delivering about 2 horsepower of mechanical power.

The following table gives a list of household electrical appliances with examples of their power ratings.

Power ratings of household electrical appliances (approx)

Electrical appliance	Power consumption (watts)
Lamp	60–100
Hair dryer	1,600
Water heater	2,500
Air conditioner	1,500
Kitchen range	8,000
Microwave	800–1,500
Refrigerator/freezer	450–550
Toaster	1,200
Washing machine	1,000
Clothes dryer	4,400
Vacuum cleaner	1,200
Computer	500
Television	200
VCR	25

Watt, James (1736–1819)

Scottish engineer who developed the steam engine in the 1760s, making Thomas Newcomen's engine vastly more efficient by cooling the used steam in a condenser separate from the main cylinder. He eventually made a double-acting machine that supplied power with both directions of the piston and developed rotary motion. The modern unit of power, the **watt**, is named after him.

Watt also devised the horsepower as a description of an engine's rate of working. Looking to cash in on his mechanical advances, Watt developed a rational method to compare the capability of his engines to the rate at which horses worked, so that farmers and industrialists would cough up the money they would normally spend on their animal power. After many experiments, he concluded that one 'horsepower' was 33,000 lb raised through 1 ft each minute. The English-speaking world used horsepower to describe the capability of an engine until recent years. Note that one horsepower equals 1.34 kilowatts.

Blowing fuses

From time to time, household electrical systems shut down because of an overload of power demand on the circuit. This usually results from operating a number of power-intense appliances at the same time. The fuse or circuit-breaker box monitors the electrical current (measured in amperes) flowing around the circuit. Fuses are rated by the number of amperes of current they can tolerate before the piece of metal inside them melts and breaks the circuit. A 30-amp fused circuit will tolerate 30 amperes of current before it blows, or shuts down.

The total power load, P watts, which each circuit can support, may be calculated by multiplying the threshold current, A amperes, by the voltage, V volts, delivered by the electricity company:

 $P = A \times V$

For a 15 ampere fused circuit with 240 volts, the maximum power load that can be supported is 3,600 watts.

Energy saving

To find ways of saving energy, it is useful to determine the energy consumption of different electrical appliances. Almost all electrical appliances are labeled with a power consumption rating, typically measured in **watts** (W) or **kilowatts** (kW).

The amount of energy consumed depends on how long the appliance is using electricity, so the typical units are **kilowatt hours** (kWh). The formula for calculating the energy consumed E given the power P and time t is:

 $E = P \times t$

If an electrical appliance has a power consumption rate P kW, then t hours of use will equate to a consumption of $(P \times t)$ kWh of energy. For example, burning a 100 W light bulb for 10 hours uses 1,000 watts or 1 kWh. Similarly, using an electric toaster with a power consumption rating of 1 kW for 1 hour uses 1 kWh of energy.

Electrical energy is typically priced in units of kWh. By calculating the amount of kWh, it is possible to determine the financial saving implied by various actions.

Example

How much power can a 100 W light bulb burning all year long consume, assuming around-the-clock use?

Solution

100 W × 365 days = 36,500
36,500 × 24 hours = 876,000 W or 876 kWh
Given the cost of one kWh of electrical energy (say 1 kWh = $0.05), the cost of burning the light bulb all year long is:
$0.05 × 876 = $43.80.

How to read your electricity meter

Houses are generally equipped with two different types of electric meters: digital display and dial meters. Each show your accumulated kilowatt-hour usage. Parts of the country are now introducing energy conservation surcharges in addition to the standard usage charges, so it is worth it to familiarize yourself with your electric company's bill and work out the math yourself to get a true picture of what you are paying for your electricity.

Digital meters

A digital meter is easy enough to read. Simply write down the numbers shown from left to right. Subtract this reading from your previous reading to get your usage rate.

Dial meters

The most important thing to remember is that the dials next to each other go around in opposite directions. To get your meter reading, you need to check the direction of the top four or five dials. If you have an additional dial beneath, ignore it – it is only there for testing purposes.

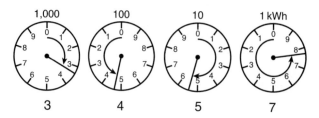

Read the dials from left to right. Write down the number that the pointer has just passed, regardless of whether the pointer is closer to the next number. If for example, the pointer is anywhere between 4 and 5, write down 4. The meter reading example shown will be 3 4 5 7.

Note – If the pointer is between 9 and 0, write down 9.

It is advisable to read your meter regularly, at about the same time each month or week. Then follow this formula to determine your kilowatt-hour usage:

- Subtract the previous reading from the current reading.

- Multiply the difference by the conversion formula used by your electricity company to convert units to kilowatt-hours.

- Multiply your kilowatt-hours by the rate charged by your electricity company to find the cost of your usage for the period you are assessing. Remember you may also have to pay a service charge and an energy conservation surcharge on top of your usage.

Example

If last month's electric meter reading was 8371 and this month is 9648, how many units of energy have been used and how much will you be charged if your rate is 11.04 cents per unit?

Solution

9648 − 8371 = 1,277 units
1,277 × $0.11 = $140.98
If you had additional charges of $19.30 and were charged 6% tax on the total, your bill for the period would be:

$140.98 + $19.30 = $160.28
0.06 × $160.28 = $ 9.62
$169.90   Total amount due

How to read your gas meter

Digital meters

To read a digital type meter, simply read the numbers from left to right. The meter reading in the example is 6842 (hundreds of cubic feet). Gas usage is usually converted into units of **therms**.

Dial or "clock" meters

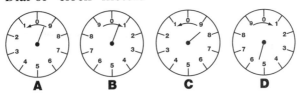

| A | B | C | D |

Your gas meter registers the amount of gas consumed in units of 100 cubic feet. When reading your dial meter, always remember that dials next to each other go around in opposite directions. Read the dials from left to right and write down the number that the hand has passed. This meter reads 9085.

Note – If the pointer is between two figures, write down the lower number. However, if the pointer is between 9 and 0, write down 9.

You will now need to subtract your previous reading from your current reading to work out the number of cubic feet of gas used.

Sliding scales

Electric and gas bills are often calculated on a sliding scale. A sliding scale refers to a variable pricing structure based on different levels of usage.

Example

A gas bill indicates a period usage of 32 therms. The first 15 therms of usage is priced at $1.08552 per therm and the remainder at $1.26821. What is the total cost for usage?

Solution

Cost of gas used
15 × $1.08552 = $16.28
<u>17</u> × $1.26821 = <u>$21.56</u>
32                      $37.84 total cost of gas used

Do It Yourself

The key to successful do-it-yourself projects is sound measurement and estimation. These next few sections will give you hints and tips on how to measure just about anything around your house for whatever your latest home improvement project might be.

Dimensions

The **dimension** of something is its actual measurement or size. When people refer to a "two by four", they mean a board that is two inches deep by four inches wide. Those are its dimensions (excepting its length, which of course can vary).

Measuring room areas

To purchase the right amount of material to have a room carpeted, or a wall tiled or wallpapered, it is necessary to calculate the total surface area of the floor or walls of a room. A number of formulas exist for simple geometrical shapes and these may be used to help compute areas for more complicated shapes. By breaking the surface into a number of smaller fragments, it is usually possible to calculate these areas separately and to add them together to get the total area.

Rectangular rooms

If the room is rectangular in shape, then the area A is simply the length l multiplied by the breadth b, that is:

$A = l \times b$

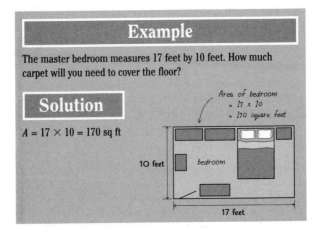

Example

The master bedroom measures 17 feet by 10 feet. How much carpet will you need to cover the floor?

Solution

$A = 17 \times 10 = 170$ sq ft

Area of bedroom
= 17 x 10
= 170 square feet

10 feet

bedroom

17 feet

Odd-shaped rooms

Perhaps you have an L-shaped or T-shaped room. No problem. Simply break the room down into squares and rectangles if you can, figure out their individual areas and then add the areas together to get the total area.

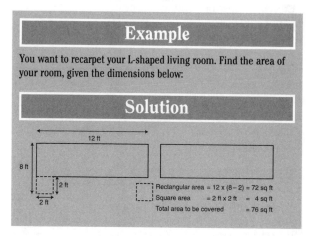

Example

You want to recarpet your L-shaped living room. Find the area of your room, given the dimensions below:

Solution

12 ft

8 ft

2 ft

2 ft

Rectangular area = 12 x (8 – 2) = 72 sq ft
Square area   = 2 ft x 2 ft = 4 sq ft
Total area to be covered   = 76 sq ft

Some rooms may have an extra semicircular alcove for a bay window. The area of a full circular disc is given by π times the radius r squared:

 $A = \pi \times r^2$

and the area of a semicircular disc is simply half this:

$A = \dfrac{\pi \times r^2}{2}$

For irregular shaped rooms, it may be easiest to first divide the floor area into a number of triangles. The area A of a triangle is given by half the length b of its base multiplied by its height h (the vertical distance from the base of the opposite apex):

$A = \dfrac{h \times b}{2}$

For information on how to calculate the areas of various shapes, see *Brushing Up*, pages 26–31.

Comparing house prices

Now that you know how to calculate the floor space in your house, you can compare two properties of different sizes to calculate the cost per unit floor area. The cost per unit area may be calculated using:

$$\text{cost per unit area} = \frac{\text{price}}{\text{area}}$$

Example

Suppose that house A has a price of $100,000 and a total floor area of 1,100 sq ft and house B costs $120,000 with a floor area of 1,400 sq ft. Assuming the same quality of building and location, which house is the better value?

Solution

House A = $100,000 ÷ 1,100 sq ft = $90.90 per sq ft
House B = $120,000 ÷ 1,400 sq ft = $85.70 per sq ft
The result implies that house B is better value for money.
Note there are many factors associated with the purchase and valuation of a house. Your personal preferences will determine whether or not this sort of calculation is useful to you.

How much wallpaper?

Making sure you have enough wallpaper is one of the most nail-biting jobs in the home. Too much and you've wasted money; not enough is a major inconvenience. The table below will give you a pretty basic rule of thumb on how many rolls you will need to paper your walls. Simply match the height of your walls to the width, to find out how many rolls you will probably need. Remember that certain patterns need to be matched carefully and will require extra rolls. For more complicated designs, it is best to get an expert's advice.

Number of wallpaper rolls needed for given height and width of walls

Height (feet)	Width (feet)								
	23	28	33	38	43	48	53	58	63
8	4	4	5	6	6	7	8	9	9
9	4	5	5	6	7	8	8	9	9
9–12	5	6	7	8	9	10	11	12	13
12	7	9	10	12	13	15	16	18	19

What volume of paint?

To calculate the volume of paint required, it is best to start by measuring the total area of the surfaces that are to be painted. Most paint cans have a coverage estimate and the number of cans needed may be calculated by dividing this estimate into the total area. The average amount of paint needed to cover 400 square feet would be one gallon.

To estimate paint coverage for a 10 by 12 room, simply determine its size in square footage; in this case it is 120 square feet. Then divide it by 400 to determine the number of gallons needed.

How many tiles?

Given the total area of a floor or wall, it is straightforward to calculate how many tiles this will take and how much it will cost to tile this area. Suppose the total surface area is A, the area of each tile is t, and the cost per tile is P. The number of tiles required is:

 $N = A / t$

and the total price is $N \times P$. The same calculation can be used to measure the amount and price of carpet and floorboards.

Number of tiles needed to cover a given area

Tile size		Quantity required	
US (in.)	Metric (mm)	Per sq yard	Per sq meter
4 × 4	100 × 100	84	100
4.25 × 4.25	108 × 108	72	86
6 × 6	150 × 150	36	44
8 × 4	200 × 100	41	50
8 × 6	200 × 150	27	33
8 × 8	200 × 200	20	25
9 × 6	225 × 150	24	29
9 × 9	225 × 225	16	20
10 × 6	250 × 150	22	27
10 × 10	250 × 250	13	16
12 × 8	295 × 295	14	17
12 × 12	300 × 300	9	11
13 × 13	330 × 330	8	9

Measuring curtain fabric

Begin by calculating the position and length of the pole used for holding up the curtains. Measure the distance between the curtain pole and either the windowsill or the floor. Allow an extra 6–10 in. for hems and heading, depending on the material weight. The width of the fabric depends on the type of heading; twice the length of the pole for pencil and pinch pleats and triple the length of the pole for sheer fabrics. Add an extra 1.5 in. for each side seam and each internal seam.

Bed sizes

Given that we toss and turn between 40 and 60 times a night and will spend the next three out of ten years in bed, selecting the right mattress size is no small matter. Below is an average mattress size chart. Variations between manufacturers will occur.

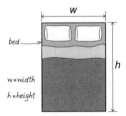

bed

w = width
h = height

Average mattress sizes

Size	Width	Dimensions (inches)
Twin/Single	3'3"	39 × 75
Long Twin	3'3"	39 × 80
Full/Double	4'6"	54 × 75
Queen	5'0"	60 × 80
Eastern King	6'4"	76 × 80
California King	6'0"	72 × 84

Outside Help
Gardening design

Planning and designing your dream garden begins with making the best use of the space you have available. Using your knowledge of measuring different shapes, you can create separate areas for planting, playing, and lush green lawns.

Example

Suppose you have a yard that is 25 feet by 40 feet. You want to a make a circular herb garden, build a sandbox for the children, and cover the rest with lawn. How much space (to the nearest square foot) will you have for lawn and sandbox if the diameter of the herb garden is 15 feet?

Solution

Total area of the yard =
25 ft × 40 ft = 1,000 sq ft
Diameter of herb garden = 15 ft
Radius of herb garden = 7.5 ft
Area of the herb garden = πr^2 =
$\qquad$ 3.14 × 7.5² =
$\qquad$ 3.14 × 56.25
$\qquad$ = 176.63 sq ft
So rounding up, the herb garden will take up approximately

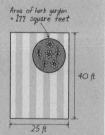

Area of herb garden = 177 square feet

40 ft

25 ft

177 square feet of the yard's 1,000 square feet area, leaving more than 800 square feet for you to create an incredibly large and exciting sandbox or soccer field for your children!

Green fingers

Going organic? Why not consider growing your own herbs and vegetables in the backyard? Most people avoid it simply because they don't know how to do it. So here is some basic advice to start you on your way to cultivating green fingers!

When you purchase seeds, bulbs, or plants, you are usually supplied with information on optimal growth conditions. Here is some of the information you might expect about growing broccoli:

Expected yield per plant	1.5 lb
Minimum distance between plants	24 inches
Minimum distance between rows	10 inches
Approximate time between sowing and picking	12 weeks
Germination time	7–12 days
Picking starts	August

Example

How much space (to the nearest square foot) would you need to produce 6 lb per week for 13 weeks, August to October, assuming you plant four rows, and the minimum distance of 10 inches between rows is allowed on either side of the row?

Solution

To produce 6 lb of broccoli for one week, you would need four plants, since the expected yield for each plant is 1.5 lb. If you wish to produce that amount for 13 weeks, the minimum number of plants required is: $4 \times 13 = 52$ plants.
Total length of a row is 52 plants multiplied by the distance between each plant:
$52 \times 24 = 1,248$ in. or 104 ft
divide the length by 4 rows:
$104 / 4 = 26$ ft
Assuming that 10 in. is left on either side of the four rows, then you would have 5 spaces multiplied by 10 in.
$5 \times 10 = 50$ in. or 4.17 ft
So the total area required to produce the desired yield is
26 ft $\times$ 4.17 ft = 108.42 sq ft or approx. 110 sq ft.

Swimming pool volume

If you are lucky enough to have a swimming pool in your yard, you may need to know its total capacity. To calculate the volume V of a rectangular swimming pool of length l, breadth b, and equal depth d all over, the formula is simply the following:

 $V = l \times b \times d$

If the swimming pool has a shallow end of depth d_1 and a deep end of depth d_2, then the total volume is

 $V = l \times b \times \dfrac{(d_1 + d_2)}{2}$

Right Angles with the Help of Pythagoras

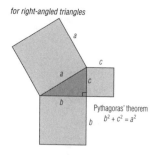

for right-angled triangles

a

c

a

c

b

Pythagoras' theorem
$b^2 + c^2 = a^2$

b

When measuring or building a structure it is useful to be able to construct right angles for perfect squares and rectangles. Pythagoras' theorem states that the sum of the squares of the sides of a right-angled triangle equals the square of its hypotenuse (the longest side, which is opposite the right angle). If the sides are b and c and the hypotenuse is a, then this theorem may be written as:

 $b^2 + c^2 = a^2$

For example, if $b = 3$, $c = 4$, and $a = 5$, then $b^2 + c^2 = 9 + 16 = 25$, and $a^2 = 25$. The combination 3, 4, and 5 is useful for measuring out a right angle and is often used by builders. Another useful set of numbers, which satisfy the formula, is 6, 8, and 10.

For example, Pythagoras' theorem can be used to measure a square hole in a door for a cat flap. If a side of the square is 10 in., then the right-angled triangle formed by any two sides of the square and a diagonal has sides $b = 10$ in., $c = 10$ in., and therefore the length of the hypotenuse which equals the diagonal of the square is given by:

$$a = \sqrt{b^2 + c^2} = \sqrt{10^2 + 10^2} = 14.14 \text{ in.}$$

Note that the diagonals of a rectangle should be of equal lengths.

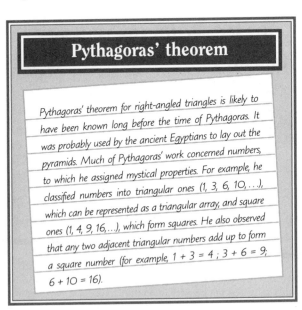

Pythagoras' theorem

Pythagoras' theorem for right-angled triangles is likely to have been known long before the time of Pythagoras. It was probably used by the ancient Egyptians to lay out the pyramids. Much of Pythagoras' work concerned numbers, to which he assigned mystical properties. For example, he classified numbers into triangular ones (1, 3, 6, 10, . . .), which can be represented as a triangular array, and square ones (1, 4, 9, 16, . . .), which form squares. He also observed that any two adjacent triangular numbers add up to form a square number (for example, $1 + 3 = 4$; $3 + 6 = 9$; $6 + 10 = 16$).

Diagonals chart

The following table lists the hypotenuse a for a range of values of b and c specified in the far left column and top row. For example, $b = 7.5$, $c = 2.5$, gives a value of $a = 7.91$.

List of values of hypotenuse a for a range of values of b and c

b	c									
	0.5	1.0	1.5	2.0	2.5	3.0	3.5	4.0	4.5	5.0
0.5	0.71	1.12	1.58	2.06	2.55	3.04	3.54	4.03	4.53	5.02
1.0	1.12	1.41	1.80	2.24	2.69	3.16	3.64	4.12	4.61	5.10
1.5	1.58	1.80	2.12	2.50	2.92	3.35	3.81	4.27	4.74	5.22
2.0	2.06	2.24	2.50	2.83	3.20	3.61	4.03	4.47	4.92	5.39
2.5	2.55	2.69	2.92	3.20	3.54	3.91	4.30	4.72	5.15	5.59
3.0	3.04	3.16	3.35	3.61	3.91	4.24	4.61	5.00	5.41	5.83
3.5	3.54	3.64	3.81	4.03	4.30	4.61	4.95	5.32	5.70	6.10
4.0	4.03	4.12	4.27	4.47	4.72	5.00	5.32	5.66	6.02	6.40
4.5	4.53	4.61	4.74	4.92	5.15	5.41	5.70	6.02	6.36	6.73
5.0	5.02	5.10	5.22	5.39	5.59	5.83	6.10	6.40	6.73	7.07
5.5	5.52	5.59	5.70	5.85	6.04	6.26	6.52	6.80	7.11	7.43
6.0	6.02	6.08	6.18	6.32	6.50	6.71	6.95	7.21	7.50	7.81
6.5	6.52	6.58	6.67	6.80	6.96	7.16	7.38	7.63	7.91	8.20
7.0	7.02	7.07	7.16	7.28	7.43	7.62	7.83	8.06	8.32	8.60
7.5	7.52	7.57	7.65	7.76	7.91	8.08	8.28	8.50	8.75	9.01
8.0	8.02	8.06	8.14	8.25	8.38	8.54	8.73	8.94	9.18	9.43
8.5	8.51	8.56	8.63	8.73	8.86	9.01	9.19	9.39	9.62	9.86
9.0	9.01	9.06	9.12	9.22	9.34	9.49	9.66	9.85	10.06	10.30
9.5	9.51	9.55	9.62	9.71	9.82	9.96	10.12	10.31	10.51	10.74
10.0	10.01	10.05	10.11	10.20	10.31	10.44	10.59	10.77	10.97	11.18

b	c									
	5.5	6.0	6.5	7.0	7.5	8.0	8.5	9.0	9.5	10.0
0.5	5.52	6.02	6.52	7.02	7.52	8.02	8.51	9.01	9.51	10.01
1.0	5.59	6.08	6.58	7.07	7.57	8.06	8.56	9.06	9.55	10.05
1.5	5.70	6.18	6.67	7.16	7.65	8.14	8.63	9.12	9.62	10.11
2.0	5.85	6.32	6.80	7.28	7.76	8.25	8.73	9.22	9.71	10.20
2.5	6.04	6.50	6.96	7.43	7.91	8.38	8.86	9.34	9.82	10.31
3.0	6.26	6.71	7.16	7.62	8.08	8.54	9.01	9.49	9.96	10.44
3.5	6.52	6.95	7.38	7.83	8.28	8.73	9.19	9.66	10.12	10.59
4.0	6.80	7.21	7.63	8.06	8.50	8.94	9.39	9.85	10.31	10.77
4.5	7.11	7.50	7.91	8.32	8.75	9.18	9.62	10.06	10.51	10.97
5.0	7.43	7.81	8.20	8.60	9.01	9.43	9.86	10.30	10.74	11.18
5.5	7.78	8.14	8.51	8.90	9.30	9.71	10.12	10.55	10.98	11.41
6.0	8.14	8.49	8.85	9.22	9.60	10.00	10.40	10.82	11.24	11.66
6.5	8.51	8.85	9.19	9.55	9.92	10.31	10.70	11.10	11.51	11.93
7.0	8.90	9.22	9.55	9.90	10.26	10.63	11.01	11.40	11.80	12.21
7.5	9.30	9.60	9.92	10.26	10.61	10.97	11.34	11.72	12.10	12.50
8.0	9.71	10.00	10.31	10.63	10.97	11.31	11.67	12.04	12.42	12.81
8.5	10.12	10.40	10.70	11.01	11.34	11.67	12.02	12.38	12.75	13.12
9.0	10.55	10.82	11.10	11.40	11.72	12.04	12.38	12.73	13.09	13.45
9.5	10.98	11.24	11.51	11.80	12.10	12.42	12.75	13.09	13.44	13.79
10.0	11.41	11.66	11.93	12.21	12.50	12.81	13.12	13.45	13.79	14.14

Food and Cooking

Smart Shopping

If ever there is a place where knowing your numbers counts, it is in the supermarket. Smart shoppers rely on their ability to process numbers quickly to make sound judgments on the value of the products they purchase. Unit costs, package sizes, expiration dates, price promotions, nutritional values, recipe requirements, and budgets are all part of the mix of numbers you'll need to consider on the average trip to the supermarket.

Unit costs

Most supermarkets now label their products with the total weight and the price per unit weight in addition to the total price. Similarly, liquid products are labeled with the total capacity and price per unit capacity. To find the unit price of an item, use the following equation:

 $$\text{unit price} = \frac{\text{price}}{\text{quantity}}$$

The unit price allows you to compare different brands and make a choice between various products of different sizes. Often, it is often more economical to buy larger quantities in order to take advantage of cheaper unit prices. Beware of expiration dates, however. A double-sized package of cheese may appear to save money in the short term; but, if it goes moldy before being eaten, then you have lost your savings advantage.

Example

A 128 oz bottle of apple juice costs $4.59, a 9-pack of 6.75 oz boxes costs $3.05, and a 64 oz bottle costs $2.39. Which offers the best value for money?

Solution

First, you need to determine the standard unit of volume among the three choices. In this example, while the volume is given in ounces, it's easier to convert to quarts for a quick mental comparison of unit costs. Since we know that there are 32 ounces to a quart, the 64 oz bottle equals 2 quarts and the 128 oz bottle equals 4 quarts. The third option is a 9-pack of 6.75 oz boxes. Rounding up to the nearest whole digit, you can quickly multiply the volume of each individual pack (@7oz) by the number of boxes (9) for a total of 63 oz or approximately 2 quarts, almost the equivalent volume of the first bottle.

Now it is easy to calculate the unit price for each option using the unit price formula:

64 oz bottle/2 quarts = $2.39 ÷ 2 = $1.20
9 × 6.75 boxes/approx. 63 oz/approx 2 quarts = $3.05 ÷ 2 = $1.53
128 oz bottle/4 quarts = $4.59 ÷ 4 = $1.15

So the 128 oz bottle offers more value for money.

Remember to be consistent when evaluating unit costs. Comparing prices in cents per quart with prices in cents per ounce is misleading. In the store, you need to check the unit labels carefully to make sure the units are equivalent, allowing you to make the right comparison between products.

Packaging conversions

An easy way to convert kilograms to pounds is to double the number of kilograms and add 10%. To convert from pounds to kilograms, divide the number of pounds by two and then take away an additional 10%.

$$\text{pound} = 2\text{ kg} + (2\text{ kg} / 100)$$
$$\text{kilogram} = \frac{\text{lb}}{2} - \left(\frac{\text{lb}}{2} / 100\right)$$

While not exact, your estimates will be close enough to give you a fair comparison of prices, assuming similar quantities. If not, you'll need to work out the unit costs based on a standardized unit.

The table below gives a number of useful weight conversions between the US system and the metric system. For a complete list of conversion rates and formulas, refer to the *Brushing Up* section on pages 31–34.

Useful weight conversions

US or Imperial	Metric
1 ounce	28 grams
0.035 ounce	1 gram
3.5 ounces	100 grams
¼ pound	113 grams
½ pound	227 grams
1 pound	454 grams
1.10 pounds	500 grams
2.2 pounds 35 ounces	1 kilogram

Nutrition

Nutrition labels

Most pre-packaged food products now feature nutrition labels to give you some idea of what's inside and how good it is for you. Included on the label is the "percent daily value" for the vitamins, minerals, and other nutrients in the product.

Example of package of macaroni and cheese

Nutrition Facts

Serving size 1 cup (228 g)

Servings per container 2

Amount per serving

Calories 250 calories from fat 110

	% Daily Value*
Total fat 12 g	18
Saturated Fat 3 g	15
Cholesterol 30 mg	10
Sodium 470 mg	20
Total carbohydrate 31 g	10
Dietary fiber 0 g	0
Sugars 5 g	
Protein 5 g	

Vitamin A 4% * Vitamin C 2%

Calcium 20% * Iron 4%

*Percent daily values are based on a 2,000 calorie diet

Energy is measured in **calories** and **joules**. We count calories as a way of assessing how much food we need to keep our bodies functioning well. A **joule** (symbol J) is an SI unit of work and energy. Specifically, it is the measurement for work done (energy transferred) by the force of one newton acting over one meter. One calorie = 4.184 joules.

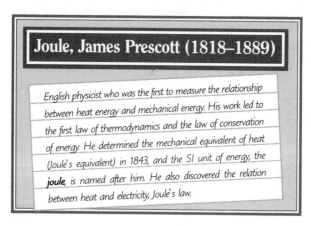

Joule, James Prescott (1818–1889)

English physicist who was the first to measure the relationship between heat energy and mechanical energy. His work led to the first law of thermodynamics and the law of conservation of energy. He determined the mechanical equivalent of heat (Joule's equivalent) in 1843, and the SI unit of energy, the *joule*, is named after him. He also discovered the relation between heat and electricity, Joule's law.

Nutritive value of foods

The following table gives the energy value of various types of foods. Both kilojoules (kJ) and calories (cal) have been calculated from the average protein, fat, and carbohydrate content per 100-gram portion.

Nutritional value of selected foods

Food	Energy		Protein	Fat	Saturated fat	Carbohydrate
	(cal)	(kJ)	(g)	(g)	(g)	(g)
Grain and grain products						
Bread, brown	218	927	8.5	2.0	0.4	44.3
Bread, white	233	988	8.0	2.4	0.4	44.1
Flour, white	341	1,450	9.4	1.3	0.2	77.7
Flour, whole wheat	310	1,318	12.7	2.2	0.3	63.9
Oats, rolled, raw	357	1,508	13.5	8.0	1.4	57.8
Rice, brown, boiled	141	597	2.6	1.1	0.3	32.1
Rice, white, boiled	138	587	2.6	1.3	0.3	30.9
Spaghetti, white, boiled	104	442	3.6	0.7	0.1	22.2
Dairy products and eggs						
Butter	737	3,031	0.5	81.7	54.0	0.0
Cheddar cheese	412	1,708	25.5	34.4	21.7	0.1
Cottage cheese	98	413	13.8	3.9	2.4	2.1
Cream, heavy	449	1,849	1.7	48.0	30.0	2.7
Cream, light	198	817	2.6	19.1	11.9	4.1
Eggs, boiled	147	612	12.5	10.8	3.1	0.0
Low-fat spread	390	1,605	5.8	40.5	11.2	0.5
Margarine, polyunsaturated	739	3,039	0.2	81.6	16.2	1.0
Milk, 2%	49	204	3.4	1.7	1.0	5.0
Milk, 1%	42	175	3.3	0.1	0.1	5.0
Milk, whole	266	75	3.2	3.9	2.4	4.8
Yogurt, whole milk, plain	79	333	5.7	3.0	1.7	7.8
Fruit						
Apples	47	199	0.4	0.1	0.0	11.8
Apricots	158	674	4.0	0.6	0.0	36.5
Avocados	190	784	1.9	19.5	4.1	1.9
Bananas	95	403	1.2	0.3	0.1	23.2
Cherries	48	203	0.9	0.1	0.0	11.5
Grapefruit	30	126	0.8	0.1	0.0	6.8
Grapes	260	57	0.4	0.1	0.0	15.4
Mangoes	57	245	0.7	0.2	0.1	14.1
Melon	28	119	0.6	0.1	0.0	6.6
Oranges	37	158	1.1	0.1	0.0	8.5
Peaches	33	142	1.0	0.1	0.0	14.0
Pears	40	169	0.3	0.1	0.0	10.0
Plums	36	155	0.6	0.1	0.0	8.8
Raspberries	25	109	1.4	0.3	0.1	4.6
Strawberries	27	113	0.8	0.1	0.0	6.0
Meat and fish						
White fish, steamed, flesh only	98	417	22.8	0.8	0.2	0.0
Chicken, breast only, raw	110	460	23.1	1.24	0.33	0.0

continued

Food	Energy		Protein	Fat	Saturated fat	Carbohydrate
	(cal)	(kJ)	(g)	(g)	(g)	(g)
Meat and fish						
Beef, ground, raw	310	1297	16.6	26.6	10.8	0.0
Pork, lean only, raw	147	615	20.7	7.1	2.5	0.0
Vegetables						
Cabbage	26	109	1.7	0.4	0.1	4.1
Celery	7	32	0.5	0.2	0.0	0.9
Corn, fresh	122	519	2.9	1.2	0.2	26.6
Cucumber	10	40	0.7	0.1	0.0	1.5
Lettuce	14	59	0.8	0.5	0.1	1.7
Mushrooms	13	55	1.8	0.5	0.1	0.4
Onions	36	150	1.2	0.2	0.0	7.9
Parsnips	66	278	1.6	1.2	0.2	12.9
Peas	69	291	6.0	0.9	0.2	9.7
Peppers	15	65	0.8	0.3	0.1	2.6
Potatoes, new	70	298	1.7	0.3	0.1	16.1
Spinach	21	90	301	0.8	0.1	0.5
Sweet potatoes	84	358	1.1	0.3	0.1	20.5
Tofu, soybean, steamed	73	304	8.1	4.2	0.5	0.7
Watercress	22	94	3.0	1.0	0.3	0.4
Zucchini	18	74	1.8	0.4	0.1	1.8

The difference between calories and kilocalories

In the USA, energy in food is expressed in kilocalories. The true calorie, sometimes referred to as a "small calorie", is one thousandth of a kilocalorie. While the term "calorie" technically applies to the "small calorie", in common usage, such as reference to food energy, the term "calorie" is actually a kilocalorie.

How fat free?

Supermarkets are full of food products that boast miraculously low fat quantities to entice their health-conscious consumers. An amount of caution should be exercised, however, before gloating over the health benefits provided by such products. A milk container for example, carrying the label "less than 2% fat" is clearly understood to contain up to 2% fat. An alternative label advertising "98% fat free" could be misunderstood by some people as implying that the product has been processed so as to remove 98% of its normal fat content. Suppose that the normal fat content for any full-fat milk is 10%. One might assume that 98% of that 10% has been removed, leaving a mere 0.2% fat – a very attractive but unfortunately false conclusion. The correct quantity of fat is still a full 2%.

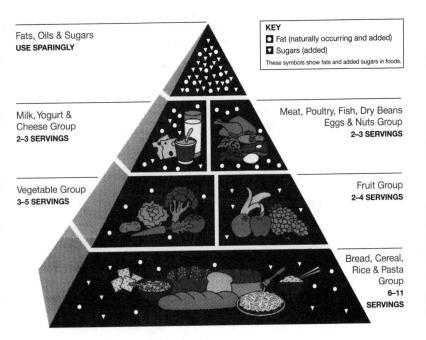

KEY
- ◻ Fat (naturally occurring and added)
- ▽ Sugars (added)

These symbols show fats and added sugars in foods.

Fats, Oils & Sugars
USE SPARINGLY

Milk, Yogurt & Cheese Group
2–3 SERVINGS

Meat, Poultry, Fish, Dry Beans Eggs & Nuts Group
2–3 SERVINGS

Vegetable Group
3–5 SERVINGS

Fruit Group
2–4 SERVINGS

Bread, Cereal, Rice & Pasta Group
6–11 SERVINGS

US Department of Agriculture and the US Department of Health and Human Services

Recommended daily intake of nutrients

RDA (Recommended Daily Allowance) is the quantity of a nutrient that is needed on a regular basis to keep most individuals fit and healthy. If a food source is giving you 25% RDA of a particular nutrient, it is giving you one quarter of the daily intake required for the average healthy person.

The RDA table here is meant as a general guide only. A qualified nutritionist should always be consulted if you have a particular medical condition or any concerns or doubts.

Recommended daily allowances
(– = Not applicable)

	Energy (cal)	Protein (g)	Calcium (mg)	Iron (mg)	Vitamin A (µg)[1]	Thiamin/ vitamin B_1 (mg)	Riboflavin vitamin B_2 (mg)	Niacin/ vitamin B_3 (mg)	Vitamin C (mg)	Vitamin D (µg)
Men										
18–34										
Moderately active	2,900	72	500	10	750	1.2	1.6	18	30	–
Very active	3,350	84	500	10	750	1.3	1.6	18	30	–
35–64										
Moderately active	2,750	69	500	10	750	1.1	1.6	18	30	–
Very active	3,350	84	500	10	750	1.3	1.6	18	30	–
65–74	2,400	60	500	10	750	1.0	1.6	18	30	–
>74	2,150	54	500	10	750	0.9	1.6	18	30	–
Women										
18–54										
Most occupations	2,150	54	600	12[3]	750	0.9	1.3	15	30	–
Very active	2,500	62	600	12[3]	750	1.0	1.3	15	30	–
Pregnant	2,400	60	1,330	13	750	1.0	1.6	18	60	10[2]
Lactating	2,750	69	1,200	15	1,200	1.1	1.8	21	60	10[2]
55–74	1,900	47	500	10	750	0.8	1.3	15	30	–
>74	1,680	42	500	10	750	0.7	1.3	15	30	–

[1] 1µg (microgram) = 0.001 mg (milligram).

[2] Most people who go out in the sun need no additional dietary source of vitamin D. It is recommended that children, adolescents, and housebound adults take 10 µg vitamin D daily during the winter season.

[3] These iron recommendations may not cover heavy menstrual losses.

Food coloring

Remember how your mother would never dream of serving cauliflower with mashed potatoes and chicken? Not enough color, she would say! And she was right – color is an integral part of our enjoyment of food. Ancient civilizations, like the Romans, understood that people "ate with their eyes" and used saffron and other spices to enrich the color of their food. Butter has been colored yellow since the 1300s. Today, many foods are made mouth-watering by the addition of color additives. Below is a list of approved color additives for food use.

Color Additives Certifianble For Food Use

Name/Common Name	Hue	Common food uses
FD&C Blue No 1 Brilliant Blue FCF	Bright blue	Beverages, dairy products powders, jellies, confections, condiments, icings, syrups, extracts
FD&C Blue No 2 Indigotine	Royal blue	Baked goods, cereals, snack foods, ice cream, confections, cherries
FD&C Green No 3 Fast Green FCF	Sea green	Beverages, puddings, ice cream, sherbet, cherries, confections, baked goods, dairy products
FD&C Red No 40 Allura Red AC	Orange-red	Gelatins, puddings, dairy products, confections, beverages, condiments
FD&C Red No 3 Erythrosine	Cherry-red	Cherries in fruit cocktail and in canned fruits for salads, confections, baked goods, dairy products, snack foods
FD&C Yellow No 5 Tartrazine FD&C Yellow No 6 Sunset Yellow	Lemon yellow	Custards, beverages, ice cream, confections, preserves, cereals

Courtesy of the US Food and Drug Administration

In The Kitchen

Adjusting recipes for different numbers of people

The most common number of servings given for recipes is usually four or six. Often, though, we find ourselves catering for a different number of people. To adapt a recipe to suit the number (x) of portions you need, simply divide the quantity of each ingredient by the number of servings the recipe is for to get the exact quantity per ingredient per person, then multiply each of these by x.

Example

You are cooking for six, but your recipe for coq au vin (given below) is meant for four. What quantities do you need for each ingredient to serve six people?

Solution

Divide each ingredient quantity by four, then times it by six. The new recipe quantities would be:

coq au vin for four	coq au vin converted for six		
3 lbs chicken	3 lb ÷ 4	= 0.75lb	× 6 = 4.5 lbs chicken
10 oz potatoes	10 oz ÷ 4	= 2.5 oz	× 6 = 13 oz potatoes
4 oz carrots	4 oz ÷ 4	= 1 oz	× 6 = 6 oz carrots
2 oz onions	2 oz ÷ 4	= 0.5 oz	× 6 = 3 oz onions
32 oz red wine	32 oz ÷ 4	= 8 oz	× 6 = 48 oz red wine

Capacity conversions

Many recipes consist of a variety of measurements, some of which you will need to convert for practical reasons. If you're in a rush, a quick rule of thumb for converting quarts to liters is to subtract 5%. To convert liters to quarts, add 5%.

liter = quart × 0.95
quart = liter × 1.05

Just remember the adage **"A liter's a quart and a liter bit more!"**

The following tables give conversions of both liquid and dry measurements.

Liquid measure conversion

Gallons	*Quarts*	*Pints*	*Cups*	*Fluid ounces*	*Liters*	*Tablespoons*	*Teaspoons*
1	4	8	16	128	3.79		
½	2	4	8	64	1.89		
¼	1	2	4	32	0.95		
	½	1	2	16	0.47		
	¼	½	1	8	0.24		
			½	4	0.12	8	24
			¼	2	0.06	4	12
			⅛	1	0.03	2	6
			½	.015	1	3	

Dry measure conversion

Cups	*Fluid ounces*	*Tablespoons*	*Teaspoons*	*Milliliters*
1	8	16	48	237
¾	6	12	36	177
⅔	5 ⅓	10 ⅔	32	158
½	4	8	24	118
⅓	2 2/2	5 ⅓	16	79
¼	2	4	12	59
⅛	1	2	6	30
1/16	½	1	3	15
1/48	⅙	¾	1	5

Temperature conversions

If you are using a cookbook that was printed outside the USA, recipes will often call for oven temperatures in Celsius, or (in Britain) gas marks. To convert from Celsius to Fahrenheit, multiply by 9, divide by 5 and add 32. To convert from Fahrenheit to Celsius, take 32 away; multiply by 5 and divide by 9.

$$F = (C \times 9 \div 5) + 32$$
$$C = (F - 32) \times 5 \div 9$$

The following table includes the most common oven cooking temperatures in Celsius and Fahrenheit, alongside a list of gas marks and a rating for comparison when cooking.

Oven temperature conversion

| Gas mark | Electric | | Rating |
	(°F)	(°C)	
½	250	120	
1	275	140	
2	300	150	Slow
3	325	170	
4	350	180	
5	375	190	Moderate
6	400	200	
7	425	220	Hot
8	450	230	
9	500	260	Very hot

Safe cooking

The cause of most food-related poisoning is the bacterium known as salmonella. The destruction of salmonella occurs during the cooking process and is used as the pasteurization standard.

Cooking meats

Meat is particularly prone to contamination. The chart below provides safe temperatures for cooking meat using an internal thermometer.

Safe temperatures for meat using internal meat thermometer

| Meat | | Core temp | |
		(°F)	(°C)
Beef	rare	140	60
Beef	medium	160	71
Beef	well-done	170	77
Pork	done	165	74
Ham, pre-cooked	done	140	60
Chicken, whole	done	175	79–80
Turkey, whole	done	180	82
Poultry pieces	done	170	77

Oven cooking times and temperatures

The following table provides a quick and easy reference for oven cooking and baking selected food products. Remember, though, that many recipes are different, as is every cook's idea of a perfect result. You may find it necessary to make adjustments until you have achieved the desired effect.

Cooking times and temperatures for foods

	Time (min)	Temperature (°F)	Temperature (°C)
Pies, breads and cakes			
Scones	10	435	220
Gingerbread	12–15	375	190
Chocolate chip cookies	10	325	163
Chocolate brownies	40–45	375	190
Pound cake	45	375	190
Home-made pizza	20	425	220
Bread (1 lb loaf)	35	425	220
Bread rolls	20	425	220
Fruit cobbler	25	375	191
Quiche	15	400	200
Cinnamon rolls	15–18	375	190
Meat and fish products			
Roast beef	120	350	180
Rack of lamb	75	400	200
Chicken pieces	40	400	200
Fish, whole	25	400	200
Misc products			
Baked potatoes	90	400	200
Stuffed peppers	30	375	190
Soufflé	30	180	350
Lasagne	45	350	180

Weighing with the help of Archimedes

Archimedes' principle states that a body immersed in a fluid displaces an amount of fluid with weight equal to the weight of that body.

Cooks can use this principle to weigh water-resistant substances such as imported butter that isn't sold in ¼-lb sticks. By weighing the displaced water instead of the butter, you can avoid getting grease on the weighing scales.

Archimedes was a good friend of King Heiro of Syracuse. King Heiro often called upon Archimedes to figure out some of his more difficult problems. On one occasion, Heiro requisitioned a goldsmith to make him a crown out of an exact amount of gold. When Heiro received the crown, he feared the goldsmith might have cheated him, so he summoned Archimedes to prove whether the amount of gold in the crown was correct. That night Archimedes filled the bathtub to the brim with water and got in. He realized that the mass of the water that spilled out of the tub was equal to his mass. The next day Archimedes told the king of his discovery (which today is called buoyancy). Archimedes then put the crown in a tub of water filled to the top and found that the crown indeed did not have enough gold in it. The goldsmith was then immediately beheaded.

object is more dense than water
object sinks

object is less dense than water
object floats

bathtub full of water — this tub is empty

king's crown dropped into bathtub

overspilled water in this tub = the weight of the crown

Alcohol Content of Drinks

The alcohol content of a beverage is usually measured as the percentage of absolute alcohol by volume, or as "proof." In the USA, proof is twice the amount of absolute alcohol by volume in distilled spirits, measured at 60°F. So a beverage that is 50% alcohol is "100 proof" and a beverage that is 40% alcohol is "80 proof". In Australia and the UK, 100 proof spirit contains 57% alcohol by volume.

Alcohol content (%) of selected beverages

Beverage	Alcohol content (%)
Beers (lager)	3.2–4.0
Ales	4.5
Stout	6.0–8.0
Malt liquor	3.2–7.0
Sake	14.0–16.0
Table wines	7.1–14.0
Fortified wines	14.0–24.0
Brandies	40.0–43.0
Whiskies	40.0–75.0
Vodkas	40.0–50.0
Gin	40.0–48.5
Rum	40.0–95.0
Tequila	45.0–50.5

Common measurements of alcoholic beverages (US)

Common measurements for alcoholic beverages	
"pony shot"	0.5 jigger; 0.75 fluid ounces
"shot"	0.666 jigger; 1 fluid ounce
"large shot"	1.25 ounces
"jigger"	1.5 shots; 1.5 fluid ounces
pint	16 shots; 0.625 fifths
fifth	25.6 shots; 25.6 ounces; 1.6 pints; 0.8 quarts; 0.75706 liters
quart	32 shots; 32 ounces; 1.25 fifths
magnum	2 quarts; 2.49797 wine bottles
bottle wine	0.800633 quarts; 0.7577 liters

Drink equivalence

The average drink contains one-half ounce of absolute alcohol, sometimes called the "**drink equivalent.**" The alcohol content in a typical 12-ounce can of beer is approximately equal to the amount of alcohol in a 4- to 5-ounce serving of wine, or in a "shot" of whiskey.

Examples of drink equivalence

12 ounces of 4% beer	0.48 ounces of absolute alcohol
5 ounces of 10% wine	0.50 ounces of absolute alcohol
1.25 ounces of 40% vodka (80 proof)	0.50 ounces of absolute alcohol
1.25 ounces of 43% whiskey (86 proof)	0.52 ounces of absolute alcohol

Blood alcohol concentration

Blood alcohol concentration (BAC) is the amount of alcohol in your bloodstream, measured in percentages. A BAC of 0.10 percent means that a person has one part alcohol per 1,000 parts blood in their system. The table below describes the physical effects experienced by the average person at various BAC levels.

Blood alcohol concentration

BAC%	Effects
0.02	Effect on body, including feeling of warmth
0.04	Feeling of relaxation, impaired judgment, inhibitions decrease
0.08	Obvious intoxication in most people, clumsiness, lack of inhibitions
0.10	Obvious intoxication in all people, equivalent to ½ pint whisky in blood stream, memory loss
0.15	Very intoxicated, vomiting, slurred speech, impaired movement
0.25	Reduced response to stimuli, inability to stand, incontinence, sleepiness
0.35	Unconsciousness, little response to stimuli, low body temperature, fall in blood pressure
0.45	Fatal dose in most people

Effect of number of drinks on individuals within weight classes

Weight (lbs)	Number of drinks – 1.25 oz 80 proof liquor, 12 oz can of beer, or 4 oz of wine over a two-hour period							
90–109	1	2	3	4	5	6	7	8
110–129	1	2	3	4	5	6	7	8
130–149	1	2	3	4	5	6	7	8
150–169	1	2	3	4	5	6	7	8
170–189	1	2	3	4	5	6	7	8
190–209	1	2	3	4	5	6	7	8
210–229	1	2	3	4	5	6	7	8
230 & up	1	2	3	4	5	6	7	8

☐	0.01% – .04%	possibly DUI (driving under the influence of alcohol)
▨	0.05% – .07%	likely DUI
▦	0.08% – up	definitely DUI

Wine years

The vintage wine chart below gives a general guide to wines from around the world for the best vintages of the past ten years. The chart provides a numeric rating for each vintage by region.

Ratings:

41–50	Excellent
31- 40	Above average to excellent
21–30	Average
11–20	Below average
1–10	Poor

Vintage wine chart

Regions	1999	1998	1997	1996	1995	1994	1993	1992	1991	1990
France Bordeaux white	45	48	41	43	43	40	37	36	36	48
France Bordeaux red	44	42	41	41	46	45	43	37	37	49
France Loire Valley white	42	42	41	45	44	36	45	37	32	48
France Champagne	NV	43	43	46	45	NV	42	NV	NV	47
Italy Piedmont	45	44	48	47	44	43	43	38	41	49
Italy Tuscany	44	40	47	36	46	42	43	40	43	47
Germany Rhine	47	42	44	46	38	45	43	40	42	47
Spain Rioja	43	42	43	41	45	49	36	41	38	43
Spain Catalonia	43	39	43	48	47	45	46	40	47	43
Australia Hunter Valley	44	47	44	45	42	43	43	43	44	44
California Cabernet	44	41	47	45	47	46	46	46	46	42
California Chardonnay	44	44	46	43	46	44	45	46	42	45
California Zinfandel	45	43	42	44	43	48	45	45	46	45
California Pinot Noir	45	43	45	44	44	46	44	44	43	43

NV = non-vintage

Shopping
and Leisure

Numbers are often considered dry, characterless, and utilitarian. But where would so many of our most treasured leisure activities be without them? You may hate them in the dressing room, love them on the discount rack, rush to them on the sports page, or be totally unaware of them when you sing, but they're there – behind your camera lens, lifting your golf clubs, and relaxing your spirit. In this section, we'll take a look at how!

Shopping

For the vast majority of people, purchasing something expensive these days often requires assistance from a credit card. Being able to run a few numbers in your head when you shop will stop you from buying something you can't afford or give you the go-ahead to spend guilt-free.

Understanding credit cards

There are a few terms you need to become familiar with when getting to grips with credit cards or department store financing. First, there is the **minimum payment**, or the minimum amount you are expected to pay each month. Usually equal to approximately 2% of your average balance due, it means that if your average daily balance for a certain month is $1,000, your minimum payment for that month will be somewhere around $20. Sounds good until you match that against your finance charge. A **finance charge** is the interest you are expected to pay on the money you owe. Below is a chart that describes a credit card purchase of $1,000 at the start of the year. In this example, the credit card company charges interest at an APR of 19.4%.

Credit card purchase of $1,000 – interest and balance during one year

Month	Ave daily balance for month ($)	Interest charged at APR 19.4% (or 1.616% monthly) ($)	Statement balance ($)	Minimum payment (2% per month) ($)	New balance ($)
January	1,000	16.16	1,016.16	20.32	995.84
February	995.84	16.09	1,011.93	20.24	991.69
March	991.69	16.03	1,007.72	20.15	987.57
April	987.57	15.96	1,003.53	20.07	983.46
May	983.46	15.89	999.35	19.99	979.36
June	979.37	15.83	995.20	19.90	975.30
July	975.29	15.76	991.05	19.82	971.23
August	971.23	15.70	986.93	19.74	967.19
September	967.19	15.63	982.82	19.66	963.16
October	963.16	15.56	978.72	19.57	959.15
November	959.15	15.50	974.65	19.49	955.16
December	955.16	15.44	970.60	19.41	951.19

As you can see, the minimum payment and the finance charge are so close that by year-end, you have made payments totaling $238.36, but have only paid back $48.81 of the principal that you owe. This is how credit card companies make their money. They charge low minimum payments because they know it will take you longer to repay your loan and they will have longer to make money from you.

Finance charges are usually calculated on your average daily balance for the month. The APR can be fixed or variable, with a low fixed rate the best option for overall value. Look for a card with a grace period of 25 days or more. A **grace period** is the time between your purchase and when the credit card company actually begins to charge interest on the purchase. If you manage to pay off your full balance each month, you may not accrue any interest charges at all.

Sears and Roebuck

In 1886, a Minneapolis railway station agent named Richard Sears (left) seized an opportunity to earn extra income by selling watches locally from a Chicago jewelry company. The resale business was brisk and within a year, Sears moved his company to Chicago where he

Pictures courtesy of Corbis

employed a watchmaker named Alvah Roebuck (right). Their alliance proved fruitful, and in 1893, the firm became known as Sears, Roebuck and Co. Sears gave farmers a cost-saving alternative to purchasing goods from their high-priced rural stores. Its slogan "Shop at Sears and Save" captured the spirit of the day and remains vital to its modern ethos. In 1901, Sears sold common and preferred stock on the open market and has been publicly owned ever since. In 1925, the first retail store was opened in Chicago and by 1931, retail sales topped mail-order sales for the first time. It remains one of the biggest and best-known retailers in the US today.

Discounts and price promotion

What's a better bargain – 25% off, or three for the price of two? To determine what you will pay for a **discounted sale** item, subtract the percentage discount from 100%, so 30% from 100% equals 70%. Then convert 70% to its decimal equivalent, 0.70 and multiply it by the item's original selling price to get the discounted price.

For **multi-buys**, stores offer you a chance to get one or more items free if you purchase several others at the same time. If P is the total price you are expected to pay, and N is the number of items you will be taking home, you can figure the average price per item (the real price you are paying for each one) by using the following formula:

average price per item = P/N

Example

Your favorite sock shop is having a three for the price of two sale. You select three pairs of socks with an original price of $6 each. What is the average price per pair of socks?

Solution

On a three for two, you will only be expected to pay for two pairs of socks, so:

$P = \$6 + \$6 = \$12$.

You will be taking home 3 pairs of socks, so your average price per pair of socks is:

$P \div N = \$12 \div 3 = \$4$

Below is a quick reference chart to help you determine discounts and price promotions in a flash. Keep in mind that multi-buys force you to purchase in multiple quantities, and that your overall bill might be significantly (and prohibitively) more expensive.

Prices and discounts

Offer discount	Multiply by	$40 Pants ($)	$75 Dress ($)	$6 Socks ($)	$20 Tie ($)
10% off	0.90	36.00	67.50	5.40	18.00
20% off	0.80	32.00	60.00	4.80	16.00
25% off	0.75	30.00	56.25	4.50	15.00
30% off	0.70	28.00	52.50	4.20	14.00
3 for 2	0.67	26.80	50.25	4.02	13.40
40% off	0.60	24.00	45.00	3.60	12.00
2 for 1	0.50	20.00	37.50	3.00	10.00
50% off	0.50	20.00	37.50	3.00	10.00

Clothing sizes

Now that you know how much you have to spend and how to shop for a bargain, all you have left to do is pick out the right size! The following tables give conversions between the different measuring systems used in the USA, UK, and continental Europe for clothes and shoe sizes.

Size conversions

USA	UK	Europe*
Women's Dresses		
6	8	34/36
8	10	36/38
10	12	38/40
12	14	40/42
14	16	42/44
16	18	44/46
18	20	46/48
20	22	48/50
22	24	50/52

* German and French sizes given

USA	UK	Europe
Women's Shoes		
4½	3	36
5	3½	36–37
5½	4	37
6	4½	37–38
6½	5	38
7	5½	38–39
7½	6	39
8	6½	39–40
8½	7	40
9	7½	40–41
9½	8	41
10	8½	41–42
10½	9	42
11	9½	42–43

USA	UK	Europe
Men's Suits		
36	36	46
38	38	48
40	40	50
42	42	52
44	44	54
46	46	56

USA	UK	Europe
Men's Shirts		
14	14	36
14½	14½	37
15	15	38
15½	15½	39
16	16	40
16½	16½	41
17	17	42
17½	17½	43

USA	UK	Europe
Men's Shoes		
5½	5	38
6	5½	38–39
6½	6	39
7	6½	40
7½	7	40–41
8	7½	41
8½	8	41–42
9	8½	42–43
9½	9	43
10	9½	43–44
10½	10	44
11	10½	45
11½	11	45–46
12	11½	46

USA	UK	Europe
Children's Shoes		
0	0	15
1	1	16–17
2	2	18
3	3	19
4	4	20–21
5	5	22
6	6	23
7	7	24
8	8	25–26
9	9	27
10	10	28
11	11	29
12	12	30–31
13	13	32

Children's clothing

USA	UK height(in.)	Age (years)	Europe height (cm)	Age (years)
4	43	4–5	125	7
6	48	6–7	135	9
8	55	9–10	150	12
10	58	11	155	13
12	60	12	160	14

What do those bar codes really mean?

Items are now manufactured with a bar code on the package that looks like this:

9 770961 887071

A bar code is a numerical identification system that allows stores to keep track of bar-coded items using a scanner and computer. The system produces a running inventory of stock for the store, which allows them to re-order on a daily basis if required. Stores can then use the information to predict customers' buying habits and adjust their stock to meet those requirements.

Electronic scanners interpret the bar part of the bar code. The bars are actually the product's identification number in coded form. Some bar code systems use 8 numbers, some use 13. Though the numbers may be grouped any number of ways, the computer reads the codes in a specific fashion.

13-digit bar code

Digits	Identify
First two digits	Country code
Next five digits	Manufacturer
Next five digits	Particular product
Final digit	Checksum

The final digit is called a **checksum**. The purpose of a checksum is to ensure that the scanner has read the first 12 digits correctly.

The Numerical Photographer

In order to create a picture, you expose film to a certain amount of light for a certain amount of time. The light's energy reacts to the silver in the film, creating a chemical reaction, which forms the basis of the negative. The more light admitted, the more silver is activated. A camera uses two things to control the amount of light (exposure) that the film receives: aperture and shutter speed.

Aperture

Aperture describes the opening in a camera lens that allows different amounts of light to pass through it. A ring of small overlapping metal leaves, known as the diaphragm, regulates the size opening. The f-stop setting on a camera reduces or enlarges the aperture. F-numbers refer to the ratio of the focal length of the lens to the diameter of the aperture. Each setting lets in half as much light as the preceding setting.

f-stop settings

f-stop number	f-number	aperture area
$f/1.4$	1.41	$1/2$
$f/2$	2.00	$1/4$
$f/2.8$	2.83	$1/8$
$f/4$	4.00	$1/16$
$f/5.6$	5.66	$1/32$
$f/8$	8.00	$1/64$
$f/11$	11.31	$1/128$
$f/16$	16.00	$1/256$
$f/22$	22.63	$1/512$
$f/32$	32.00	$1/1024$
$f/45$	45.25	$1/2048$

Most cameras have fixed focal lengths and use different apertures to achieve the same or similar exposures. Longer lenses require larger openings to admit the same amount of light, so the f-stop on a camera with a 50 mm lens would have smaller relative openings than a camera with a 135 mm lens.

To determine the relative aperture among lenses of differing focal lengths, use the following formula:

 $$f\text{-stop} = \frac{\text{lens focal length}}{\text{aperture diameter}}$$

$$f\text{-}8 = \frac{135 \text{ mm}}{16.8}$$

By dividing the focal length by the f-stop number you can determine the aperture size opening:

 $$\frac{50 \text{ mm}}{f/8} = 6.25$$

Aperture also controls how much of an image will be in focus. The plane of critical focus is the area on which you are focusing; the depth of field determines the plane of critical focus. High depth of field allows objects in the background and foreground to appear in focus. Low depth of field concentrates on a single object or distance plane, causing objects that are closer or further away to be out of focus. Knowing what will appear in focus is one of the basic considerations in taking a photograph. For the aspiring professional, here are a few helpful equations to help you focus!

Hyperfocal distance

The following formula can help you to find the maximum focus range, or **hyperfocal**, for any aperture and lens focal length combination, based on an acceptable sharpness for an 8 × 10 inch print. If you set your focus at the hyperfocal distance, you will achieve a maximum depth of field from H/2 (hyperfocal distance divided by 2) to infinity.

 $H = (L^2) / (f \times c)$

H = hyperfocal distance (mm)
L = focal length of lens (mm)
f = f-stop
c = diameter of circle of least confusion (mm)
for 35 mm format c = 0.03
for 6 × 6 cm format c = 0.06
for 4 × 5 in. format c = 0.15

Remember you will probably need to convert your answer to feet and/or inches.

Near field–far field calculations

You can determine the near focus and far focus limits of a photograph using the following equations that rely on you knowing the hyperfocal distance. You will probably need to use a calculator for these as the products in millimeters tend toward very large numbers.

Near focus limit

$$\text{near focus (mm)} = \frac{H \times D}{H + (D - L)}$$

Where:
H = hyperfocal distance (mm)
D = distance of focus (mm)
L = focal length of lens (mm)

Far focus limit

$$\text{far focus (mm)} = \frac{H \times D}{H - (D - L)}$$

Where:
H = hyperfocal distance (mm)
D = distance of focus (mm)
L = focal length of lens (mm)

Shutter speed

The shutter on a camera blocks light from exposing the film until you are ready to do so. When you press the camera's button, the shutter opens and closes quickly, allowing just enough light in to create the picture. Shutter speed also controls motion, allowing you to freeze action or convey a feeling of movement.

Most cameras use standard shutter speeds. Each speed setting is half the time of the next one. The speed number acts as the denominator of a fraction of a second indicating how long the shutter will stay open.

Shutter speed

Shutter setting	Shutter speed
1	$^1/_1$ or one second
2	$^1/_2$ or half a second
4	$^1/_4$ or one-quarter of a second
8	$^1/_8$ or one-eighth of a second
15	$^1/_{15}$ or one-fifteenth of a second
30	$^1/_{30}$ or one-thirtieth of a second
60	$^1/_{60}$ or one-sixtieth of a second
500	$^1/_{500}$ or one five-hundredth of a second

The combination of aperture and shutter speed affects the amount of light entering a camera and the sharpness of the picture. Changing one directly impacts on the other. Keep in mind that the same amount of light will be let in by an f/16 aperture at the shutter speed of 1 (or one second) as an f/11 at a shutter speed of 2 (or a $^1/_2$ second). Learning how to adjust one to the other to create the effect you want is central to good photography.

Film

Selecting the right film for your subject and lighting conditions can mean the difference between a good and a great picture. Point-and-shoot cameras do it automatically by reading the DX coding on the metal strips located on the film canister. If your camera is manual, however, you will need to adjust the speed yourself. Film speeds in the USA are listed as ASA (American Standards Association) rated films. In the UK, film speeds are listed as ISO (International Standards Organization) rated films, and are basically identical to the ASA ratings.

The sensitivity of the chemical emulsion on the film is what determines film speed. It also determines the sharpness and grain of your photographs. Slower speed films are less sensitive, with smaller chemical grains that create sharper pictures. Faster film speeds have larger grains, making the photo less defined. Higher speeds tend to be more useful in low light situations.

Uses of films of various speeds

ISO number	Speed	Use
24, 64, 100, and 200	Slow	Best for outdoor or well-lit shots. Produces sharp pictures, so good for enlargement purposes.
400	Medium	All-purpose film for daylight and low light shots. Not as sharp as slower speed films.
800, 1,000, 1,600, and 3,200	Fast	Good for very low light and night-time pictures. Not recommended for picture enlargement, as it produces fuzzier pictures than slower film.

Mathletics

Where else are numbers so hotly debated but in the world of sports? Here are just a few examples of where numbers count!

Golf clubs

Don't know your seven iron from your driver? Well, despite golf being a very individual game, those clubs are numbered for a reason. First off, there are two types of clubs: woods and irons. Woods usually have large, thick heads made of a solid wood, sometimes laminated, though some woods now have hollow metal heads. Woods are used for the longest shots.

Irons, on the other hand, have thin, blade-like heads of steel. Irons are used when accuracy is desired more than distance. Though sometimes considered an iron, the putter is usually sold separately from irons and is now designed in different styles to suit the individual player.

Woods and irons are numbered from one to nine. Each club has a different slope, known as **loft**, on the front of its head (see the illustration on page 119). The higher the number of the club, the greater its loft and the higher and shorter the ball will travel.

The no. 1 wood, called the **driver**, is designed to hit the ball the furthest and is used off the tee. It has the least amount of loft of any club except the putter. Players at the top of their game will average about 250 yards on a drive. The other woods, used to hit off the fairways, are the no. 2 (rarely used today), no. 3, no. 4, and no. 5 woods.

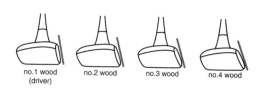

no.1 wood
(driver)   no.2 wood   no.3 wood   no.4 wood

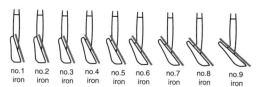

no.1   no.2   no.3   no.4   no.5   no.6   no.7   no.8   no.9
iron   iron   iron   iron   iron   iron   iron   iron   iron

Diagram of woods and irons showing the comparative loft of each.

In every sport where an instrument is used to hit a ball, there is something known as the "sweet spot". The sweet spot is the point on a bat, club, or racket where the least amount of resistance or vibration is incurred. When you hit the ball just right, you have hit the sweet spot. A tennis racket has two sweet spots. One relates to vibration. When the ball hits the racket, it vibrates in response, sending waves of vibrations up and down the racket (the stinging or shaking you feel in your hand). If you hit that sweet spot, known as the "node," you'll feel nothing. There is also the center of percussion (COP). When a ball hits the COP, your hand won't feel any force pushing or pulling against it. The COP is located about 6–8 in. from the end of the racket. When you hit a ball outside of the COP, the energy of your swing goes into moving the racket in your hands, not pushing the ball so that it flies farther and faster away. If you find the COP, less of the racket's energy goes to your hands, sending the ball a longer distance.

Sweet spot

tennis racket
sweet spot
6–8 in
tennis ball

Baseball

Statistics to a baseball fan is like milk to a baby. Passionate followers of baseball check league standings daily, but it is the players' individual stats that make numbers come alive and give afficionados something to talk about!

Player statistics

The table below ranks individual players according to their batting averages. Batting averages are determined by the number of official hits divided by the number of official at bats. Official hits are earned when a player reaches a base after safely hitting the ball. They do not include errors or fielders' choices made by the opposing team. Official at bats start with the number of times a player appears at the plate, minus walks, hit by pitches, and sacrifices.

Assume a player has 12 official hits, and the following at bats:

50 plate appearances
   – 5 walks
   – 1 hit by pitch
   – 2 sacrifices (1 fly, 1 bunt)
= 42 official at bats

12 hits ÷ 42 at bats = 0.286

Not bad if you consider the average batting average in the pros is 0.265.

Major League Baseball player statistics June 2001

	Player	TEAM	POS	G	AB	R	H	RBI	AVG
1	M Ramirez	BOS	DH	65	249	44	89	66	0.357
2	L Gonzalez	ARI	OF	69	261	60	93	62	0.356
3	M Alou	HOU	OF	51	203	33	72	44	0.355
4	I Suzuki	SEA	OF	66	304	61	108	32	0.355
5	R Aurilia	SF	SS	65	254	44	90	25	0.354
6	A Pujols	STL	3B	68	247	44	87	62	0.352
7	L Walker	COL	OF	63	237	61	82	66	0.346
8	J Giambi	OAK	1B	67	230	40	79	54	0.343
9	J Gonzalez	CLE	OF	63	245	47	84	57	0.343
10	T Helton	COL	1B	68	247	70	84	79	0.340

POS = position, G = games, AB = at bats, R = runs, H = hits, RBI = runs batted in, AVG = batting average

Music

Math and music are closely intertwined. As early as 500 BC, followers of Pythagoras had discovered that musical harmonies corresponded to simple ratios in number. The close links between music and mathematics are too numerous to mention, but here are some basic examples of numbers in music.

Music is a secret arithmetical exercise and the person who indulges in it does not realize that he is manipulating numbers.

Gottfried Leibniz

Rhythm

Rhythm is one of the basic ingredients of music. Rhythm measures time. We use bars and time signature to regulate rhythm for different pieces of music. A piece of music is divided into many measures, or **bars**, with each bar representing the same amount of time. A bar is split into equal portions called **beats**.

Time signature is found at the beginning of the piece and looks like a fraction without the dividing bar. The bottom number describes what type of note (half, quarter, eighth, and so on) gets a single beat, or count, and the upper number tells how many of those notes are in a bar. So, a time signature of $\frac{3}{4}$ indicates three quarter notes per bar and means that there are three beats in a bar and a quarter note gets one beat.

Musical styles and their time signatures

waltz	3/4
polonaise	6/8
polka	2/4
gigue	6/8
sarabande	3/4
chaconne	3/4
passacaglia	3/4
allemande	4/4
tango	2/4, 4/4, 4/8 (before 1955)

Notes

Different symbols are used in musical notation to represent how long a note should be held. A dot after any note increases the note's length by half. This table illustrates the notes and their fractional equivalents.

Notes and their fractional equivalents

Note symbol	Name	Fraction of measure	No. notes that fit in measure
	Whole	$1/1$	$1 = 2^0$
	Half	$1/2$	$2 = 2^1$
	Quarter	$1/4$	$4 = 2^2$
	Eighth	$1/8$	$8 = 2^3$
	Sixteenth	$1/16$	$16 = 2^4$

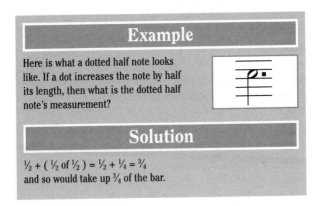

Example

Here is what a dotted half note looks like. If a dot increases the note by half its length, then what is the dotted half note's measurement?

Solution

$1/2 + (1/2 \text{ of } 1/2) = 1/2 + 1/4 = 3/4$
and so would take up $3/4$ of the bar.

Rest

Musicians insert rest signs to indicate an interval of silence. This table shows you the counts of varied rests.

Rest Symbol	Name	Fraction of measure	No. of rests that fit in measure
	Whole	$1/1$	$1 = 2^0$
	Half	$1/2$	$2 = 2^1$
	Quarter	$1/4$	$4 = 2^2$
	Eighth	$1/8$	$8 = 2^3$
	Sixteenth	$1/16$	$16 = 2^4$

Tone

An important element of music is tone. A tone's pitch is related to the frequency (number of vibrations per second, usually shown in hertz, Hz) that a listener picks up and interprets as high or low note sounds. The higher the frequency, the higher the pitch. The standard pitch adopted internationally in the 20th century is 440 Hz and is used to tune instruments.

Tuning a piano

A piano's keyboard has 88 keys, in a repeating pattern of 12 keys, 7 white, and 5 black. The standard middle A on a piano is 440 Hz. Here is a table describing the frequency of the middle scale of a piano.

Middle scale of a piano

Scale	Frequency (Hz)
A	220.0
A#	233.1
B	246.9
C	261.1
C#	277.2
D	293.7
D#	311.1
E	329.6
F	349.2
F#	370.0
G	392.0
G#	415.3
A	440.0

The Mozart effect

One of the most notable links between music and academic subjects (particularly mathematics) is the "Mozart effect." The Mozart effect claims that exposure to classical music, especially by Mozart, improves academic performance. Children who have been exposed to Mozart's music apparently score better on tests of spatial visualization and abstract reasoning than those who have not.

Health

In today's rapidly evolving world, medicine plays a huge role in preventing, diagnosing, and treating disease, both physical and mental. The basis of medicine is anatomy (the structure and form of the body) and physiology (the study of the body's functions). Each time we visit the doctor or have tests taken, we are subject to a series of numbers and information of which we have little understanding. This section looks at how numbers affect our bodies and how using numbers to our advantage can actually help us enjoy longer, healthier lives.

Body Temperature

Body temperature is the measure of heat within the body (core temperature) as recorded by a thermometer. Body temperature is controlled by the hypothalamus in the brain, which acts as a thermostat to lose or gain heat. Heat is conserved by constriction of the blood vessels closest to the skin, causing the blood to flow in deeper vessels. To lose heat, the blood vessels under the skin dilate, and sweating occurs.

In a healthy adult, body temperature is normally 98.6°F. Any significant departure from this temperature is potentially serious, although fever is a necessary response to infection.

Classification of different body temperatures

	Temperature (°F)
Healthy adult	98.6
Hyperthermia	above 105.8
Hypothermia	below 95

Heart Beat

The cardiac cycle is the sequence of events during one complete cycle of a heartbeat. This consists of contraction of the atria, a pause, followed by contraction of the two ventricles, then a longer pause. The contraction phase is called **systole** and the relaxation phase is called **diastole**. The whole cycle is repeated 70–80 times a minute under resting conditions.

Typical number of heartbeats per minute

	Heart beats per minute
Average heart beat	70–72
Normal range	50–90
Newborn range	130–150

Blood Pressure

A **blood pressure gauge.**

Blood pressure refers to the pressure of the blood against the inner walls of blood vessels, particularly the arteries, due to the muscular pumping activity of the heart. The left ventricle of the heart pumps blood into the arterial system. This pumping is assisted by waves of muscular contraction by the arteries themselves, but resisted by the elasticity of the inner and outer walls of the same arteries. Pressure is greatest when the heart ventricle contracts (systole) and lowest when the ventricle relaxes (diastole), and pressure is maintained solely by the elasticity of the arteries.

Blood pressure is measured in millimeters of mercury (mmHg) and is typically recorded with the systolic pressure written first, followed by the diastolic pressure. For example, 110 mmHg systolic and 75 mmHg diastolic measurements are written as 110/75, and often described as 110 over 75.

Normal human blood pressure varies with age, but in a young healthy adult it is around 120/80 mmHg. There is a tendency for systolic pressure to increase with age as the arteries become less elastic. It may rise to more than 200 mmHg in people with untreated hypertension (high blood pressure). Diastolic pressure is a more accurate predictor of hypertension.

The World Health Organization (WHO) has established the following standards for assessment of high blood pressure.

Standards for assessment of high blood pressure

Category	Systolic (mmHg)	Diastolic (mmHg)
Optimal	<120	<80
Normal	<130	85
High normal	130–139	85–90
High (hypertension)	140	>95

Comparing Blood Glucose Levels

Glucose is blood sugar. It is our basic energy source. This table compares blood glucose levels, giving you some idea of the range and level at which you should maintain your blood sugar levels.

Blood glucose levels

Avg glucose (millimoles per liter)[1]	Level
5.5	Excellent
5–6	Good
8–11	Good/Fair
11–14	Fair
14–16	Fair/Poor
16–17	Poor
17+	Poor/Critical

[1] A millimole is one thousandth of a "mole" which is an SI unit used by scientists to measure very small amounts of a substance.

Glucose and weight management

For a healthy body to function in peak condition, blood glucose levels should remain steady throughout the day. This can be achieved by eating certain products that will break down and release glucose at different rates between meals. In order to attain this balance, more frequent and smaller meals are recommended. Knowing how quickly various foods are broken down by the body will allow you to select an eating regime that will increase, decrease, or keep steady your blood sugar level depending on your activity level and health requirements. This is particularly important for diabetics who need to avoid erratic blood sugar levels.

The rate that foods break down into glucose in two or three hours after eating is called the **glycemic index rating**. It compares the speed at which a food raises blood sugar against pure glucose, which has a glycemic index rating of 100. The closer a food is to 100, the faster it is broken down into blood sugar in the body. The lower the corresponding index number is, the slower the breakdown into glucose, and the better the potential is for you controlling blood sugar levels and insulin secretion.

Foods and their glycemic index rating

Foods	Glycemic index rating
Beverages	
Soy milk	30
Orange drink	66
Soft drink, e.g. cola	68
High energy drink	95
Breads and cakes	
Cake, sponge	46
Cake, banana, made with sugar	47
Pastry	59
Pizza, cheese	60
Muffins	62
Croissant	67
Crumpet	69
Doughnut	76
Waffles	76
Raisin bread	47
Oat bran bread	48
Multi-grain bread	48
Pitta bread, white	57
Hamburger bun	61
Barley flour bread	67
Wheat bread, high fiber	68
Wheat bread, whole wheat flour	69
Wheat bread, white	71
Bagel, white	72
Bread stuffing	74
French baguette	95
Breakfast cereals	
Oatmeal	49
Nutri-grain	66
Cornflakes	83

Foods	Glycemic index rating
Grains	
Barley, pearl	25
Rye	34
Wheat kernels	41
Bulgar wheat	48
Barley, cracked	50
Buckwheat	54
Rice, brown	59
Rice, white	88
Couscous	65
Cornmeal	69
Biscuits and crackers	
Oatmeal cookies	55
Sugar cookies	59
Shortbread	64
High fiber rye crispbread	65
Water crackers	71
Rice cakes	77
Saltines	72
Dairy foods	
Chocolate milk	34
Milk, full fat	27
Milk, skimmed	32
Yogurt, low fat	33
Yogurt	38
Ice cream, low fat	50
Ice cream	61

continued

Foods and their glycemic index rating – *continued*

Foods	Glycemic index rating
Fruit and fruit products	
Cherries	22
Grapefruit	25
Apricots, dried	30
Pear	37
Apple	38
Plum	39
Apple juice	41
Peach	42
Orange	44
Grapes	46
Pineapple juice	46
Peach, canned	47
Grapefruit juice	48
Orange juice	55
Kiwi	52
Banana	62
Fruit cocktail	55
Mango	56
Sultanas	56
Apricots, fresh	57
Apricots, canned, syrup	64
Raisins	64
Melon, cantaloupe	65
Pineapple	66
Watermelon	72
Beans	
Soy beans, canned	14
Soy beans	18
Lentils	29
Kidney beans	29
Butter beans	31
Split peas	32
Lima beans	32
Chick peas	33
Kidney beans	27
Green beans	38
Black-eyed beans	41
Chick peas, canned	42
Baked beans, canned	48
Kidney beans, canned	52
Lentils, green, canned	52
Broad beans (fava beans)	79

Foods	Glycemic index rating
Pasta	
Fettuccine	32
Vermicelli	35
Spaghetti, whole wheat	37
Ravioli, meat filled	39
Spaghetti, boiled 5 min.	36
Spirals, (fusilli)	43
Macaroni	45
Linguine	50
Instant noodles	47
Tortellini, cheese	50
Macaroni and cheese	64
Gnocchi	67
Vegetables	
Peas, dried	22
Peas, fresh	48
Corn, fresh	55
Pumpkin	75
Potato, boiled	61
Beets	64
Potato, mashed	73
Carrots	49
Turnip	72
French fries	75
Potato, instant	83
Potato, baked	93
Parsnips	97
Snack foods	
Peanuts	15
Chocolate bar	40
Jams and marmalades	49
Chocolate	49
Potato chips	54
Popcorn	55
Granola bars	61
Soups	
Tomato soup	38
Lentil soup	44
Split pea soup	60
Black bean soup	64

Human Body Composition

The following table lists the elements that are present in the human body. Other elements that are found in the body include magnesium, iron, manganese, copper, iodine, and traces of cobalt and zinc.

Elements and substances present in the body

Element or substance	% of Body weight
Oxygen	65
Carbon	18
Hydrogen	10
Nitrogen	3
Calcium	2
Phosphorus	1.1
Potassium	0.35
Sulphur	0.25
Sodium	0.15
Chlorine	0.15

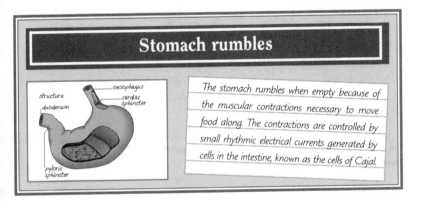

Stomach rumbles

structure
oesophagus
cardiac sphincter
duodenum
pyloric sphincter

The stomach rumbles when empty because of the muscular contractions necessary to move food along. The contractions are controlled by small rhythmic electrical currents generated by cells in the intestine, known as the cells of Cajal.

Body mass index

The body mass index (BMI) takes both the weight and height into account when assessing whether an individual is underweight or obese. BMI equals a person's weight in pounds divided by height in inches squared:

 BMI = 703 × weight (pounds) / height^2 (inches^2)

For example, a person who is 5'10" and weighs 145 lbs has a BMI of 703 × 145 ÷ 70^2 = 20.8.

Normal values for the BMI in adults are between 20 and 25. Values below 20 indicate that an individual is underweight and values above 30 indicate that an individual is obese. However, the BMI is only a general guide, and allowances should be made for build and gender.

BMI values

Weight (lb)	5'	5'1"	5'2"	5'3"	5'4"	5'5"	5'6"	5'7"	5'8"	5'9"	5'10"	5'11"	6'	6'1"	6'2"	6'3"	6'4"
75	14.6	14.2	13.7	13.3	12.9	12.5	12.1	11.7	11.4	11.1	10.8	10.5	10.2	9.9	9.6	9.4	9.1
90	17.6	17.0	16.5	15.9	15.4	15.0	14.5	14.1	13.7	13.3	12.9	12.6	12.2	11.9	11.6	11.2	11.0
95	18.6	18.0	17.4	16.8	16.3	15.8	15.3	14.9	14.4	14.0	13.6	13.2	12.9	12.5	12.2	11.9	11.6
100	19.5	18.9	18.3	17.7	17.2	16.6	16.1	15.7	15.2	14.8	14.3	13.9	13.6	13.2	12.8	12.5	12.2
105	20.5	19.8	19.2	18.6	18.0	17.5	16.9	16.4	16.0	15.5	15.1	14.6	14.2	13.9	13.5	13.1	12.8
110	21.5	20.8	20.1	19.5	18.9	18.3	17.8	17.2	16.7	16.2	15.8	15.3	14.9	14.5	14.1	13.7	13.4
115	22.5	21.7	21.0	20.4	19.7	19.1	18.6	18.0	17.5	17.0	16.5	16.0	15.6	15.2	14.8	14.4	14.0
120	23.4	22.7	21.9	21.3	20.6	20.0	19.4	18.8	18.2	17.7	17.2	16.7	16.3	15.8	15.4	15.0	14.6
125	24.4	23.6	22.9	22.1	21.5	20.8	20.2	19.6	19.0	18.5	17.9	17.4	16.9	16.5	16.0	15.6	15.2
130	25.4	24.6	23.8	23.0	22.3	21.6	21.0	20.4	19.8	19.2	18.7	18.1	17.6	17.2	16.7	16.2	15.8
135	26.4	25.5	24.7	23.9	23.2	22.5	21.8	21.1	20.5	19.9	19.4	18.8	18.3	17.8	17.3	16.9	16.4
140	27.3	26.5	25.6	24.8	24.0	23.3	22.6	21.9	21.3	20.7	20.1	19.5	19.0	18.5	18.0	17.5	17.0
145	28.3	27.4	26.5	25.7	24.9	24.1	23.4	22.7	22.0	21.4	20.8	20.2	19.7	19.1	18.6	18.1	17.7
150	29.3	28.3	27.4	26.6	25.7	25.0	24.2	23.5	22.8	22.2	21.5	20.9	20.3	19.8	19.3	18.7	18.3
155	30.3	29.3	28.4	27.5	26.6	25.8	25.0	24.3	23.6	22.9	22.2	21.6	21.0	20.4	19.9	19.4	18.9
160	31.2	30.2	29.3	28.3	27.5	26.6	25.8	25.1	24.3	23.6	23.0	22.3	21.7	21.1	20.5	20.0	19.5
165	32.2	31.2	30.2	29.2	28.3	27.5	26.6	25.8	25.1	24.4	23.7	23.0	22.4	21.8	21.2	20.6	20.1
170	33.2	32.1	31.1	30.1	29.2	28.3	27.4	26.6	25.8	25.1	24.4	23.7	23.1	22.4	21.8	21.2	20.7
175	34.2	33.1	32.0	31.0	30.0	29.1	28.2	27.4	26.6	25.8	25.1	24.4	23.7	23.1	22.5	21.9	21.3
180	35.2	34.0	32.9	31.9	30.9	30.0	29.1	28.2	27.4	26.6	25.8	25.1	24.4	23.7	23.1	22.5	21.9
185	36.1	35.0	33.8	32.8	31.8	30.8	29.9	29.0	28.1	27.3	26.5	25.8	25.1	24.4	23.8	23.1	22.5
190	37.1	35.9	34.8	33.7	32.6	31.6	30.7	29.8	28.9	28.1	27.3	26.5	25.8	25.1	24.4	23.7	23.1
195	38.1	36.8	35.7	34.5	33.5	32.4	31.5	30.5	29.6	28.8	28.0	27.2	26.4	25.7	25.0	24.4	23.7
200	39.1	37.8	36.6	35.4	34.3	33.3	32.3	31.3	30.4	29.5	28.7	27.9	27.1	26.4	25.7	25.0	24.3
210	41.0	39.7	38.4	37.2	36.0	34.9	33.9	32.9	31.9	31.0	30.1	29.3	28.5	27.7	27.0	26.2	25.6
225	43.9	42.5	41.2	39.9	38.6	37.4	36.3	35.2	34.2	33.2	32.3	31.4	30.5	29.7	28.9	28.1	27.4
240	46.9	45.3	43.9	42.5	41.2	39.9	38.7	37.6	36.5	35.4	34.4	33.5	32.5	31.7	30.8	30.0	29.2
250	48.8	47.2	45.7	44.3	42.9	41.6	40.4	39.2	38.0	36.9	35.9	34.9	33.9	33.0	32.1	31.2	30.4
275	53.7	52.0	50.3	48.7	47.2	45.8	44.4	43.1	41.8	40.6	39.5	38.4	37.3	36.3	35.3	34.4	33.5
300	58.6	56.7	54.9	53.1	51.5	49.9	48.4	47.0	45.6	44.3	43.0	41.8	40.7	39.6	38.5	37.5	36.5
325	63.5	61.4	59.4	57.6	55.8	54.1	52.5	50.9	49.4	48.0	46.6	45.3	44.1	42.9	41.7	40.6	39.6
350	68.4	66.1	64.0	62.0	60.1	58.2	56.5	54.8	53.2	51.7	50.2	48.8	47.5	46.2	44.9	43.7	42.6

Ideal Weights

The ideal weights for men and women are given in the following table.

Ideal weights

Height		Weight	
(ft)	*(m)*	*(lb)*	*(kg)*
Men			
5'2"	1.57	123–145	56.0–66.0
5'3"	1.60	125–148	56.7–67.1
5'4"	1.63	126–150	57.4–68.2
5'5"	1.65	129–155	58.5–70.2
5'6"	1.68	131–160	59.5–72.4
5'7"	1.70	133–163	60.2–73.8
5'8"	1.73	135–167	61.3–75.9
5'9"	1.75	137–170	62.0–77.3
5'10"	1.78	139–175	63.1–79.5
5'11"	1.80	141–179	63.8–81.0
6'0"	1.83	144–183	65.4–83.1
6'1"	1.85	146–186	66.4–84.5
6'2"	1.88	150–192	68.0–87.1
6'3"	1.90	153–197	69.4–89.3
Women			
4'10"	1.47	99–129	45.0–58.4
4'11"	1.50	100–131	45.3–58.4
5'0"	1.52	101–133	45.7–60.5
5'1"	1.55	103–137	46.7–62.2
5'2"	1.57	105–139	47.4–63.2
5'3"	1.60	108–144	48.9–65.3
5'4"	1.63	111–149	50.5–67.4
5'5"	1.65	114–152	51.6–68.8
5'6"	1.68	117–157	53.2–71.0
5'7"	1.70	120–160	54.3–72.4
5'8"	1.73	123–164	55.9–74.5
5'9"	1.75	125–167	56.9–75.5
5'10"	1.78	129–170	58.6–77.2

Waist-to-hip ratio

The waist-to-hip ratio WHR (for adults only) is calculated by the formula:

$$\text{WHR} = \frac{\text{waist size (inches)}}{\text{hip size (inches)}}$$

Research shows that people who carry more weight around the waist (apple-shaped bodies) face more health risks than those who carry more weight around the hips (pear-shaped bodies). For men a desirable WHR is less than 0.9, which means that the waist should be 90% diameter of the hips. For middle-aged and elderly women the WHR is recommended to be less than 0.8.

Waist-to-hip ratios

Waist (inches)	Hip (inches)								
	28	30	32	34	36	38	40	42	44
20	0.71	0.67	0.63	0.59	0.56	0.53	0.5	0.48	0.45
22	0.79	0.73	0.69	0.65	0.61	0.58	0.55	0.52	0.5
24	0.86	0.8	0.75	0.71	0.67	0.63	0.6	0.57	0.55
26	0.93	0.87	0.81	0.76	0.72	0.68	0.65	0.62	0.59
28	1	0.93	0.88	0.82	0.78	0.74	0.7	0.67	0.64
30	1.07	1	0.94	0.88	0.83	0.79	0.75	0.71	0.68
32	1.14	1.07	1	0.94	0.89	0.84	0.8	0.76	0.73
34	1.21	1.13	1.06	1	0.94	0.89	0.85	0.81	0.77
36	1.29	1.2	1.13	1.06	1	0.95	0.9	0.86	0.82
38	1.36	1.27	1.19	1.12	1.06	1	0.95	0.9	0.86
40	1.43	1.33	1.25	1.18	1.11	1.05	1	0.95	0.91
42	1.5	1.4	1.31	1.24	1.17	1.11	1.05	1	0.95
44	1.57	1.47	1.38	1.29	1.22	1.16	1.1	1.05	1
46	1.64	1.53	1.44	1.35	1.28	1.21	1.15	1.1	1.05
48	1.71	1.6	1.5	1.41	1.33	1.26	1.2	1.14	1.09
50	1.79	1.67	1.56	1.47	1.39	1.32	1.25	1.19	1.14

Cholesterol Levels

Cholesterol is a white, crystalline, steroid alcohol found throughout the body, especially in fats, blood, nerve tissue, and bile. It is also found in foods such as eggs, meat, and butter. A high level of cholesterol in the blood is thought to contribute to atherosclerosis (hardening of the arteries).

Low-density lipoprotein cholesterol (**LDL-cholesterol**), when present in excess, can enter the tissues and become deposited on the surface of the arteries, causing atherosclerosis. High-density lipoprotein cholesterol (**HDL-cholesterol**) acts as a scavenger, transporting fat and cholesterol from the tissues to the liver to be broken down. This is often known as "good" cholesterol.

Reducing the amount of alcohol and fat in the diet can alter total cholesterol levels in the blood. Substituting saturated fat for polyunsaturated fat can also reduce the LDL-cholesterol. HDL-cholesterol can be increased by exercise. The table below gives values for normal, borderline, and high levels of cholesterol.

Levels of cholesterol

Total cholesterol level	**(milligrams per deciliter)**
Normal	<200 mg/dl
Borderline	200–239 mg/dl
High	>240 mg/dl
LDL-cholesterol level	**(milligrams per deciliter)**
Normal	<130 mg/dl
Borderline	130–160 mg/dl
High	>160 mg/dl
HDL-cholesterol level	**(milligrams per deciliter)**
Normal	<35 mg/dl
Borderline	35–45 mg/dl
High	>45 mg/dl

Combating cholesterol

The Inuit people rarely suffer from heart disease. One explanation for this may be the high amount of fish, notably salmon, in their diet, which reduces the level of blood cholesterol.

Cholesterol and fat content of foods

This table lists a number of foods with their corresponding cholesterol levels and fat content.

Cholesterol levels and fat content of foods

Food	Cholesterol (milligrams)	Fat (grams)
Egg (one large)	213	5
Cheese (1 oz)		
Brie	28	8
Cheddar	30	9
Cottage cheese	5	1
Fast Food		
Cheese pizza (one slice)	9	3
French fries	0	12
Cheeseburger	141	44
Meat and Poultry (3.5 oz – cooked)		
Steak	96	15
Tenderloin (lean)	84	9
Chicken (with skin)	84	11
Chicken (without skin)	85	5
Turkey (with skin)	89	12
Turkey (without skin)	85	7
Shellfish (3 oz – raw)		
Crab	35	0.5
Scallops	28	0.6
Shrimp	167	0.6
Lobster	61	<1

A Snellen chart.

Visual Acuity Test

Visual acuity is measured with a Snellen chart, which displays letters of progressively smaller size. "Normal" vision is 20/20. When a person has 20/20 vision, it means that each of his or her eyes can see what an average person sees at a distance of 20 ft. If a test subject sees the same line of letters at 20 ft that the average individual sees at that distance, his or her vision is considered normal.

20/40 vision means that the test subject sees at 20 ft what the average person sees at 40 ft. For people with 20/40 vision, objects must be at half the normal distance in order to see them clearly.

A person with 20/20 vision is able to see letters 1/10th as large as someone with 20/200 vision.

By contrast, 20/15 vision is better than 20/20. A person with 20/15 vision can see objects at 20 ft that a person with 20/20 vision can only see at 15 ft.

Levels of vision

20/20	Normal vision. Required to read the small print in newspaper, or numbers in the telephone book.
20/40	Able to pass driver's licence test in most places. Most printed material is at this level.
20/80	Able to read alarm clock at 10 feet. News headlines are this size.
20/200	Legal blindness. Able to see STOP traffic signs.

Decibel Scale

Sound describes the physiological sensation received by the ear, originating in a vibration that communicates itself as a pressure variation in the air and travels in every direction, spreading out as an expanding sphere. All airbound sound waves travel with a speed dependent on the temperature. Under ordinary conditions, this is about 1,070 ft per second. The pitch of the sound depends on the number of vibrations imposed on the air per second (frequency), but the speed is unaffected. The loudness of a sound is dependent primarily on the amplitude of the vibration of the air.

Sounds and decibels

Decibels	Typical sound
0	threshold of hearing
10	rustle of leaves in gentle breeze
10	quiet whisper
20	average whisper
20–50	quiet conversation
40–45	hotel; theater (between performances)
50–65	loud conversation
65–70	traffic on busy street
65–90	train
75–80	factory (light/medium work)
90	heavy traffic
90–100	thunder
110–140	jet aircraft at takeoff
130	threshold of pain
140–190	space rocket at takeoff

Human hearing

The lowest note audible to a human being has a frequency of about 20 Hz (vibrations per second), and the highest one of about 20,000 Hz; the lower limit of this range varies little with the person's age, but the upper range falls steadily from adolescence onwards.

Driving

Owning a car requires familiarity with all sorts of numbers from purchasing and performance to upkeep and more. In this section we will take a look at the numbers that make your car run and give you the tools to make informed choices.

Ford, Henry (1863–1947)

© Corbis

In 1896, American engineer Henry Ford constructed a self-propelled vehicle called the Quadricycle. It had 4 heavy bicycle-wire wheels, a tiller steering mechanism, and a gasoline engine. In 1903 Ford established the Ford Motor Company to refine and sell his fledgling designs. In 1908 he introduced the Model T, the first reasonably priced, reliable and efficient automobile, responsible for initiating a whole new era of personal transportation in the US. To meet demand, Ford opened a large factory in Michigan where he introduced the concept of precision manufacturing: standardized and interchangeable parts, division of labor, and moving assembly lines. By 1918 half of all cars in America were Model Ts. The company's continuous innovations during the past century have made it one of the largest and most enduring automobile manufacturers in the world.

Engines and Cylinders

Behind every motorized vehicle is an internal combustion engine of some sort. Every engine has cylinders, each of which contains a piston. The fuel in your car is pushed into the cylinders, where it is compressed and ignited, forcing the pistons to move up and down. This produces the mechanical energy that is directed to the car wheels and makes the car move.

Generally, the more cylinders in your engine, the more powerful your car will be. Cylinders have valves on them that allow the engine to breathe in and out. The more valves on each cylinder the more powerful and efficient that engine should be. Most automotive engines today consist of four, six, or eight cylinders. The cylinders are arranged either in a straight line or with two banks of in-line cylinders forming a V pattern.

Displacement

The size, or capacity, of an engine is measured by the displacement of its cylinders. Displacement is the volume through which the piston moves from high to low position. The volume is calculated from the bore $2r$ (diameter of the cylinder) and stroke h (length of the piston's travel). We rely on the standard formula for a cylindrical volume to determine displacement:

Displacement of one cylinder (volume) =
$$\pi \times r^2 \times h = 3.14 \times \left(\frac{bore}{2}\right)^2 \times (stroke)$$

Total displacement is the combined displacement of all the engine's cylinders.

Example

A four-cylinder engine has a 86.0 mm bore and a 97 mm stroke, what is its total displacement in cubic centimeters and cubic inches?

Solution

Displacement of one cylinder (volume) = $\pi \times r^2 \times h$

$= 3.14 \times \left(\dfrac{86}{2}\right)^2 \times 97$

$= 3.14 \times 1,849 \times 97$

$= 563,168$ cubic millimeters or 563 cubic centimeters (cc)

$= 563$ cc $\times 4$ (no. of cylinders) $= 2,252$ cc $= 137$ cubic inches.

A two-liter engine effectively takes in two liters of fuel/air mixture for every revolution. Likewise, a four-liter engine of similar design should produce twice the power of the two-liter engine.

Displacement can be given in liters, cubic centimeters, or cubic inches. Here is a handy table for converting one to the other:

Conversion of liters to cubic centimeters or cubic inches

To convert	
Liters to cubic inches	multiply by 61
Liters to cubic centimeters	multiply by 1,000
Cubic centimeters to liters	divide by 1,000
Cubic centimeters to cubic inches	divide by 1,000, then multiply by 61
Cubic inches to liters	divide by 61
Cubic inches to cubic centimeters	divide by 61, then multiply by 1,000

Compression ratio

You will often hear the compression ratio mentioned in discussions about car engines. The compression ratio measures the amount that the air/fuel mixture is squeezed or compressed in one cylinder. As the piston moves towards the top of the stroke, it compresses the fuel into the space known as the combustion chamber. This is a formula for the compression ratio where D is the cylinder's displacement and V is the volume of the combustion chamber:

 compression ratio $= \dfrac{D + V}{V} = \dfrac{\text{maximum chamber volume}}{\text{minimum chamber volume}}$

Compressing the air/fuel mixture is important for developing power. Higher compression produces more pressure on the piston when the fuel mixture burns, and more power. A typical compression ratio for a passenger car engine is between 8:1 and 9:1. Higher performance vehicles can be anywhere from 11:1 to 13:1.

Brake horsepower

The important overall measure of the power of an engine is its brake horsepower (bhp). Brake horsepower is the actual power delivered by the engine. The test for brake horsepower is conducted by placing a braking device on the engine's output shaft, and then measuring the resistance at high revolutions per minute (rpm). Combined with the friction horsepower (power lost to friction and other mechanical losses), BHP becomes the indicated horsepower.

BHP + friction horsepower = indicated horsepower

An engine with a one-liter capacity usually has between 50 and 70 bhp. Turbo-charged engines can double the performance of a one-liter engine.

Acceleration

A car's movement (unlike an airplane's) depends on the friction created between its moving tires and the ground it is driving on. A car's acceleration can be measured using the standard formula for acceleration:

$$\text{acceleration} = \frac{\text{change in velocity}}{\text{time}} = \frac{v_2 - v_1}{\text{time}}$$

The change in velocity (rate of motion) is equal to the difference between the initial velocity and the final velocity. The standard measurement of acceleration for cars is the time it takes to go from 0 to 60 miles per hour (mph). If a car accelerates at 5 mph per second, then it will go from 0 to 10 in 2 seconds and 0 to 15 in 3 seconds until it reaches 60 mph in 12 seconds.

Example

It takes a car 10 seconds to go from 0 to 60 mph. What is the car's rate of acceleration expressed in miles per second?

Solution

$$\text{Acceleration} = \frac{\text{change in velocity}}{\text{time}}$$

$$= \frac{60 - 0}{10} = \frac{60}{10} = 6 \text{ mph per second}$$

Speed

Speed is defined as the rate at which an object moves. The average speed v of an object may be calculated by dividing the distance s it has traveled by the time t taken to do so, and may be expressed as:

$$v = \frac{s}{t}$$

Example

A drive to Hartford from New York City is 120 miles. If it takes an hour and 45 minutes to get there, what is the average speed of the car journey?

Solution

Solution: $v = \dfrac{s}{t} = \dfrac{120}{1.75} = 68.5$ miles per hour

In the above it is easier to convert time into a decimal equivalent of an hour rather than changing it into minutes, otherwise you will have to multiply your answer by 60 in order to get the miles per hour speed.

The SI units of speed are meters per second or kilometers per hour and these may be converted to and from miles per hour and feet per second using the following table.

Speed conversion table

Convert	To	Multiply by
Miles per hour	kilometers per hour	1.609344
Feet per second	meters per second	0.3048
Kilometers per hour	miles per hour	0.621371
Meters per second	feet per second	3.28084

Stopping distances

The stopping distance is the minimum distance in which a vehicle can be brought to rest in an emergency from the moment that the driver notices danger ahead. It is the sum of the thinking distance and the braking distance. Stopping distances increase with wet and slippery roads, poor brakes and tires, and tired drivers. On a dry road, a reliable car with good brakes and tires and an alert driver will stop in the distances shown in the following table.

Stopping distances

Speed	Thinking distance	Braking distance	Overall stopping distance	Number of car lengths
20 mph	20 ft/6 m	20 ft/6 m	40 ft/12 m	3
30 mph	30 ft/9 m	45 ft/14 m	75 ft/23 m	6
40 mph	40 ft/12 m	80 ft/24 m	120 ft/36 m	9
50 mph	50 ft/15 m	125 ft/38 m	175 ft/53 m	13
60 mph	60 ft/18 m	180 ft/55 m	240 ft/73 m	18
70 mph	70 ft/21 m	245 ft/75 m	315 ft/96 m	24

Gas Mileage

Gas mileage is the distance that you travel per one unit of gasoline and is expressed as either miles per gallon (mpg) or kilometers per liter (kpl). The sensible way to calculate your mileage is to let your tank run as low as is safe and sensible. When you refill your tank, write down the mileage on your odometer and note the total number of gallons you have purchased. Again, let your gas tank run low, as close as you can to the previous level. When you are ready to refill your tank, note the mileage on your odometer. Subtract your first reading from your second reading and then divide your answer by the number of gallons you purchased when you filled your tank to find out your average gas mileage. The equation for this is:

$$\text{Gas mileage} = \frac{\text{distance traveled}}{\text{gas volume}}$$

Example

A trip from Chicago to Cleveland is approximately 350 miles.
A round trip consumes 25 gallons of gas.
What is the car's average gas mileage for the trip?

Solution

Distance traveled =
350×2 (round trip) = 700 mi

$$\text{gasoline mileage} = \frac{700}{25} = 28 \text{ mpg}$$

Fuel consumption

Different measures of fuel consumption may be converted with the help of the following table. If you wish to convert US or imperial measurements into a metric measurement, then multiply by the corresponding decimal number in column two. If you wish to convert from metric to US or imperial, multiply your measurement by the corresponding decimal number in column three.

Fuel consumption conversion table

Fuel consumption			
miles per gallon (US)	0.4251	2.3521	kilometers per liter
miles per gallon (imperial)	0.3540	2.824859	kilometers per liter
gallons per mile (US)	2.3521	0.4251	liters per kilometer
gallons per mile (imperial)	2.824859	0.3540	liters per kilometer

Fuel efficiency

A number of the most fuel-efficient vehicles are listed for different size categories below. The fuel efficiency is expressed in miles per gallon (mpg) for both city and highway driving. Cars are rated annually and the list is published by the US Department of Energy.

Some fuel efficiency figures

Category	Vehicle	City (mpg)	Highway (mpg)
Best Two Seaters	Honda Insight 3 cyl. 1 L, Manual	61	68
	Mercedes-Benz SLK230 Kompressor 4 cyl. 2.3 L, Automatic	23	30
Best Subcompact Cars	VW New Beetle (Diesel) 4 cyl. 1.9L, Manual	42	49
	Honda Civic HX 4 cyl. 1.7L, Manual	36	44
Best Compact Cars	Toyota Prius 4 cyl. 1.5L, Automatic	52	45
	VW Golf/Jetta (Diesel) 4 cyl. 1.9L, Manual	42	49
Best Midsize Cars	Mazda 626 4 cyl. 2L, Manual	26	32
	Honda Accord 4 cyl. 2.3L, Manual	26	32
Best Large Cars	Chevrolet Impala 6 cyl. 3.4L, Automatic	21	32
	Toyota Avalon 6 cyl. 3L, Automatic	21	29

Annual Car Costs

There are two different costs associated with owning and running a car. The first group is the operating costs, or the actual costs of using the car. Operating costs include the purchase of gasoline, oil, tires, and payment for repairs, replacements, and servicing to keep it in usable condition. Ownership costs are charges for owning the car and using it on public roads. These costs include registration, insurance, and for most people now, emergency roadside service. Depreciation of car value can also be considered an ownership cost.

There are far too many variables to create a standard formula for car costs within categories, but the table below gives an estimated breakdown of costs for one year for several types of cars.

Annual car cost estimates based on 15,000 total miles driven per year

	Standard 4-cyl. (2.2 liter) compact	Standard 6-cyl. (3.0 liter) midsize	SUV 6-cyl. (4.3 liter) 2WD 2-door
Operating costs	**per mile**	**per mile**	**per mile**
Gas and oil	*5.0 cents*	*6.3 cents*	*7.2 cents*
Maintenance	*2.9 cents*	*3.1 cents*	*3.4 cents*
Tires	*1.3 cents*	*1.4 cents*	*1.4 cents*
Cost per mile	**9.2 cents**	**10.8 cents**	**12.0 cents**
Ownership costs	**per year**	**per year**	**per year**
Insurance	*$912*	*$856*	*$1312*
License, registration, taxes	*$175*	*$223*	*$396*
Depreciation (15,000 miles)	*$2,819*	*$3,294*	*$3,556*
Finance charge (20% down; loan @ 9.0%/4yrs)	*$598*	*$802*	*$929*
Cost Per Year	**$4,504**	**$5,175**	**$6,193**
Cost Per Day	**$12.34**	**$14.18**	**$16.97**
Total Cost Per Mile			
Cost per mile × 15,000	*$1,380*	*$1,620*	*$1,800*
Cost per day × 365	*$4,504*	*$5,175*	*$6,193*
Total Cost Per Year	**$5,884**	**$6,795**	**$7,993**
Total Cost Per Mile	**39.2 cents**	**45.3 cents**	**53.3 cents**

To claim or not to claim

In order to drive on public roads, cars must be insured for your own protection as well as the protection of other drivers on the road. To encourage safe driving, insurance companies offer discounts known as **no-claims bonuses** to motorists with clean driving records who did not make any claims against their insurance policy the previous year. You can often save hundreds per year with these no-claims bonuses in force, so you may want to consider whether or not it is in your best interests to make a claim for minor accidents.

Example

You bang your bumper and find it will cost $350 to fix. You have an annual policy deductible of $250. Should you could claim on your insurance or not?

Solution

Since you still have to pay the first $250 before the insurance picks up the balance, you need to determine how much your insurance will rise if you lose your no-claims bonus. Assuming it rises by $100 or more when it comes due, you will have in effect paid out $350 that year anyway. The real financial damage is the effect of losing your no-claims bonus on the cost of your insurance for subsequent years. Once your insurance goes up, it rarely comes back down. Check with your insurance representative to discuss whether it is sensible to pay for a minor scratch yourself. He or she should be able to help you calculate the numbers for your particular policy and advise you.

Depreciation

The single greatest cost to owning a car is depreciation. Though it varies from make to make, there are still some approximations that can be made if your car is relatively popular, and has an average sticker price. After the fifth year, your car's value will be based more on how well you have maintained it and how many miles you have driven it, rather than how old it is.

Depreciation in value of a car

Year of ownership	Depreciation (%)
First	35
Second	17
Third	13
Fourth	11
Fifth	8

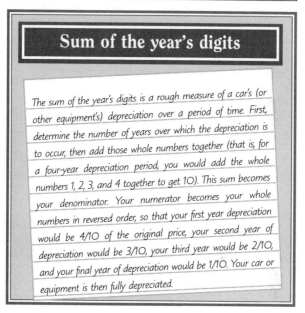

Sum of the year's digits

The sum of the year's digits is a rough measure of a car's (or other equipment's) depreciation over a period of time. First, determine the number of years over which the depreciation is to occur, then add those whole numbers together (that is, for a four-year depreciation period, you would add the whole numbers 1, 2, 3, and 4 together to get 10). This sum becomes your denominator. Your numerator becomes your whole numbers in reversed order, so that your first year depreciation would be 4/10 of the original price, your second year of depreciation would be 3/10, your third year would be 2/10, and your final year of depreciation would be 1/10. Your car or equipment is then fully depreciated.

Cars and the Environment

Cars are responsible for almost a quarter of the world's carbon dioxide (CO_2) emissions. Since the 1960s, car manufacturers have had pressure put on them to develop vehicles that would be less harmful to the environment. Experiments with steam cars (cumbersome), diesel engines (slow and heavy, though economical), solar-powered cars, and hybrid cars using both electricity (in town centers) and gasoline (on the open road) have met with less than satisfying results. Innovations in standard car and engine design have improved overall efficiency, but with more cars on the road, the overall impact has been negligible.

Two of the most pressing concerns are a car's CO_2 emissions and their contribution to the **greenhouse effect** and waste control at the end of a car's life cycle, both of which are discussed here. Checking how a car rates in these categories will be as important as any other consideration when purchasing a car in the future.

CO_2 emissions

Carbon dioxide (CO_2) emissions measure the amount of CO_2 discharged at the exhaust pipe. CO_2 is a chief contributor to the "greenhouse effect" and its by-product, global warming – one of the greatest threats to our world environment.

Before you make your next car purchase, ask about the car's CO_2 emission level. State and federal laws exist to control CO_2 emissions, with New York and California among the most stringent. If a specific vehicle meets the requirements of the state and federal government, then the manufacturer may call that car or truck a Low Emission Vehicle or LEV. That's the one you want.

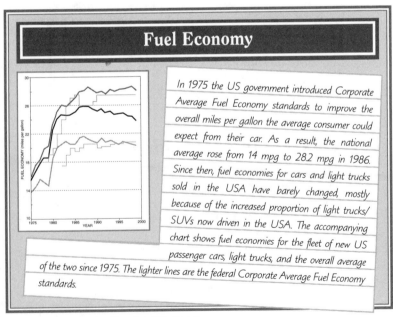

Fuel Economy

In 1975 the US government introduced Corporate Average Fuel Economy standards to improve the overall miles per gallon the average consumer could expect from their car. As a result, the national average rose from 14 mpg to 28.2 mpg in 1986. Since then, fuel economies for cars and light trucks sold in the USA have barely changed, mostly because of the increased proportion of light trucks/ SUVs now driven in the USA. The accompanying chart shows fuel economies for the fleet of new US passenger cars, light trucks, and the overall average of the two since 1975. The lighter lines are the federal Corporate Average Fuel Economy standards.

Figure courtesy of the American Council for an Energy-Efficient Economy

Traveling

Getting your bearings when you travel means knowing your numbers. The wonderful thing about numbers is that they can be translated into any language with relative ease. Getting to grips with the right numbers can mean the difference between a good and a great trip! Here are a few handy tips and tables to make your explorations a breeze.

Measuring Global Distances

Points on the earth's surface are commonly expressed in latitude and longitude, imaginary lines used to locate position on the globe. Latitude is the angular distance of a place from the equator. Lines of latitude are drawn parallel to the equator, with 0° at the equator and 90° at the north and south poles. Lines of longitude are drawn at right angles to these, with 0° (the prime meridian) passing through Greenwich, London.

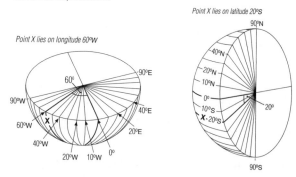

Lines of latitude and longitude.

If two points lie on the same meridian (i.e., they have the same longitude), then it is easy to determine the distance between them. Note that a full circle contains 360 degrees and each degree contains 60 minutes. Suppose that the earth's diameter is D, then its circumference is πD, where π = 3.14 approximately. This means that each degree of separation is equivalent to $\pi D/360$. By converting the angular separation to decimal degrees, it is therefore possible to relate this distance to the earth's diameter. The additional information that D = 12,756 km/7,923 mi, may be used to express this distance in either kilometers or miles.

distance between cities =
angular difference × $\dfrac{\text{earth's circumference}}{360°}$

Example

The angular separation between Rome (41°N 12°E) and Copenhagen (55°N 12°E) is 14°. How far apart are they?

Solution

If the angular separation of the two cities is 14°, then the distance between them is:

$14 \times \dfrac{(3.14 \times 7,923)}{360} = 14 \times 69.1 = 967.4$ mi

It is also possible to find the distances between cities with approximately the same latitude but the formula is more complicated, given that the distance between one degree of latitude changes the closer you move towards the poles. At the equator the distance between 1° of latitude or longitude is the same, approximately 69 mi/111 km, but at 60° latitude the east–west distance equivalent to a one degree difference of longitude is approximately 56 mi/35 km.

The following table gives the correct multipliers for different latitudes, valid for both northern and southern hemispheres.

Multipliers for different latitudes

Latitude (degrees)	Distance equivalent of 1° of longitude		
	(mi)	(km)	(nautical miles)
0	69.17	111.32	60.11
10	68.13	109.64	59.20
20	65.03	104.65	56.51
30	59.95	96.48	52.10
40	53.06	85.39	46.11
50	44.55	71.70	38.71
60	34.67	55.80	30.13
70	23.73	38.19	20.62
80	12.05	19.39	10.47
90	0.00	0.00	0.00

To find the difference between cities with approximately the same latitude, determine the difference between their lines of longitude, either by subtracting the larger number from the smaller if both are in the same hemisphere, or by adding together their longitudes if they lie in different hemispheres.

Example

New York City and Madrid lie close to the 40th parallel. New York has a longitude of 73° 58' W while Madrid has a longitude of 3° 42' E. Using the table above, what is the approximate distance between the two cities?

Solution

First calculate the difference between the two cities' longitude. Because they are in different hemispheres, take the sum of their angles. First round New York to 74° W and Madrid to 4° E and then add the two numbers together: 74 + 4 = 78°. Using the multiplier for 40° above, you can calculate the difference between the cities as $78 \times 53.06 \cong 4{,}138$ mi or $78 \times 85.39 \cong 6{,}660$ km.

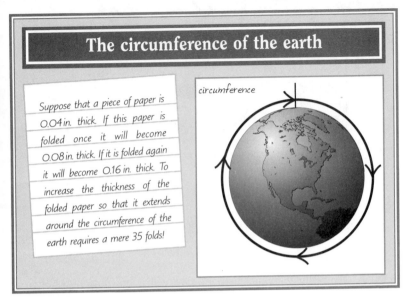

The circumference of the earth

Suppose that a piece of paper is 0.04 in. thick. If this paper is folded once it will become 0.08 in. thick. If it is folded again it will become 0.16 in. thick. To increase the thickness of the folded paper so that it extends around the circumference of the earth requires a mere 35 folds!

circumference

Maps

Maps are created to approximate distances in the real world and rely on ratios in order to establish a relationship between distances on the map and distances on the earth's surface. To draw this relationship, a scale is used. Maps covering larger areas might use a scale of 1 inch to represent 100 miles on the ground; maps covering smaller distances might choose a scale of 1 inch to represent 10 miles. Road maps generally use a scale of 1 inch equivalent to 2 miles. All maps supply a scale so that you can determine the actual distance by measuring its proportional equivalent on the map.

Example

If a map uses a scale of 2 in. equal to 5 miles, and the distance from your home to work on the map measures 7 in., how far is it to your office?

Solution

If 2 in. on the map is equivalent to 5 miles, then 1 in. is equivalent to $\frac{5}{2}$ miles, so $7 \times \frac{5}{2}$ equals 17.5 real miles.

Air Miles

In today's global economy, international travel is no longer a perk, it is a requirement. Airlines hoping to encourage loyalty among their users have developed frequent-flyer programs. Participants in these programs earn the equivalent air miles to their destinations, the aim of which is to accumulate enough air miles to be awarded free plane tickets or special promotional prizes depending on the particular airline's reward system. The table on pages 156–57 should give you some idea how many air miles you might expect to earn when flying from one destination to another.

Average commercial flying times between selected major cities (hours)

	Athens	Copenhagen	Frankfurt	London	Madrid	Moscow	NY	Paris	Rome
Athens		$4\frac{1}{2}$	$3\frac{1}{4}$	$3\frac{3}{4}$	$4\frac{1}{2}$	$4\frac{3}{4}$	12	$3\frac{1}{4}$	$1\frac{3}{4}$
Copenhagen	4		$1\frac{1}{2}$	$1\frac{1}{2}$	$3\frac{1}{2}$	3	$8\frac{3}{4}$	$1\frac{3}{4}$	$3\frac{1}{4}$
Frankfurt	3	$1\frac{1}{2}$		$1\frac{1}{2}$	$2\frac{1}{2}$	3	9	$1\frac{1}{4}$	$1\frac{3}{4}$
London	$3\frac{1}{2}$	$1\frac{3}{4}$	$1\frac{1}{2}$		$2\frac{1}{4}$	$3\frac{1}{2}$	$7\frac{1}{2}$	1	$2\frac{1}{2}$
Madrid	$4\frac{1}{2}$	$3\frac{1}{4}$	$2\frac{3}{4}$	2		$5\frac{1}{4}$	$8\frac{1}{2}$	$1\frac{3}{4}$	$2\frac{1}{4}$
Moscow	5	3	$3\frac{1}{4}$	$3\frac{3}{4}$	$5\frac{1}{4}$		$12\frac{1}{4}$	$4\frac{1}{4}$	$4\frac{1}{4}$
New York	$10\frac{3}{4}$	8	$8\frac{1}{4}$	$6\frac{3}{4}$	$7\frac{1}{4}$	$10\frac{3}{4}$		7	$8\frac{3}{4}$
Paris	$3\frac{1}{4}$	$1\frac{3}{4}$	$1\frac{1}{4}$	1	$1\frac{3}{4}$	4	8		$1\frac{3}{4}$
Rome	$1\frac{3}{4}$	$3\frac{1}{4}$	$1\frac{3}{4}$	$2\frac{1}{2}$	$2\frac{1}{4}$	$4\frac{1}{4}$	$10\frac{1}{4}$	$1\frac{3}{4}$	

Air distances between major world cities (in miles)

(– means not applicable.)

City	Bangkok	Beijing	Berlin	Cairo	Cape Town	Caracas
Bangkok	–	2,046	5,352	4,523	6,300	10,555
Beijing	2,046	–	4,584	4,698	8,044	8,950
Berlin	5,352	4,584	–	1,797	5,961	5,238
Cairo	4,523	4,698	1,797	–	4,480	6,342
Cape Town	6,300	8,044	5,961	4,480	–	6,366
Caracas	10,555	8,950	5,238	6,342	6,366	–
Chicago	8,570	6,604	4,414	6,141	8,491	2,495
Hong Kong	1,077	1,217	5,443	5,066	7,376	10,165
London	5,944	5,074	583	2,185	5,989	4,655
Los Angeles	7,637	6,250	5,782	7,520	9,969	3,632
Madrid	6,337	5,745	1,165	2,087	5,308	4,346
Melbourne	4,568	5,643	9,918	8,675	6,425	9,717
Mexico City	9,793	7,753	6,056	7,700	8,519	2,234
Montreal	8,338	6,519	3,740	5,427	7,922	2,438
Moscow	4,389	3,607	1,006	1,803	6,279	6,177
New York	8,669	6,844	3,979	5,619	7,803	2,120
Paris	5,877	5,120	548	1,998	5,786	4,732
Rio de Janeiro	9,994	10,768	6,209	6,143	3,781	2,804
Rome	5,494	5,063	737	1,326	5,231	5,195
San Francisco	7,931	5,918	5,672	7,466	10,248	3,902
Singapore	883	2,771	6,164	5,137	6,008	11,402
Stockholm	5,089	4,133	528	2,096	6,423	5,471
Tokyo	2,865	1,307	5,557	5,958	9,154	8,808
Washington, DC	8,807	6,942	4,181	5,822	7,895	2,047

City	Chicago	Hong Kong	London	Los Angeles	Madrid	Melbourne
Bangkok	8,570	1,077	5,944	7,637	6,337	4,568
Beijing	6,604	1,217	5,074	6,250	5,745	5,643
Berlin	4,414	5,443	583	5,782	1,165	9,918
Cairo	6,141	5,066	2,185	7,520	2,087	8,675
Cape Town	8,491	7,376	5,989	9,969	5,308	6,425
Caracas	2,495	10,165	4,655	3,632	4,189	9,673
Chicago	–	7,797	3,958	1,745	4,189	9,673
Hong Kong	7,797	–	5,990	7,240	6,558	4,595
London	3,958	5,990	–	5,439	785	10,500
Los Angeles	1,745	7,240	5,439	–	5,848	7,931
Madrid	4,189	6,558	785	5,848	–	10,758
Melbourne	9,673	4,595	10,500	7,931	10,758	–
Mexico City	1,690	8,788	5,558	1,542	5,643	8,426
Montreal	745	7,736	3,254	2,427	3,448	10,395
Moscow	4,987	4,437	1,564	6,068	2,147	8,950
New York	714	8,060	3,469	2,451	3,593	10,359
Paris	4,143	5,990	214	5,601	655	10,430
Rio de Janeiro	5,282	11,009	5,750	6,330	5,045	8,226
Rome	4,824	5,774	895	6,326	851	9,929
San Francisco	1,859	6,905	5,367	347	5,803	7,856
Singapore	9,372	1,605	6,747	8,767	7,080	3,759
Stockholm	4,331	5,063	942	5,454	1,653	9,630
Tokyo	6,314	1,791	5,959	5,470	6,706	5,062
Washington, DC	596	8,155	3,674	2,300	3,792	10,180

continued

Air distances between major world cities (in miles) – *continued*

City	Mexico City	Montreal	Moscow	New York	Paris	Rio de Janeiro
Bangkok	9,793	8,338	4,389	8,669	5,877	9,994
Beijing	7,753	6,519	3,607	6,844	5,120	10,768
Berlin	6,056	3,740	1,006	3,979	548	6,209
Cairo	7,700	5,427	1,803	5,619	1,998	6,143
Cape Town	8,519	7,922	6,279	7,803	5,786	3,781
Caracas	2,234	2,438	6,177	2,120	4,732	2,804
Chicago	1,690	745	4,987	714	4,143	5,282
Hong Kong	8,788	7,736	4,437	8,060	5,990	11,009
London	5,558	3,254	1,564	3,469	214	5,750
Los Angeles	1,542	2,427	6,068	2,451	5,601	6,330
Madrid	5,643	3,448	2,147	3,593	655	5,045
Melbourne	8,426	10,395	8,950	10,359	10,430	8,226
Mexico City	–	2,317	6,676	2,090	5,725	4,764
Montreal	2,317	–	4,401	331	3,432	5,078
Moscow	6,676	4,401	–	4,683	1,554	7,170
New York	2,090	331	4,683	–	3,636	4,801
Paris	5,725	3,432	1,554	3,636	–	5,684
Rio de Janeiro	4,764	5,078	7,170	4,801	5,684	–
Rome	6,377	4,104	1,483	4,293	690	5,707
San Francisco	1,887	2,543	5,885	2,572	5,577	6,613
Singapore	10,327	9,203	5,228	9,534	6,673	9,785
Stockholm	6,012	3,714	716	3,986	1,003	6,683
Tokyo	7,035	6,471	4,660	6,757	6,053	11,532
Washington, DC	1,885	489	4,876	205	3,840	4,779

City	Rome	San Francisco	Singapore	Stockholm	Tokyo	Washington, DC
Bangkok	5,494	7,931	883	5,089	2,865	8,807
Beijing	5,063	5,918	2,771	4,133	1,307	6,942
Berlin	737	5,672	6,164	528	5,557	4,181
Cairo	1,326	7,466	5,137	2,096	5,958	5,822
Cape Town	5,231	10,248	6,008	6,423	9,154	7,895
Caracas	5,195	3,902	11,402	5,471	8,808	2,047
Chicago	4,824	1,859	9,372	4,331	6,314	596
Hong Kong	5,774	6,905	1,605	5,063	1,791	8,155
London	895	5,367	6,747	942	5,959	3,674
Los Angeles	6,326	347	8,767	5,454	5,470	2,300
Madrid	851	5,803	7,080	1,653	6,706	3,792
Melbourne	9,929	7,856	3,759	9,630	5,062	10,180
Mexico City	6,377	1,887	10,327	6,012	7,035	1,885
Montreal	4,104	2,543	9,203	3,714	6,471	489
Moscow	1,483	5,885	5,228	716	4,660	4,876
New York	4,293	2,572	9,534	3,986	6,757	205
Paris	690	5,577	6,673	1,003	6,053	3,840
Rio de Janeiro	5,707	6,613	9,785	6,683	11,532	4,779
Rome	–	6,259	6,229	1,245	6,142	4,497
San Francisco	6,259	–	8,448	5,399	5,150	2,441
Singapore	6,229	8,448	–	5,936	3,300	9,662
Stockholm	1,245	5,399	5,936	–	5,053	4,183
Tokyo	6,142	5,150	3,300	5,053	–	6,791
Washington, DC	4,497	2,441	9,662	4,183	6,791	–

Average Monthly Temperatures

In a world where the amount of travel between countries is increasing, and escaping abroad for the weekend is commonplace, it is useful to have some guidelines about the temperatures so that logical decisions can be made about which clothes to pack for the trip. The table below gives the average monthly temperatures in degrees Fahrenheit (°F) of a number of major cities worldwide.

Average monthly temperatures (°F) of major cities throughout the year

City	January	April	July	October
Athens, Greece	48°	60°	81°	67°
Atlanta, Georgia	42°	62°	78°	62°
Beijing, China	25°	56°	80°	51°
Buenos Aires, Argentina	74°	63°	50°	60°
Cairo, Egypt	56°	70°	83°	71°
Chicago, Illinois	20°	49°	73°	54°
Dallas, Texas	44°	66°	86°	68°
Dublin, Ireland	40°	46°	59°	50°
Geneva, Switzerland	34°	50°	68°	51°
Hong Kong	59°	70°	82°	77°
Honolulu, Hawaii	71°	74°	81°	79°
Johannesburg, S Africa	68°	61°	52°	65°
Lima, Peru	74°	72°	62°	65°
London, England	40°	48°	64°	51°
Los Angeles, California	56°	60°	71°	67°
Madrid, Spain	40°	54°	75°	57°
Melbourne, Australia	73°	58°	49°	58°
Mexico City, Mexico	54°	65°	64°	60°
Miami, Florida	67°	75°	82°	78°
Milan, Italy	35°	56°	74°	57°
Montreal, Canada	13°	42°	70°	47°
New York, New York	28°	52°	76°	58°
Paris, France	37°	51°	66°	52°
Rio de Janeiro, Brazil	79°	75°	70°	71°
Rome, Italy	47°	57°	76°	63°
San Francisco, California	48°	55°	62°	60°
San Juan, Puerto Rico	75°	76°	80°	80°
Seoul, Korea	26°	52°	77°	56°
Sydney, Australia	72°	65°	53°	63°
Taipei, Taiwan	60°	70°	84°	74°
Tel Aviv, Israel	57°	67°	82°	77°
Tokyo, Japan	38°	55°	77°	62°
Vienna, Austria	30°	49°	67°	50°
Washington, DC	35°	57°	79°	59°

Average Monthly Rainfall

In addition to temperature, rainfall can have a large effect on holiday enjoyment. The following table can be used to optimize trips by choosing the most suitable destination and time to go. The levels of rainfall are given in inches. Indeed, as the table demonstrates, travel to some destinations may call for an umbrella irrespective of the time of year. Dubai is the driest capital with only 4 inches of annual rain whereas New York is the wettest capital with 44.4 inches of annual rain.

Average monthly rainfall (inches) of major cities

City	Jan	Feb	Mar	Apr	May	Jun	Jul	Aug	Sep	Oct	Nov	Dec	Annual
Amsterdam	3.1	1.7	3.5	1.5	2	2.4	2.9	2.4	3.2	4.1	3	2.8	32.7
Athens	2.1	1.6	1.4	0.9	0.8	0.5	0.2	0.3	0.6	1.8	2.5	2.7	15.5
Berlin	1.6	1	1.4	1.4	1.8	2.6	1.7	1.9	1.4	1.1	1.4	1.9	19.3
Copenhagen	1.7	1.3	1.4	1.5	1.6	2	2.5	2.7	2.2	2.3	2.1	1.9	23.2
Dubai	1	0.7	0.4	0.3	0	0	0	0	0	0	0.5	1	4
Dublin	2.5	2	2	1.9	2.2	2.2	2.6	3	2.5	2.9	2.7	2.7	29.2
Edinburgh	2.2	1.6	1.9	1.5	2	2	2.5	2.7	2.5	2.4	2.5	2.4	26.2
Lisbon	3.7	3.4	3.3	2.3	1.7	0.7	0.2	0.2	1.3	2.9	3.9	3.8	27.7
London	1.9	1.5	1.6	1.7	1.9	2.1	2.3	2.3	2.2	2.4	2.3	2.1	24.2
Los Angeles	2.4	2.6	1.9	1	0.2	0	0	0.1	0.3	0.4	1.4	2.3	12.7
Madrid	1.4	1.4	1.6	1.8	1.7	1.2	0.4	0.4	1.3	1.9	2.1	1.7	16.9
New York	3.3	3.1	3.9	3.7	4.2	3.3	4.1	4.1	3.6	3.3	4.2	3.6	44.4
Paris	1.8	1.5	1.6	1.7	2.2	2.2	2.2	2.2	2.1	2.2	2.1	1.9	23.9
Prague	1	0.8	1.1	1.4	2.5	2.8	3.2	2.8	1.8	1.1	1.1	0.9	20.8
Rome	3.2	2.5	2.8	2.2	2.1	1.4	0.7	1.1	2.4	4.6	4.4	3.9	31.2
Tokyo	2	2.8	4.2	5.1	5.7	6.9	5.3	5.8	8.5	7.6	3.8	2.1	60

World Time Zones

Up until the mid-19th century, most cities still relied upon the sun to tell them approximately what time it was. When railroads made it possible to travel hundreds of miles a day, it became necessary to develop some standardized measurement of time, rather than attempting to keep track of hundreds of local times. In 1883, the USA officially divided itself in to four time zones roughly located on the 75th, 90th, 105th, and 120th meridians. The following year,

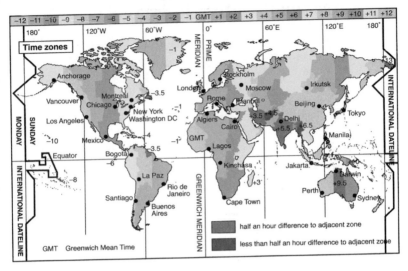

the country hosted the International Meridian Conference where an international standard was agreed. Time zones were created using the 24 standard meridians, every 15° east and west of Greenwich, England (the prime meridian), as centers of the zones. Zone boundaries tend to wander considerably from straight north–south lines with individual countries and states preferring to stay within one time zone for various reasons

In 1972, universal time, based on the earth's actual rotation, was replaced by coordinated universal time (UTC), which involves the addition (or subtraction) of leap seconds on the last day of June or December. National observatories make standard time available, and the BBC (British Broadcasting Corporation) broadcasts six pips at certain hours (five short, from second 55 to second 59, and one long, the start of which indicates the precise minute). Its computerized clock has accuracy greater than 1 second in 4,000 years. UTC replaced Greenwich Mean Time (GMT) in 1986. However, the Greenwich meridian, adopted at the 1884 International Meridian Conference, is still used to measure longitude and to calculate the world's standard time zones.

Relative times in cities throughout the world

The time indicated in the following tables is fixed by law and is called standard time; it is shown using the 24-hour clock.

Relative times in cities throughout the world at 12:00 noon, GMT

City	Time	City	Time
Abu Dhabi, United Arab Emirates	16:00	Delhi, India	17:30
Accra, Ghana	12:00	Denver (CO), USA	05:00
Addis Ababa, Ethiopia	15:00	Dhaka, Bangladesh	18:00
Adelaide, Australia	21:30	Dubai, United Arab Emirates	16:00
Alexandria, Egypt	14:00	Dublin, Republic of Ireland	12:00
Algiers, Algeria	13:00	Florence, Italy	13:00
Amman, Jordan	14:00	Frankfurt am Main, Germany	13:00
Amsterdam, Netherlands	13:00	Gdansk, Poland	13:00
Anchorage (AK), USA	03:00	Geneva, Switzerland	13:00
Ankara, Turkey	14:00	Hague, The, Netherlands	13:00
Athens, Greece	14:00	Harare, Zimbabwe	14:00
Auckland, New Zealand	24:00	Havana, Cuba	07:00
Baghdad, Iraq	15:00	Helsinki, Finland	14:00
Bahrain (also called Al Manamah), Bahrain	15:00	Hobart, Australia	22:00
Bangkok, Thailand	19:00	Ho Chi Minh City, Vietnam	19:00
Barcelona, Spain	13:00	Hong Kong, China	20:00
Beijing, China	20:00	Istanbul, Turkey	14:00
Beirut, Lebanon	14:00	Jakarta, Indonesia	19:00
Belgrade, Yugoslavia	13:00	Jerusalem, Israel	14:00
Berlin, Germany	13:00	Johannesburg, South Africa	14:00
Bern, Switzerland	13:00	Karachi, Pakistan	17:00
Bogotá, Colombia	07:00	Kiev, Ukraine	14:00
Bonn, Germany	13:00	Kuala Lumpur, Malaysia	20:00
Brazzaville, Republic of the Congo	13:00	Kuwait City, Kuwait	15:00
Brisbane, Australia	22:00	Kyoto, Japan	21:00
Brussels, Belgium	13:00	Lagos, Nigeria	13:00
Bucharest, Romania	14:00	Le Havre, France	13:00
Budapest, Hungary	13:00	Lima, Peru	07:00
Buenos Aires, Argentina	09:00	Lisbon, Portugal	12:00
Cairo, Egypt	14:00	London, England	12:00
Calcutta, India	17:30	Luanda, Angola	13:00
Canberra, Australia	22:00	Luxembourg, Luxembourg	13:00
Cape Town, South Africa	14:00	Lyon, France	13:00
Caracas, Venezuela	08:00	Madrid, Spain	13:00
Casablanca, Morocco	12:00	Manila, Philippines	20:00
Chennai (formerly Madras), India	17:30	Marseille, France	13:00
Chicago (IL), USA	06:00	Mecca, Saudi Arabia	15:00
Cologne, Germany	13:00	Melbourne, Australia	22:00
Colombo, Sri Lanka	18:00	Mexico City, Mexico	06:00
Copenhagen, Denmark	13:00	Milan, Italy	13:00
Damascus, Syria	14:00	Minsk, Belarus	14:00
Dar es Salaam, Tanzania	15:00	Monrovia, Liberia	12:00
Darwin, Australia	21:30	Montevideo, Uruguay	09:00
		Montreal, Canada	07:00

continued

Relative times in cities throughout the world at 12:00 noon, GMT – *continued*

City	Time	City	Time
Moscow, Russian Federation	15:00	St Petersburg, Russian Federation	15:00
Mumbai (formerly Bombay), India	17:30	Stockholm, Sweden	13:00
Munich, Germany	13:00	Sydney, Australia	22:00
Nairobi, Kenya	15:00	Taipei, Taiwan	20:00
New Orleans (LA), USA	06:00	Tashkent, Uzbekistan	17:00
New York (NY), USA	07:00	Tehran, Iran	15:30
Nicosia, Cyprus	14:00	Tel Aviv-Yafo, Israel	14:00
Oslo, Norway	13:00	Tenerife, Canary Islands	12:00
Ottawa, Canada	07:00	Tokyo, Japan	21:00
Panamá, Panama	07:00	Toronto, Canada	07:00
Paris, France	13:00	Tripoli, Libya	13:00
Perth, Australia	20:00	Tunis, Tunisia	13:00
Port Said, Egypt	14:00	Valparaiso, Chile	08:00
Prague, Czech Republic	13:00	Vancouver, Canada	04:00
Rawalpindi, Pakistan	17:00	Vatican City	13:00
Reykjavìk, Iceland	12:00	Venice, Italy	13:00
Rio de Janeiro, Brazil	09:00	Vienna, Austria	13:00
Riyadh, Saudi Arabia	15:00	Vladivostok, Russian Federation	22:00
Rome, Italy	13:00	Volgograd, Russian Federation	16:00
San Francisco (CA), USA	04:00	Warsaw, Poland	13:00
Santiago, Chile	08:00	Wellington, New Zealand	24:00
Seoul, South Korea	21:00	Yangon (formerly Rangoon), Myanmar	18:30
Shanghai, China	20:00	Yokohama, Japan	21:00
Singapore City, Singapore	20:00	Zagreb, Croatia	13:00
Sofia, Bulgaria	14:00	Zürich, Switzerland	13:00

The International Date Line (IDL)

An imaginary line of demarcation that separates two consecutive calendar days and approximately follows the 180° line of longitude. The date is put forward a day when crossing the line going west and back a day when going east. The IDL was chosen at the International Meridian Conference in 1884. Given that the prime meridian is located in Greenwich, England, it was logical to select a place for changing the date 12 hours or 180° from Greenwich, which fortunately runs mostly through the open Pacific. The IDL zigzags in Siberia, Hawaii, and New Zealand to incorporate parts and islands of the countries, but otherwise runs straight along the 180° meridian.

International Dialing Codes

The following table lists the international telephone codes required for dialing into a number of different countries.

Country	Dialing code	Country	Dialing code
Albania	355	Colombia	57
Algeria	213	Comoros	269
Andorra	376	Congo, Democratic	
Angola	244	Republic of	243
Anguilla	1	Congo, Republic of the	242
Antigua and Barbuda	1	Cook Islands	682
Argentina	54	Costa Rica	506
Armenia	374	Côte d'Ivoire (Ivory Coast)	225
Aruba	297	Croatia (Hrvatska)	385
Ascension Island	247	Cuba	53
Australia	61	Cyprus (No rth)	90
Austria	43	Cyprus (Republic of)	357
Azerbaijan	994	Czech Republic	420
Azores	351	Denmark	45
Bahamas	1	Diego Garcia	246
Bahrain	973	Djibouti	253
Bangladesh	880	Dominica	1
Barbados	1	Dominican Republic	1
Belarus	375	Ecuador	593
Belgium	32	Egypt	20
Belize	501	El Salvador	503
Benin	229	Equatorial Guinea	240
Bermuda	1	Eritrea	291
Bhutan	975	Estonia	372
Bolivia	591	Ethiopia	251
Bosnia Herzegovina	387	Falkland Islands	500
Botswana	267	Faroe Islands	298
Brazil	55	Fiji	679
Brunei	673	Finland	358
Bulgaria	359	France	33
Burkina Faso	226	French Guiana	594
Burundi	257	French Polynesia	689
Cambodia	855	Gabon	241
Cameroon	237	Gambia	220
Canada	1	Georgia	995
Canary Islands	34	Germany	49
Cape Verde	238	Ghana	233
Cayman Islands	1	Gibraltar	350
Central African Republic	236	Greece	30
Chad	235	Greenland Island	299
Chile	56	Grenada	1
China	86	Guadeloupe	590
Christmas Island	61	Guam	1
Cocos (Keeling) Islands	61	Guatemala	502
		Guinea-Bissau	245

continued

Country	Dialing code	Country	Dialing code
Guinea (Republic of)	224	Monaco	377
Guyana	592	Mongolia	976
Haiti	509	Montserrat	1
Honduras	504	Morocco	212
Hong Kong	852	Mozambique	258
Hungary	36	Myanmar (Burma)	95
Iceland	354	Namibia	264
India	91	Nauru	674
Indonesia	62	Nepal	977
Iran	98	Netherlands	31
Iraq	964	Netherlands Antilles	599
Ireland	353	New Caledonia	687
Israel	972	New Zealand	64
Italy	39	Nicaragua	505
Jamaica	1	Niger	227
Japan	81	Nigeria	234
Jordan	962	Niue	683
Kazakhstan	7	Norfolk Island	672
Kenya	254	Norway	47
Kiribati	686	Oman	968
Korea (North)	850	Pakistan	92
Korea (South)	82	Palau	680
Kuwait	965	Panama	507
Kyrgyzstan	996	Papua New Guinea	675
Laos	856	Paraguay	595
Latvia	371	Peru	51
Lebanon	961	Philippines	63
Lesotho	266	Poland	48
Liberia	231	Portugal	351
Libya	218	Puerto Rico	1
Lithuania	370	Qatar	974
Luxembourg	352	Reunion	262
Macau	853	Romania	40
Macedonia	389	Rwanda	250
Madagascar	261	Russia	7
Malawi	265	St Christopher	1
Malaysia	60	St Helena	290
Maldives	960	St Lucia	1
Mali	223	St Pierre and Miquelon	508
Malta	356	St Vincent	1
Mariana Islands	1	Samoa (US)	684
Marshall Islands	692	Samoa (Western)	685
Martinique	596	San Marino	378
Mauritania	222	São Tomé and Príncipe	239
Mauritius Island	230	Saudi Arabia	966
Mayotte Island	269	Senegal	221
Mexico	52	Seychelles	248
Micronesia	691	Sierra Leone	232
Moldova	373	Singapore	65

continued

International dialing codes – *continued*

Country	Dialing code	Country	Dialing code
Slovakia	421	Tunisia	216
Slovenia	386	Turkey	90
Solomon Islands	677	Turkmenistan	993
Somalia	252	Turks and Caicos Islands	1
South Africa	27	Tuvalu	688
Spain	34	Uganda	256
Sri Lanka	94	Ukraine	380
Sudan	249	United Arab Emirates	971
Surinam	597	United Kingdom	44
Swaziland	268	United States	1
Sweden	46	Uruguay	598
Switzerland	41	Uzbekistan	7
Syria	963	Vanuatu	678
Taiwan	886	Venezuela	58
Tadzhikistan	7	Vietnam	84
Tanzania	255	Virgin Islands (British)	1
Thailand	66	Virgin Islands (US)	1
Togo	228	Yemen	967
Tokelau	690	Yugoslavia	381
Tonga	676	Zambia	260
Trinidad and Tobago	1	Zimbabwe	263

International Exchange Rates

One of the biggest challenges of international travel is figuring out how much items cost in your own currency, rather than that of the country you are visiting. To convert foreign currency into dollars, you need to check the current international exchange rate. Exchange rates are published daily in most major newspapers and can be found on any of a number of financial investment sites currently available on the Web. Here is an example table showing approximate international exchange rates for March 2001.

International exchange rates (March 2001)

Currency names	UK pound	Euro	French franc	German mark	Japanese yen	US dollar
UK pound	1.00	0.64	0.097	0.33	0.006	0.68
Euro	1.57	1.00	0.15	0.51	0.009	1.08
French franc	10.29	6.56	1.00	3.35	0.059	7.05
German mark	3.07	1.95	0.29	1.00	0.018	2.10
Japanese yen	175.11	111.49	16.99	57.00	1.00	119.94
US dollar	1.46	0.93	0.14	0.48	0.008	1.00

To determine what an item costs in your own currency, multiply the amount you have spent by the decimal percentage listed on the exchange table.

Example

You have spent £30 on a pair of earrings while on vacation in London. Using the exchange table given, what is its equivalent price in dollars?

Solution

Find US dollar in the left-hand column, scroll across to the UK pound column.

The decimal percentage is 1.46.

£30 × 1.46 = $43.80.

You have spent the equivalent of $43.80.

Tax Refunds on Foreign Purchases

You may come across something called VAT in your international travels. Value Added Tax is a national sales tax on retail goods and services. VAT rates vary from country to country. The average rate is approximately 18%. If you wish to reclaim VAT in a foreign country, take your passport with you when you shop, so that you can prove you are a foreign citizen. When making your purchase, request a VAT refund form from the sales assistant and find out if the store charges a fee for making VAT refunds. When you leave the country, go to the airport earlier than usual and have a customs officer inspect your purchases and stamp the VAT forms or invoices. Educational items such as books are generally charged a lower VAT rate.

Country	Books (%)	VAT on most products(%)
Austria	10	20
Belgium	6	21
Denmark	25	25
Finland	8	22
France	5.50	19.60
Germany	7	16
Great Britain and Northern Ireland	0	17.50
Greece	0	17.50
Ireland (Eire)	0	20
Italy	4	20
Luxembourg	3	15
Netherlands	6	19
Portugal	5	17
Spain	4	16
Sweden	25	25

Analog clock

Digital clock

The 24-hour Clock

Many of us still rely on the big hand and the little hand to tell us what time it is, but the digital age has effectively changed all that. Where once we referred solely to the 12-hour clock, differentiating morning from afternoon by the terms **a.m.** and **p.m.**, most countries and languages now use the 24-hour international standard format for time. The 24-hour clock is a measure of what time it is since the previous midnight, so if it is morning (anytime past midnight until noon), the 12-hour and 24-hour clocks will read the same. If it is afternoon (anytime past noon until midnight), then the 12-hour clock rolls back to zero, but the 24-hour clock continues counting till it reaches midnight again. To convert an afternoon time on a 24-hour clock to a 12-hour time, you simply subtract 12.

Reading Schedules

Most train and ferry schedules give you a weekday schedule and a weekend schedule. Your first task is to find the day you need and the direction in which you intend to travel. The first city listed is usually the first point of departure for the route; the last city listed is the last stop or final destination. It is imperative that you are looking at the right schedule in the right order. Here is an example of how to read a train schedule (see page opposite).

Example

It is 8:00 a.m. Sunday morning and you have just received a call from your mother in Poughkeepsie. You need to attend a family lunch there at 12 noon, but you have tickets booked for the theater in New York in the evening at 7:30 p.m. It takes you 30 minutes to get to the station and get tickets. Which trains can you use that will get you to the family lunch and back again in time to make the theater curtain?

Solution

First check to see you are looking at the Sunday schedule and the part headed "To Poughkeepsie." If you leave your house at 8:20 a.m. you should be able to catch the 8:49 train and arrive in Poughkeepsie at 10:43 a.m. Since your mother lives only 20 minutes away from the station you can take the 9:53 a.m. train and still arrive in time.

For the return journey, you need to be sure you are in time for the theater. The 4:33 p.m. train arrives at 6:26 p.m. but you decide this does not leave you enough time to find the theater and get to your seat, so you decide to take the 3:33 p.m. train back to New York.

SATURDAY, SUNDAY & HOLIDAYS

To Poughkeepsie	8813	8817	8821
Grand Central Terminal	AM 8 49	AM 9 53	AM 10 53
Harlem 125th Street	R 9 00	R 10 04	R 11 04
Morris Heights / University Heights			
Marble Hill / Spuyten Duyvil / Riverdale	9 08	10 12	11 12
Ludlow / Yonkers / Glenwood / Greystone	9 15	10 19	11 19
Hastings / Dobbs Ferry / Ardsley / Irvington			
Tarrytown / Philipse Manor / Scarborough	9 28	10 30	11 30
Ossining / Croton-Harmon Ar	9 33	10 37	11 37
Croton-Harmon Lv	9 38	10 42	11 42
Cortlandt	9 46	10 50	11 50
Peekskill	9 51	10 55	11 55
Manitou	9 57		
Garrison	10 02	11 05	12 05
Cold Spring	10 06	11 08	12 08
Beacon	10 17	11 17	12 17
New Hamburg	10 24	11 24	12 24
Poughkeepsie	10 43	11 43	12 43

To New York	8840	8844	8848
Poughkeepsie	PM 3 33	PM 4 33	PM 5 33
New Hamburg	3 43	4 43	5 43
Beacon	3 50	4 50	5 50
Breakneck Ridge		4 55	
Cold Spring	3 58	5 00	5 58
Garrison	4 02	5 04	6 02
Manitou		5 09	
Peekskill	4 13	5 18	6 12
Corlandt	4 18		6 17
Croton Harmon Ar.		5 23	
Croton-Harmon Lv.	4 29	5 34	6 27
Ossining	4 33	5 38	6 31
Scarborough / Philipse Manor			
Tarrytown	4 41	5 46	6 39
Irvington / Ardley / Dobbs Ferry / Hastings			
Greystone		5 57	
Glenwood / Yonkers / Ludlow	4 52		6 50
Riverdale		6 03	
Spuytan Duyvil / Marble Hill	4 58		6 56
University Heights / Morris Heights		6 10	
Harlem – 125th Street	H 5 10	H 6 15	H 7 08
Grand Central Terminal	5 21 PM	6 26 PM	7 19 PM

Reference Marks

C – Connecting service

R – Stops only to receive customers

H – Stops primarily to discharge customers. Train may depart 5 minutes earlier than the time shown.

Computing

Hide all you want, but there's no escaping the Digital Age. All those numbers that the enthusiasts throw around actually mean something, and much as you would like to gloss over them, it's in your best interest to make friends with them. In this section we will take the gentle approach to understanding the numbers that rule our desktops.

Computer Basics

A computer is a programmable electronic device that processes data and performs calculations and other symbol-manipulation tasks. There are three types: the digital computer, which manipulates information coded using binary numbers; the analog computer, which works with electrical currents and voltages; and the hybrid computer, which has characteristics of both analog and digital computers.

Binary number system

Digital computer programs run on codes based on binary numbers. The binary system uses numbers to base two, meaning the digits 1 and 0. The binary digits (known as bits) are used to represent instructions and data in all modern digital computers. The values of the binary digits are stored or transmitted as open/closed switches, magnetized/ unmagnetized disks and tapes, and high/low voltages in circuits.

To appreciate how this works, you need to understand binary. Our usual number system is "base-ten:" there are ten digits (0–9) and ten is written as "10" to show there is one value of ten and no value of units. The binary system is a "base-two" system, so "10" would show that there is one value of 2 and no value of 1, and so it represents the number 2. The value of any position in a binary number doubles (1, 2, 4, 8) with each move from right to left, just as in our normal number system it increases by the power of 10 (10, 100, 1,000). So "111" in the binary system means there is one value of 4, one value of 2, and one value of 1, add these together and you get 7. "101" means there is one value of 4, no value of 2, and one value of 1, which, added together makes 5.

Decimal to binary conversions for the numbers 1 to 10

Decimal		Binary							
10's	1's	128	64	32	16	8	4	2	1
0	1	0	0	0	0	0	0	0	1
0	2	0	0	0	0	0	0	1	0
0	3	0	0	0	0	0	0	1	1
0	4	0	0	0	0	0	1	0	0
0	5	0	0	0	0	0	1	0	1
0	6	0	0	0	0	0	1	1	0
0	7	0	0	0	0	0	1	1	1
0	8	0	0	0	0	1	0	0	0
0	9	0	0	0	0	1	0	0	1
1	0	0	0	0	0	1	0	1	0

Example

Find the equivalent decimal system value for 1011 in the binary number system.

Solution

Since the binary number extends four places, you would add up your values like this:

$$(1 \times 8) + (0 \times 4) + (1 \times 2) + (1 \times 1) = 11$$

Babbage, Charles (1792–1871)

English mathematician who devised a precursor of the computer. He designed an analytical engine, a general-purpose mechanical computing device for performing different calculations according to a program input on punched cards (an idea borrowed from the Jacquard loom). This device was never built, but it embodied many of the principles on which today's digital computers are based.

Bethmann/Corbis

Boolean logic

In his work *The Mathematical Analysis of Logic (1847)*, English mathematician George Boole established the basis of modern mathematical logic and computer design. Boole's system is essentially two-valued. By subdividing objects into separate classes, each with a given property, his algebra makes it possible to treat different classes according to the presence or absence of the same property. Hence it involves just two numbers, 0 and 1 – the binary system used in the computer.

Algorithms

An algorithm is a procedure or series of steps that can be used to solve a problem. In computer science, an algorithm describes the logical sequence of operations to be performed by a program. A flow chart is a visual representation of an algorithm. The word derives from the name of 9th-century Arab mathematician Muhammad ibn-Musa al-Khwarizmi.

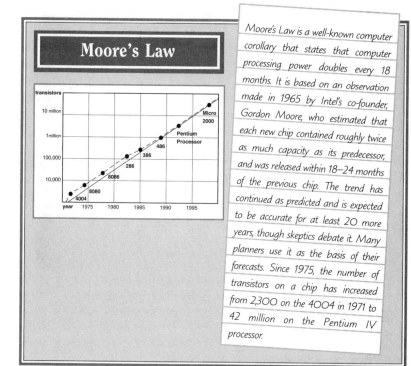

Moore's Law

Moore's Law is a well-known computer corollary that states that computer processing power doubles every 18 months. It is based on an observation made in 1965 by Intel's co-founder, Gordon Moore, who estimated that each new chip contained roughly twice as much capacity as its predecessor, and was released within 18–24 months of the previous chip. The trend has continued as predicted and is expected to be accurate for at least 20 more years, though skeptics debate it. Many planners use it as the basis of their forecasts. Since 1975, the number of transistors on a chip has increased from 2,300 on the 4004 in 1971 to 42 million on the Pentium IV processor.

Computer Memory Storage

In computing, memory is the part of a system used to store data and programs either permanently or temporarily. There are two main types: immediate access memory and backing storage. Data is recorded in the form of bits (the binary digits 0 or 1). A byte is the most common unit of memory capacity and equals 8 bits. A list of typical units of memory capacity is given in the following table.

Typical units of memory capacity

1 byte	8 bits
1 KB	1,024 or 1,000 bytes*
1 MB	1,048,576 or 1,000,000 bytes
1 GB	1,073,741,824 or 1,000,000,000 bytes

*In the metric system, the prefix "kilo" denotes multiplication by 1,000.
However, computer memory is based on the binary number system, and the most convenient binary equivalent of 1,000 is 2^{10}, or 1,024.

Typical memory capacities

Device	Typical memory capacity
Hard disk	1–50 GB
Floppy disk	0.5–2 MB
Zip drive	100 MB
CD-ROM	680 MB
DVD	8.5 GB
RAM	16–256 MB

Computer Clock Rate

The computer clock rate is the frequency of a computer's internal electronic clock. Every computer contains an electronic clock, which produces a sequence of regular electrical pulses used by the control unit to synchronize the components of the computer and regulate the retrieve-execute cycle by which program instructions are processed. Clock rates are measured in megahertz (MHz) or millions of pulses a second. Microcomputers commonly have clock rates of up to 1,000 MHz.

Central Processing Unit

A main component of a computer, the central processing unit (CPU) executes individual program instructions and controls the operation of other parts. It is sometimes referred to as the central processor or, when contained on a single, integrated circuit, a microprocessor.

The CPU has three main components: the **arithmetic and logic unit** (ALU), where all calculations and logical operations are carried out; a **control unit**, which decodes, synchronizes, and executes program instructions; and the **immediate access memory**, which stores the data and programs on which the computer is currently working. All these components contain **registers**, which are memory locations reserved for specific purposes.

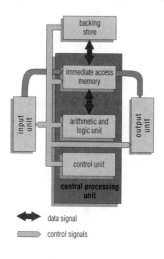

The relationship between the three main areas of a computer's CPU.

Apple Versus PC Power

An Apple computer's CPU (central processing unit) is different from the standard Intel or Intel-based PC CPU, running at almost twice the speed of its PC-size counterpart. So be careful when comparing statistics between an Apple computer and a PC. You will get the same performance level from an Apple of lower MHz as one from a higher speed PC. The accompanying chart gives a rough estimate of equivalent performance levels between the Apple G3 series and the Intel Pentium III chip.

Equivalent performance levels between the Apple G3 series and the Intel Pentium III chip

Apple G3 PowerPC series	Intel Pentium III chip
PowerPC 750 350 MHz	500 MHz
PowerPC 750 400 MHz	750–800 MHz
G3 PowerPC 750 450 MHz	850–900 MHz
G3 PowerPC 750 500 MHz	1 GHz (1,000 MHz)
G4 PowerPC 7400 400 MHz	950 MHz
G4 PowerPC 7400 450 MHz	1 GHz (1,000 MHz)
G4 PowerPC 7400 500 MHz	1.5 GHz (1,500 MHz)

Modems and Modem Speeds

A modem is a device for transmitting computer data over telephone lines. Modems are used for linking remote terminals to central computers and enable computers to communicate with each other anywhere in the world. The more speed or **bandwidth** (rate of data transmission, measured in bits per second) you have at your computer's disposal, the faster your download times.

Your modem in reality has two speeds: connect speed and computer speed. Connect speed is the rate at which the remote modem and your modem connect. Typical speeds are 28.8 kbps (kilobits per second), 33.6 kbps, 48 kbps, and 56 kbps. Computer speed on the other hand is the rate at which your computer and modem communicate. This rate is normally higher than your connection rate. It can be 57.6 kbps, 115.2 kbps, or even 230.4 kbps. Practically speaking, it is the connect speed that is important since it determines how quickly data will get transmitted to you from an external source.

ISDN (Integrated Services Digital Network) is an internationally developed telecommunications system for sending signals in digital format, thereby greatly increasing the amount of information that can be carried. With ISDN's Basic Rate Access, a **multiplexer** divides one voice telephone line into three channels. Two of the bands offer 64 kilobits per second, and can carry one voice conversation or 50 simultaneous data calls at 1,200 bits per second. The third band operates at 16 kilobits per second.

DSL is an abbreviation for Digital Subscriber Loop (or Line). Examples include ADSL (asymmetric digital subscriber loop) which is the standard for transmitting video data through existing copper telephone wires.

The following table shows the modem speeds from 9600-bits per second to dual-channel ISDN and DSL (Digital Subscriber Loop) connection speed.

Modem throughput speed

Connection	Modem throughput speed					
	Bits/sec	*Bytes/sec*	*Bytes/min*	*KB/min*	*MB/hour*	*Mins/MB*
9600 Modem	9,600	1,200	72,000	70.31	4.12	14.56
14.4 Modem	14,400	1,800	108,000	105.47	6.18	9.71
V.34 Modem	28,800	3,600	216,000	210.94	12.36	4.85
33.6 Modem	33,600	4,200	252,000	246.09	14.42	4.16
V.90 Modem	42,000	5,250	315,000	307.62	18.02	3.33
V.90 Modem	50,000	6,250	375,000	366.21	21.46	2.80
ISDN (1 B)	64,000	8,000	480,000	468.75	27.47	2.18
ISDN (2 B)	128,000	16,000	960,000	937.50	54.93	1.09
DSL 256K	256,000	32,000	1,920,000	1,875.00	109.86	0.35

Note that these numbers are for uncompressed data (gif's, jpg's, zip, and exe files), just to give an idea on raw data throughput. Because graphic images on Web pages are already compressed, Web browsing generally works out to approximately 1.5 to 2 times faster than the above listed rates. So divide these times by 2 to approximate real-world download times.

Sample download times

This table gives estimated download time for text, pictures, and videos.

Estimated download time for text, pictures, and videos

Modem speed	Text (2.2 KB)	Picture (300 KB)	Video (2.4 MB)
2,400 bps	7.33 sec	16.6 min	2.42 hrs
9,600 bps	1.83 sec	4.17 min	33.3 min
14,400 bps	1.22 sec	2.78 min	22.2 min
28,800 bps	0.61 sec	1.39 min	11.1 min

Internet

The Internet is a global computer network connecting governments, companies, universities, and millions of private users. The Internet itself began in the mid-1980s with funding from the US National Science Foundation as a means to allow US universities to share the resources of five regional supercomputing centers.

Electronic mail, electronic conferencing, and educational and chat services are all supported across the Internet, as is the ability to access remote computers and send and retrieve files.

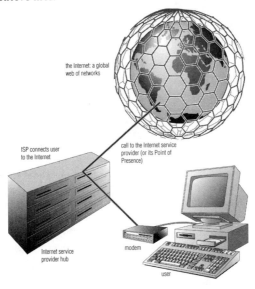

the Internet: a global web of networks

ISP connects user to the Internet

call to the Internet service provider (or its Point of Presence)

Internet service provider hub

modem

user

The Internet is accessed by millions of users via a modem to the service provider's hub, which handles all connection requests. Once connected, the user can access a whole range of information from many different sources, including the World Wide Web.

TCP/IP

At the heart of the Internet is a set of common standards known as Internet **protocols** or **TCP/IP** (Transmission Control Protocol/Internet Protocol). A computer of any type can connect with the Internet and successfully exchange data as long as it can run those protocols.

TCP/IP is composed of layers:

- **IP** – moves packets of data from node to node (a node is a processing location – in this case, your computer to another computer). Packets are forwarded based on a four-byte destination address (the IP number). The Internet authorities assign ranges of numbers to different organizations who in turn assign numbers internally.

- **TCP** – verifies the correct delivery of data from your computer to the server. Data can be lost during transmission between networks. TCP provides additional support to detect errors or lost data and to trigger retransmission until the data is received correctly.

- **Sockets** – subroutines (sections of a program) that provide access to TCP/IP on most computer systems.

Internet numbers

An Internet number is actually a 32-bit number, commonly represented as four numbers joined by periods (.), like 191.37.245.155., and known as a **dotted quad**. Each piece of an Internet address (like 191) is called an octet. The first two or three pieces (for example 191.37.245) represent the network that a system is on, also known as its *subnet*. IP addresses and domain names are assigned and monitored by Internet authorities such as the Network Information Center (NIC).

Turing, Alan Mathison (1912–1954)

English mathematician and logician (shown here far left). In 1936 he described a "universal computing machine" that could theoretically be programmed to solve any problem capable of solution by a specially designed machine. This concept, now called the Turing machine, foreshadowed the digital computer. Turing is believed to have been the first to suggest (in 1950) the possibility of machine learning and artificial intelligence. His test for distinguishing between real (human) and simulated (computer) thought is known as the Turing test: with a person in one room and the machine in another, an interrogator in a third room asks questions of both to try to identify them. When the interrogator cannot distinguish between them by questioning, the machine will have reached a state of humanlike intelligence.

Alan Turing Archives

Section Three

Magical Math

Fascinating Figures

One – might be the loneliest number, but everyone wants to be no. 1 in the rankings! Being one of a kind makes you unique. Favorite fairy tales begin with "Once upon a time … ." An *ace* is a single spot, a favorite playing card, winning serve, hole in one, skilled performer. To *have an ace in the hole*, *an ace up your sleeve*, or *hold all the aces* means you have the advantage or the power. Words related to one include *unit, unity, single, solo*. Words beginning with *uni-* usually mean *one* of something, as in *unicycle* (one wheel) and *unicorns* (one horn). *Mono-* also means *one* of something, as in *monorail* (single rail track), *monosyllabic* (one syllable), or *monogamy* (having only one partner).

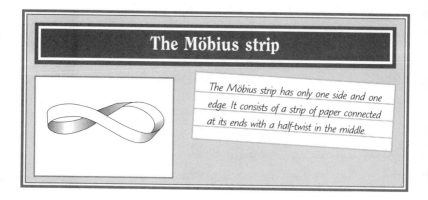

The Möbius strip

The Möbius strip has only one side and one edge. It consists of a strip of paper connected at its ends with a half-twist in the middle.

Two – has the honor of being the only even prime number. It can make one less lonely (two's company) or more miserable (cut in two, missing half, terrible twos). Words that are associated with the number two are *deuce*, *dual*, a *duet*, *couple*, and *pair*. People have two hands, two feet, two eyes, two ears. There are two sexes and two sides to an argument, both giving rise to the phrase, "it takes two to tango". Two is often joined with other words to form a compound that means divided into, consisting of, or having, two parts or divisions, as in *two-sided*. *Bi-* also means two as in *bicycle* (two wheels) and *bifocals* (glasses with lenses for both close work and distance). The *binary* number system is written to the base two.

Three – is the first odd prime number. In Christian theology, three is the union of God the Father, the Son, and the Holy Spirit. There were three kings who visited the baby Jesus, three little pigs, three angels (Charlie's), and three musketeers. We live in a three-dimensional world. We're in the third millennium AD. A *hat trick* is three goals in ice hockey. A braid is formed with three strands of hair. There can be three terms in the school year. The prefix *tri-* means three: *triplex*, *tricycle*, *tripod*. A *triangle* is a geometric figure and a musical instrument.

Four – is a square number. There are four seasons to a year, four suits in a pack of cards, four points on a compass, four-wheel drive, and four musketeers (if you include d'Artagnan!). The prefixes *tetra-* and *quadri-* mean four: *quadrilateral* (having or formed by four sides) or *tetrahedron* (solid figure with four plane faces). The 4th of July is Independence Day. Four can be fun as in *four-poster bed*, *four-leaf clover*, or not so fun, *four-eyes* and *four-letter word*.

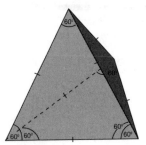

A regular tetrahedron is a pyramid on a triangular base with four sides equal in length.

Five – we have on each hand five fingers, and on each foot five toes. We *take five* when we need a breather. One of the most famous perfumes in modern times is Chanel No. 5. A *five-star* establishment is at the top of its field. Most children start grade school at the age of 5. Many men get a five o'clock shadow. A basketball team sports five players on the floor at any one time. Related prefixes are *quinque-* (quincunx) and *penta-* (pentagon). A *pentagram* is a five-pointed star.

A pentagram is formed by extending the sides of a pentagon in all directions till they intersect.

Prime numbers

Prime numbers have fascinated mathematicians since ancient times. A prime number is a number whose only factors are itself and the number one. Determining whether a large number is prime is a long and arduous process. Most prime numbers now are discovered using mega-computing power, and are cause for great celebration in the mathematics world when a new one is discovered. Here are some interesting tables relating to prime numbers.

Largest primes on record to date

Prime	Digits	Who	When
$2^{6972593}-1$	2098960	Hajratwala, Woltman, Kurowski, GIMPS	1999
$2^{3021377}-1$	909526	Clarkson, Woltman, Kurowski, GIMPS	1998
$2^{2976221}-1$	895932	Spence, Woltman, GIMPS	1997
$2^{1398269}-1$	420921	Armengaud, Woltman, GIMPS	1996
$2^{1257787}-1$	378632	Slowinski, Gage	1996
$48,594^{65536}+1$	307140	Scott, Gallot	2000
$2^{859433}-1$	258716	Slowinski, Gage	1994
$2^{756839}-1$	227832	Slowinski, Gage	1992
$667,071.2^{667071}-1$	200815	Toplic, Gallot	2000
$1,041,870^{32768}+1$	197192	Gallot	2000

The ten largest known twin primes

Twin primes are pairs of primes that differ by two. The first twin primes are {3,5}, {5,7}, and {11,13}.

The ten largest known twin primes

Prime	Digits	Who	When
$665{,}551{,}035 \cdot 2^{80025} \pm 1$	24099	Underbakke, Carmody, Gallot	2000
$1{,}693{,}965 \cdot 2^{66443} \pm 1$	20008	LaBarbera, Jobling, Gallot	2000
$83{,}475{,}759 \cdot 2^{64955} \pm 1$	19562	Underbakke, Jobling, Gallot	2000
$4{,}648{,}619{,}711{,}505 \cdot 2^{60000} \pm 1$	18075	Indlekofer, Jarai, Wassing	2000
$2{,}409{,}110{,}779{,}845 \cdot 2^{60000} \pm 1$	18075	Indlekofer, Jarai, Wassing	2000
$2{,}230{,}907{,}354{,}445 \cdot 2^{48000} \pm 1$	14462	Indlekofer, Jarai, Wassing	1999
$871{,}892{,}617{,}365 \cdot 2^{48000} \pm 1$	14462	Indlekofer, Jarai, Wassing	1999
$361{,}700{,}055 \cdot 2^{39020} \pm 1$	11755	Lifchitz	1999
$835{,}335 \cdot 2^{39014} \pm 1$	11751	Ballinger, Gallot	1998
$242{,}206{,}083 \cdot 2^{38880} \pm 1$	11713	Indlekofer, Jarai	1995

The ten largest known Mersenne primes

Mersenne primes are a special subset of prime numbers of particular fascination in mathematics and take the form $2^q - 1$, where q is also a prime.

The ten largest known Mersenne primes

Prime	Digits	Who	When
$2^{6972593} - 1$	2098960	Hajratwala, Woltman, Kurowski, GIMPS	1999
$2^{3021377} - 1$	909526	Clarkson, Woltman, Kurowski, GIMPS	1998
$2^{2976221} - 1$	895932	Spence, Woltman, GIMPS	1997
$2^{1398269} - 1$	420921	Armengaud, Woltman, GIMPS	1996
$2^{1257787} - 1$	378632	Slowinski, Gage	1996
$2^{859433} - 1$	258716	Slowinski, Gage	1994
$2^{756839} - 1$	227832	Slowinski, Gage	1992
$2^{216091} - 1$	65050	David Slowinski	1985
$2^{132049} - 1$	39751	David Slowinski	1983
$2^{110503} - 1$	33265	Welsh, Colquitt	1988

Perfect numbers

Since antiquity, certain integers have been endowed with special religious or magical significance. One of the most fascinating examples of this is what is known as a **perfect number**, a number for which the sum of all its proper factors is equal to the number itself.

The first three perfect numbers are:

- $6 = 1 + 2 + 3$

- $28 = 1 + 2 + 4 + 7 + 14$

- $496 = 1 + 2 + 4 + 8 + 16 + 31 + 62 + 124 + 248$

There is not another perfect number until 33,550,336.

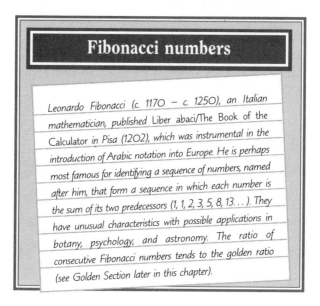

Fibonacci numbers

Leonardo Fibonacci (c. 1170 – c. 1250), an Italian mathematician, published Liber abaci/The Book of the Calculator in Pisa (1202), which was instrumental in the introduction of Arabic notation into Europe. He is perhaps most famous for identifying a sequence of numbers, named after him, that form a sequence in which each number is the sum of its two predecessors (1, 1, 2, 3, 5, 8, 13. . .). They have unusual characteristics with possible applications in botany, psychology, and astronomy. The ratio of consecutive Fibonacci numbers tends to the golden ratio (see Golden Section later in this chapter).

Palindromic numbers

A **palindrome** is a word that reads the same forward or backward, like *level* or *noon*. Similarly, palindromic numbers, like 88 and 1540451, have the same digits forward and backward.

Here's a little trick to turn almost any number into a palindromic number.

Pick a number	*184*
reverse its digits	*+ 481*
add them together	*665*
Repeat the process . . .	*+ 566*
	1231
until you get . . .	*+ 1321*
. . . a palindromic number	*2552*

This flip and add process appears not to work on the number 196, but who knows what computers might be able to discover. . .

Single numbers with curious properties

$111,111,111 \times 111,111,111 = 12,345,678,987,654,321$

$1,741,725 = 1^7 + 7^7 + 4^7 + 1^7 + 7^7 + 2^7 + 5^7$

73939133
7393913
739391
73939
7393
739
73
7

All of these numbers are primes. This is the biggest number that has such a property.

Googol

What is a **googol**? Well, a googol is simple. It's the number 1 followed by a hundred zeros. Here is what a googol looks like:

10,000,000,000,000,000,000,000,000,000,000,000,000,000,
000,000,000,000,000,000,000,000,000,000,000,000,000,000,
000,000,000,000,000

It was named by US mathematician Edward Kasner. When he needed to solve a problem using enormous numbers, he looked to his nine-year-old nephew who coined the term "googol." Dr Kasner went a step further and made up the word "googolplex" to mean the number 1 followed by a googol of zeros. The googolplex is to date the largest named number. Both the googol and the googolplex can be written using exponents: a googol is 10^{100} and a googolplex is $10^{10^{100}}$.

Golden Section

First constructed by the Greek mathematician Euclid and used in art and architecture, the **golden section** is a visually satisfying ratio of approximately 8:13 or 1:1.618. A rectangle whose sides are in this ratio is called a **golden rectangle**. A golden rectangle is one, like that shaded in the picture, that has its length and breadth in this ratio.

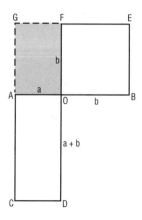

These rectangles are said to be pleasant to look at and have been used instinctively by artists in their pictures. In Leonardo da Vinci's picture *Virgin and Child*, for example, the Madonna's face fits perfectly into a golden rectangle.

© *Corel.* **The Parthenon in Athens.**

The Parthenon in Athens is a temple to the goddess Athena. It is built entirely of marble, and is a fine example of Doric architecture, in which the orders or columns do not have a base. The architects used the mathematical principle of the golden section to give it proportions pleasing to the eye.

The Magic Square

A **magic square** is an array of numbers in which the rows, columns, and diagonals add up to the same total. A simple example employing the numbers 1 to 9, with a total of 15, has a first row of 6, 7, 2, a second row of 1, 5, 9, and a third row of 8, 3, 4.

A **pandiagonal magic square** is one in which all the broken diagonals also add up to the magic constant.

The simplest of all magic squares (*figure 1*) is formed by 9 digits and in this example the sum of any row or column is 15. In *figure 2*, the numbers 1 to 5 are arranged in any order in the first row; the second commences with the fourth number from the first row and proceeds in the same relative order. The third row starts with the fourth number from the second row, and so on. *Figure 3* consists of the numbers 0

Magic Squares

2	1	5	3	4
3	4	2	1	5
1	5	3	4	2
4	2	1	5	3
5	3	4	2	1

Figure 2

6	7	2
1	5	9
8	3	4

Figure 1

15	5	0	20	10
0	20	10	15	5
10	15	5	0	20
5	0	20	10	15
20	10	15	5	0

Figure 3

17	6	5	23	14
3	24	12	16	10
11	20	8	4	22
9	2	21	15	18
25	13	19	7	1

Figure 4

to 4 multiplied by 5, and each row starts with the third number from the row above. Adding together the corresponding numbers from *figures 2* and *3* produces the magic square in *figure 4*.

Why Pi?

The number pi (π) has almost mythical connotations in the math world. It is also one of the few numbers instantly recognizable by the average person in the street. By definition, pi is the ratio of the circumference of a circle to its diameter. Its symbol is π and its value is 3.1415926 correct to seven decimal places. Common approximations are 22/7 and 3.14.

To remember the digits of pi (to seven decimal places), in this rhyme, the number of letters in each word is equal to the corresponding digit of pi (pi = 3.1415926)

May I have a large container of yogurt?

The Babylonians and Egyptians knew about pi long before Archimedes (c. 287–212 BC) who made its first theoretical calculation. Archimedes wrote a book called *The Measurement of a Circle* in which he states that pi is a number between $3\frac{10}{71}$ and $3\frac{1}{7}$. He figured this out by taking a polygon with 96 sides and inscribing a circle inside the polygon. Other great mathematicians were seduced by pi and calculated it further:

Ptolemy (*c.* 90–168)	3.1416
Tsu Ch'ung Chi (430–501)	355/113
al-Khwarizmi (*c.* 800–*c.* 850)	3.1416
al-Kashi (*c.* 1430)	14 places
Viète (1540–1603)	9 places
Roomen (1561–1615)	17 places
Van Ceulen (1540–1610)	35 places

Welsh mathematician William Jones gave pi its symbol in 1706. Its calculation is probably one of the only challenges from ancient mathematics that is still energetically pursued by modern researchers. The world record for calculating pi presently belongs to Professor Yamusada Kanada of Japan, who calculated it to 51,539,607,552 places in 1997.

So why is pi so special? For two reasons: its historical relevance and its staying power. Because of its flexibility and persistence, it shows up regularly in equations relating to DNA double helix descriptions, harmonic motion theory, superstrings, probability, and Einstein's gravitational field equation, plus it continues to prove its usefulness in often surprising ways in modern mathematics. We use it every day to measure circles, lay out our gardens, figure our hat size, decorate our cakes, and more.

What is e?

It may seem like a poor sibling to the better-known pi, but the mathematical constant e (an irrational number which starts 2.71828) is one of the most fascinating and most useful numbers in mathematics. It appears to describe the rate at which many things grow, from nature to your bank account. We bumped into the growth pattern e when we looked at compound interest (it is the number of dollars you'll have at the end of a year if you deposit $1 at 100% interest, that is $2.72) in the *Personal Finance* section. It describes the instantaneous rate of growth of something being proportional to its existing amount. It does not matter if it is a population in the wild, bacteria in a culture, or radioactive decay of radium. It is also the approximate model for inflation – exponential growth.

To calculate e exactly is impossible, but you can use the following infinite series where, the more terms you add, the closer you will get to its value.

e = 1 + 1 + 1 / 2 + 1 / (2 × 3) + 1 / (2 × 3 × 4) + 1 / (2 × 3 × 4 × 5) + 1 / (2 × 3 × 4 × 5 × 6) + ...

Pascal's Triangle

In Pascal's triangle, each number is the sum of the two numbers immediately above it, left and right – for example, 2 is the sum of 1 and 1, and 4 is the sum of 3 and 1. Furthermore, the sum of each row equals a power of 2 – for example, the sum of the 3rd row is $4 = 2^2$; the sum of the 4th row is $8 = 2^3$. French mathematician Blaise Pascal used it in his study of probability.

```
              1
            1   1
          1   2   1
        1   3   3   1
      1   4   6   4   1
    1   5  10  10   5   1
  1   6  15  20  15   6   1
1   7  21  35  35  21   7   1
```

The numbers in the rows give the binomial probability distribution (with equal probability of success and failure) of an event, such as the result of tossing a coin. For example, when you toss a coin, you have an equal chance of getting heads or tails. You will have the same chance of getting heads or tails on the second toss, but your chances of having both tosses come up heads or both tosses come up tails is actually smaller than your chances of having one toss coming up heads and one tails.

Example

What are the possible outcomes of two coin tosses?

Solution

If your first toss is heads, your second toss can be either heads or tails. If your first toss is tails, your second toss could be either heads or tails. So you would have four possible combinations: heads/heads; heads/tails; tails/heads (same thing); or tails/tails. So your probability distribution would be 1–2–1, just like row 3 in Pascal's triangle.

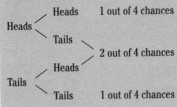

Pascal's triangle?

The 13th century Chinese text Detailed Analysis of the Mathematical Rules in the Nine Chapters/Hsiang Chieh Chiu Chang Suan Fa proved the theory known as "Pascal's triangle" 300 years before Pascal was born.

Risky Business

The above example of tossing coins leads to a fuller discussion of probability, especially in terms of our risk-taking behavior. Every year, millions of people travel to casinos or play the stock market, the national lottery, or any number of card games such as poker or blackjack, hoping to strike it rich. Probability cannot only tell you whether it is possible to win, it can tell you the likelihood of winning.

Determining the probability that a certain event will occur allows you to consider what you are up against and whether to decide to risk the odds.

Example

Imagine there are 5 red balls and 7 green balls in a sack. If you were to close your eyes and pull one out, what is the probability that you would pick a red ball?

Solution

Since there are 12 balls in total, and 5 red ones in the bunch, your chances of selecting a red ball are 5 out of 12, or 5/12. Converting 5/12 into a percentage gives you 42%, so you have a 42% chance of picking a red ball.

If you only had one ball of each color, your chances would be 1 out of 2, $\frac{1}{2}$, or 50%, making the odds equal that you would select one or the other color.

Roulette

© *Corbis*. **Roulette wheel.**

The roulette wheel is divided into 38 numbered slots divided into 18 red, 18 black, and two green slots. A round begins when the wheel is spun and a ball is dropped on the outside edge. When the wheel stops, the ball drops into 1 of the 38 slots.

Bets can be made on a single number, double numbers, 3, 4, 6, 8, 12, or 24 numbers. Naturally the odds are reduced the more numbers are selected. Bets can also be made on the number being odd or even, between 1 and 18, between 19 and 36, or being red or black; the odds are even in each of those cases.

Players bet on where they think the ball will land. If you bet your money that the ball will land on red, your chances of winning are 18 out of 38, but if you bet your money on a particular number, your chances of winning drop to 1 in 38.

While playing a color seems a reasonably safe bet, the mathematics of probability guarantee that over time the owners of the roulette wheel will make more money than the players. The odds are in their favor that you will lose 20 out of 38, making it certain that, over time, the casino will consistently turn a profit.

Card games

Probabilities of card games are trickier to calculate than those of games like roulette. A standard deck of cards contains 52 cards, broken down into four suits (hearts, clubs, diamonds, and spades). Each suit contains an ace, the number cards 1 though 10, a jack, a queen, and a king. The probability of drawing any card from the deck is 1 out of 52, but your chances of pulling a particular number or face card (regardless of suit) is 4 out of 52. Logically, with every card drawn from the deck, the number of cards remaining reduces by one. This affects subsequent probabilities, so if you draw an ace on your first card, your chances of drawing an ace on your second card reduced to 3/51.

The odds of obtaining a particular poker hand

Hand	No. of Ways	Probability	Expected Frequency
Royal flush	4	0.00000154	1 in 649,740
Straight flush	36	0.00001385	1 in 72,193
Four of a kind	624	0.0002401	1 in 4,165
Full house	3,744	0.0014406	1 in 694
Flush	5,108	0.0019654	1 in 509
Straight	10,200	0.0039246	1 in 255
Three of a kind	54,912	0.0211285	1 in 47.33
Two pair	123,552	0.0475390	1 in 21
Pair	1,098,240	0.4225690	1 in 2.37
None of the above	1,302,540	0.5011774	1 in 2
Totals	**2,598,960**	**1.0000000**	

Lottery odds

Numbers on the Pick-6 Lotto ticket are 1–49. You choose six numbers. If any three or more of your numbers match those drawn, you win. Prize awards will vary depending on the total amount of money raised that week. Usually half the money that's put into the lottery is paid out as prize money. Each number has the same chance of coming up. Numbers with an equal chance of coming up are called random numbers, so effectively there is no combination that is more or less likely to occur.

What you can control, however, is how much of the total prize money you may have a chance to split. If studies show that most people tend to select numbers related to birthdays, then selecting a number under 31 means potentially more people to share out the profits of a win.

Here is a simplified example using selected numbers:

Imagine 20 people each paying $1 and asked to select from the following six numbers:

Selected Numbers	1	5	7	13	19	33
No. of people/choices	2	5	8	1	3	1

Looking at the above example, you can see that a good strategy for winning more money via the lottery would be to play numbers that others are likely to avoid. So don't pick lucky numbers like 1, 7, and 11, or birthdays, but do go for numbers higher than 31 and for numbers in a sequence (something most people avoid because they believe they are less likely to occur, though there is no statistical evidence to support this).

Showing Off: Math Tricks

Here is a great party trick, if you have a piece of paper and a pencil, or better still a calculator at hand. Ask your friends to take their age, multiply it by 7, and then multiply that product by 1,443. What they will get is their age repeated 3 times. This works because what you are actually multiplying by is 10,101 (7 × 1,443).

Here is a tried and true way of discovering someone's age!

- Ask the person to multiply the first number of their age by 5 (so if they are 32, they would multiply 3 by 5).
- Tell them to add 3 and then double that figure.
- Then ask them to add the second number of their age to the figure and have them tell you their answer.
- Only thing you need to do now is to deduct 6 and you will have their age!

Two more slick calculating tricks:

- Pick any 3-digit whole number. (e.g. **125**)
- Repeat the digits to create a 6-digit number (125,125)
- Divide by 7 (125,125/7 = 17,875)
- Divide by 11 (17,875/11 = 1,625)
- Divide by 13 (1,625/13 = **125**)
- You're back to your original number.

- Choose any prime number greater than 3. (e.g. 17)
- Square that number (17 × 17 = 289)
- Add 14 (289 + 14 = 303)
- Divide by 12 (303/12 = 25 **remainder 3**)
- The remainder will always be 3.

Calendar

A calendar subdivides time into years, months, weeks, and days and is one of the earliest uses of numbers known. From year one, an assumed date of the birth of Jesus, dates are calculated backwards (BC 'before Christ') and forwards (AD, Latin *Anno Domini* 'in the year of the Lord').

The lunar month (period between one new moon and the next) naturally averages 29.5 days, but the Western calendar uses for convenience a **calendar month** with a complete number of days, 30 or 31 (February has 28). For adjustments, since there are slightly fewer than six extra hours a year left over, they are added to February as a 29th day every fourth year (**leap year**), century years being excepted unless they are divisible by 400. For example, 1896 was a leap year; 1900 was not.

What years are leap years?

It takes the earth a little more than 365 days to go around the sun, about 365.2422 to be exact. So what do we do with the extra few hours that add up each year? Circling the sun four times takes 1460.9688 days. Since four calendar years are only 1460 days and 0.9688 is almost a whole day, we add an extra day to our calendar (29 February) every fourth year and call it a leap year.

For hundreds of years, the Julian calendar followed this rule, adding a leap year every four years. However, because 0.9688 is not *exactly* a whole day, the Julian calendar slowly began to disagree with the actual seasons. Pope Gregory in 1582 adjusted the rules to make up for the discrepancy, and our current calendar is named after him:

The Gregorian calendar

Rule	Examples
Every fourth year is a leap year	2004, 2008, and 2012 are leap years
Every hundredth year is not a leap year	1900 and 2100 are not leap years
Every four hundred years is a leap year	2000 and 2400 are leap years

A very good year …

When can you reuse your calendar (in other words, in what years are each day and each month the same)? Okay let's assume that we are just dealing with this century (2000–2099). Here is how you calculate it:

- If year x is a leap year, you can reuse its calendar in year $x + 28$.

- If year x is the first year after a leap year, you can reuse its calendar in years $x + 6$, $x + 17$, and $x + 28$.

- If year x is the second year after a leap year, you can reuse its calendar in years $x + 11, x + 17,$ and $x + 28$.

- If year x is the third year after a leap year, you can reuse its calendar in years $x + 11, x + 22,$ and $x + 28$.

Modular or Clock Arithmetic

Modular or modulo arithmetic, sometimes known as residue arithmetic or clock arithmetic, uses only a specific number of digits, whatever the value. It sounds complex – and in its pure math applications it can be – but we use it every day, without even thinking about it when we deal with time or days of the week. The number of numbers permitted is called the **modulo** (abbreviated to **mod**), and so the days of the week are mod 7, and the hours of the day are mod 12. When we reach this number we start again. So in the mod 12, the answer to a question as to what time it will be in five hours if it is now ten o'clock can be expressed $10 + 5 = 3$.

What day of the week?

Using modular 7 (for the seven days of the week), you can calculate the day on which a particular date falls, using the following algorithm. If there are any remainders whenever you divide, discard them, keeping only the whole number:

$a = (14 - \text{month})/12$
$y = \text{year} - a$
$m = \text{month} + (12 \times a) - 2$
For Gregorian calendar:
$d = (\text{day} + y + (y / 4) - (y / 100) + (y / 400) + (31 \times m)/12)$ mod 7

Use 1–12 for the months of the year, 1–31 for the days of the months, and the full four-digit year.

To perform the final mod calculation, use this easy shortcut. Divide your answer by 7 and discard the whole number. Your answer is the first number of the remainder!

The value of d is 0 for a Sunday, 1 for a Monday, 2 for a Tuesday, and so on.

Example

On what day of the week was Christmas Day 2000?

Solution

$a = \dfrac{(14 - 12)}{12} = 0.16$ (rounded down to 0) $y = 2000 - 0 = 2000$

$m = 12 + (12 \times 0) - 2 = 10$

$d = (25 + 2000 + 2000/4 - 2000/100 + 2000/400 + (31 \times 10)/12) \bmod 7$

$= (25 + 2000 + 500 - 20 + 5 + 25) \bmod 7$

$= 2535 \bmod 7$ ($2535 \div 7 = 362$ remainder 1)

$= 1$ (your answer in modular arithmetic)

So if the value 0 corresponds to Sunday, the value 1 corresponds to Monday and Christmas (25 December) was on a Monday in the year 2000.

Fractals

Fractals are shapes that show similar features at different sizes. Their nature is characterized by the property of **self-similarity** (smaller or larger versions of itself). Generated on a computer screen, fractals are used in creating models of geographical or biological processes (for example, the creation of a coastline by erosion or accretion, or the growth of plants).

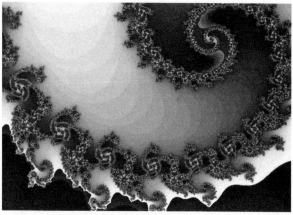

© *Corel.* **Fractal created by Benoit Mandelbrot.**

The name was coined by the French mathematician Benoit Mandelbrot, creator of the world's most famous fractal (page 199), in 1975. In his book *Fractals: Form, Chance, and Dimension*, Mandelbrot used the term **fractal** to describe a number of mathematical phenomena that seemed to exhibit chaotic or surprising behavior.

Mandelbrot also introduced the term fractal to describe irregular objects like the surface of a mountain. Using fractal geometry we can visually model much of what we see in nature, the most recognizable being trees and coastlines. Fractal art consists of mathematical images that reveal more and more detail the more they are magnified. Some areas are symmetrical, and others are random in appearance, many of which produce very beautiful images.

Knots

Knot theory is a branch of **topology** which deals with knots and links. What makes topology interesting is that it deals with those properties of a figure that remain unchanged even when the figure is transformed (bent, stretched) – for example, when a square painted on a rubber sheet is deformed by distorting the sheet.

The simple mathematical definition of a knot is a closed, one-dimensional, and non-intersecting curve in three-dimensional space. Knot theory today stretches from chemistry and molecular biology into the world of quantum mechanics and ultimately to superstring theory.

Helping Your Child Learn Math

Whether you found math terrifying or electrifying, it pays to encourage your children to take their own inquisitive approach to mathematics. Showing them that math can be fun can open up new worlds and make their school day math lessons seem a lot less boring. Spend time with kids on simple board games, puzzles, and activities that encourage strong counting and measuring skills. Helping you bake or playing in a sandbox or a bathtub can teach children math concepts like weight, density, and volume. Make a game of figuring out things – how much will the tip be at a restaurant, how long will it take to drive to Grandma's house. Here's a list of top ten tips for parents who want to help their children succeed in math.

Top Ten Tips for Parents

1) Act confident

No matter what your child needs to learn, you can help. It doesn't matter if you "weren't any good" at math. They will need to be. Demand for skills in mathematics, business and finance, science and technology are continually growing, and they will be expected to know far more than you do. Mathematics is about problem-solving, not about gene pools. The first and most valuable lesson you can teach them is how to go about finding an answer when one is not readily available.

2) Even mathematicians get the blues

Remember, it doesn't take a mathematician to teach your child math. In fact, the best brains in math are often the worst teachers. Far more important than being able to execute mathematics yourself is being able to relate to your child at their level of understanding. Go over their assignment instructions with them. Ask them for their interpretation of the assignment. Have them explain how they expect to complete the assignment and work with them on any potential problem areas.

3) Tend Your Own Mathematical Flame

There's nothing like genuine enthusiasm to encourage the same reaction in children. Perhaps you had a miserable experience learning mathematics as a child. Change your own perspective by reading inspiring stories like *Fermat's Enigma*, a wonderfully entertaining account of a mathematical riddle that eluded the greatest mathematical minds for centuries. It's great reading, great history, and totally inspiring. You can also brush off your own mathematical cobwebs by reviewing the Brushing Up section of this book, especially useful if your child is in grades K–6.

4) Know what's expected of your child

Ask your child's school for their input on what's expected of your child at each grade level. If your child is pre-school, check with your local nursery or kindergarten for their advice on what your child should be able to accomplish by the time they reach school age. Knowing what's expected of your child gives you a head start on creating an environment in which they can learn age-appropriate math skills.

5) Show them examples of math in everyday life

Whether you are in your home, in the car, or in the supermarket, you can help your child improve their math skills by helping you go about your everyday business. These are the places where you can reinforce doing math in their heads. The activities section that follows provides a full range of engaging activities that will bring out the budding mathematician in your child and make learning math more fun for both of you.

6) Extend their problem solving and reasoning ability

Encourage them to question and explore solutions to problems. Ask them to explain how they arrived at their answers. Might there have been other ways to solve the problem? Reasoning ability is the ability to think logically, to see similarities and differences, to see relationships between things, and to make choices based on those critical assessments. Getting your child to communicate mathematically and extending your child's reasoning ability will strengthen and expand their problem-solving abilities not only in math but almost everywhere else in their life.

7) Introduce them to a calculator

You may have been taught that using a calculator is a cheat, but these days it's a necessity. If you are concerned that your child may be relying on a calculator as a substitute for knowing the basics of mathematics, then test him or her regularly with age-appropriate mental math games, just to be sure. Using calculators in class is now required, so don't discourage them. Keep one in the car for handy use when you play math games on long-distance drives.

8) Know where to look when either of you gets stuck

There's a plethora of online resources and colorful, engaging exercise books that provide support for parents, teachers, or students learing math at any stage. If you have Internet access, go online and try searching for answers to a particular problem. There's a short list of highly recommended math sites on page 213. For extra support, check our your local bookstore where you'll find homework help books for your child's age/grade and specific needs.

9) Speak with their teacher regularly

Mathematics is a living breathing discipline, subject to change. How math was taught in your time and how it is taught now is most likely different. Rather than simply adding, subtracting, multiplying, and dividing, elementary school children are now exposed to broad ideas about mathematics, the seedlings of algebra, calculus, geometry, probability and statistics. Keep in touch with their teacher to see how your child is progressing at regular intervals.

10) Provide an environment that encourages them to learn more on their own

Listen to classical music. Recent studies have shown links betwen a child's exposure to classical music and increased math aptitude. Provide them with lots of measuring tools, building blocks of different shapes and sizes and art supplies. Let them play with the computer. Guide them to the many challenging interactive math games available online. Teach them about history – some of the most compelling real-life dramas are about mathematicians and what drove them to their discoveries. If you want them to learn math, point them to heroes that inspire them: Pythagoras, Archimedes, Pascal, Turing, Wiley, Hypatia, Ada Lovelace, Maria Agnesi, Sophie Germain.

Fun and Games

Activity One – Measuring Up (Grades K-2)

Using four glasses of equal size, a measuring cup and water, have your little one fill up the cup to different levels ($\frac{1}{2}$, $\frac{1}{3}$, $\frac{3}{4}$ and full) and pour the water into separate glasses. Ask them to compare the water levels. Are they the same? Which has more? Less? Have them estimate whether they could pour the water from one glass into another without the water spilling over. As your child learns more, have them empty the water into containers of different shapes and sizes. This helps them make comparisons and learn about various capacities of different-sized containers.

Activity Two – Pizza Parlor (Grades K-3)

Whether you are about to share a real pizza or prefer to draw one on a piece of paper, you can capture your child's attention by asking your child to count up the total number of slices. If there are four of you eating and 8 slices, ask your child how many pieces each of you should get. If one of you isn't hungry and gives away a piece of their pizza, ask your child to describe how many pieces of the pie each person ate (i.e. 3 out of 8). When your child gets older, you can make it more complicated by introducing different sorts of toppings or more pizzas, great exercises for introducing concepts like mixed fractions.

Activity Three – Scavenger Hunt (Grades K-6)

It's a classic. Send your children off hunting for a list of items: keys, buttons, seashells, tennis balls, baseball caps, pencils, pens, whatever. When they return, sort them by category. Then take a took at them individually by category. Are they the same? How are they different? Are there different colors? For older children, help them create a graph of their treasures. Have them count up all of the treasures and then figure out what proportion (fraction and percentage) of the total find was one particular category.

Activity Four – Nets (Grades 4-5)

Mathematically speaking, nets are flat unfolded designs of 3-D shapes. Have your child take an empty cereal box, hat box, or poster tube and ask them to image how that container looks flattened. What shapes might the flattened version be made of? Ask them to trace every side of the container to see what shapes make it up. Help them to unfold the container and lay it flat and observe how the various shapes interact to form the 3-D version. Have them rebuild the container so that it's back to its 3-D shape. Ask them what the net of other 3-D shapes like a pyramid might look like.

Activity Five – Fractals (Grades 4-6)

Fractals can be intriguing to look at for most children, but difficult to explain conceptually. This trick introduces the idea of self-similarity with simplicity and charm. Simply, ask your child to draw a tree by first drawing a big letter Y. Then have them draw two smaller y's at the end of the branches of the first Y, and then smaller y's at the ends of those branches and then smaller y's at the ends of those. In no time they will begin to see the tree branch out and take shape. Amazing!

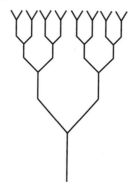

At the Grocery Store:

Have them compare prices and sizes of similar products, have them weigh your vegetables, nuts, or any items sold in bulk for you, challenge them to keep a running total (estimation) of what is in your shopping cart and award a prize for the one who comes closest to the final amount, have them pay for the goods and get the right change back.

In the Car:

License plate games can take hours off long car journeys. Challenge your children to find the license plate with the highest number, or to rearrange the numbers on a license plate so that the number is the largest (or smallest) number is can possibly be. You can also keep track of license plates by state, and make a chart of how many states are represented and what percentage of the total license plates each state makes up. What percentage of the 50 states wasn't represented?

Taking Care of the Puppy:

Taking care of a puppy is a great way to learn math. Have your child figure out how much food a puppy needs by following the age and weight guidelines provided on the package from dog food manufacturers. If a puppy is to get two cups of food per day, ask them how much the puppy should get at each meal if you intend to feed him three times a day. How much if you were to feed him two times a day? Your child can also make a growth chart of the puppy's life, and compare his size and weight to his age.

Multiplying by 9

Here's a nifty trick that will delight your little math genius. Ask your child to hold our their hands in front of them so that their thumbs point toward one another. Ask them to imagine that the left pinky is the number 1 and assign consecutive numbers from left to right so that the right pinky is number 10.

Now they are ready to multiply by 9. Simply have them put the finger down they wish to multiply by 9. All fingers to the left of the down finger represent the tens digit of the answer while all fingers to the right represent the ones digit.

Example: Multiply 4×9.

Solution: Put the finger representing 4 down (the left-hand pointer). To the left of the down finger, you have 3 fingers up, so your tens digit is 3. To the right, you have 6 fingers up, so your units digit is 6. Put them together and the answer is 36!

Appendix

Mathematical shortcuts

Shortcuts can save you time when doing calculations in your head or on the run. The tables below feature a few mathematical labor savers.

Operation	Shortcut
Multiply by 5	multiply by 10; then divide by half
Divide by 5	multiply by 2; divide by 10
Multiply by 9	multiply by 10 and subtract the other number, as in: $27 \times 9 = (27 \times 10) - 27 = 243$
Adding up consecutive even numbers for a two-digit number	divide number by 2; then multiply by the next number (that is, the sum of all even numbers between 2 and 24 = $(24/2) \times (24/2 + 1) = 12 \times 13 = 156$
Adding up consecutive odd numbers for a two-digit number	add one to the number; divide by 2; square your result to get your final answer (that is, the sum of all odd numbers between 1 and 35 = $[(35 + 1) / 2]^2 = 18 \times 18 = 324$

Divisibility table

Divisible by	If
2	Units position is even (0,2,4, ...)
3	Sum of all digits is divisible by 3 (729)
4	Number formed by last 2 digits is divisible by 4
5	Digit in units position is 0 or 5
6	Number is divisible by 2 and divisible by 3 (units digit is even and sum of digits divisible by 3)
8	Number formed by last 3 digits is divisible by 8
9	Sum of all its digits is divisible by 9
10	Units position is 0
11	Add every other digit of number and remember it. Add remaining digits to form another number. If the difference between these two new numbers is 0 or divisible by 11, then the original number is divisible by 11.
12	It is divisible by 4 and divisible by 3 (last two digits are divisible by 4 and sum of its digits is divisible by 3)

continued

Divisible by	If
15	It is divisible by 3 and divisible by 5 (units digit is 0 or 5 and sum of digits is divisible by 3).
16	Number formed by last four digits is divisible by 16.
18	It is divisible by 2 and divisible by 9 (units digit is even and sum of digits is divisible by 9).
20	Units digit is 0 and tens digit is even.
22	It is divisible by 2 and 11 (units digit is even and difference between sums of every other digit is divisible by 11).
25	Number formed by last two digits is 0, 25, 50, 75.

Roman numerals

The seven key symbols in Roman numerals, as represented today, are I (1), V (5), X (10), L (50), C (100), D (500), and M (1,000). There is no zero, and therefore no place-value, as is fundamental to the Arabic system. When a Roman symbol is preceded by a symbol of equal or greater value, the values of the symbols are added (XVI = 16). When a symbol is preceded by a symbol of less value, the values are subtracted (XL = 40). A horizontal bar over a symbol indicates a multiple of 1,000 ($\overline{X}$ = 10,000).

Roman and Arabic numerals

Roman	Arabic	Roman	Arabic
I	1	VII	7
II	2	VIII	8
III	3	IX	9
IV	4	X	10
V	5	XI	11
VI	6	XIX	19

To remember the roman numerals in order for 50, 100, 500, and 1,000 remember:

Lucky Cows Drink Milk

L, C, D, M.

SI Units

The International System of Units (Système International d'Unités, or SI) is the standard system of units used by scientists worldwide. Originally proposed in 1960, it is based on seven basic units: the meter (m) for length, kilogram (kg) for mass, second (s) for time, ampere (A) for electrical current, kelvin (K) for temperature, mole (mol) for amount of substance, and candela (cd) for luminosity.

Some quantities with their SI units and symbols

Quantity	SI unit	Symbol
Absorbed radiation dose	gray	Gy
Amount of substance	mole*	mol
Electric capacitance	farad	F
Electric charge	coulomb	C
Electric conductance	siemens	S
Electric current	ampere*	A
Energy or work	joule	J
Force	newton	N
Frequency	hertz	Hz
Illuminance	lux	lx
Inductance	henry	H
Length	meter*	m
Luminous flux	lumen	lm
Luminous intensity	candela*	cd
Magnetic flux	weber	Wb
Magnetic flux density	tesla	T
Mass	kilogram*	kg
Plane angle	radian	rad
Potential difference	volt	V
Power	watt	W
Pressure	pascal	Pa
Radiation dose equivalent	sievert	Sv
Radiation exposure	roentgen	R
Radioactivity	becquerel	Bq
Resistance	ohm	Ω
Solid angle	steradian	sr
Sound intensity	decibel	dB
Temperature	°Celsius	°C
Temperature, thermodynamic	kelvin*	K
Time	second*	s

*SI base unit.

Wind speed

The Beaufort scale is a system of recording wind velocity (speed) devised in 1806 by Francis Beaufort (1774–1857). It is a numerical scale ranging from 0 for calm to 12 for a hurricane.

The Beaufort scale

Number and description	Features	Air speed (kph)	(mph)
0 calm	smoke rises vertically; water smooth	0–2	0–1
1 light air	smoke shows wind direction; water ruffled	2–5	1–3
2 light breeze	leaves rustle; wind felt on face	6–11	4–7
3 gentle breeze	loose paper blows around	12–19	8–12
4 moderate breeze	branches sway	20–29	13–18
5 fresh breeze	small trees sway, leaves blown off	30–39	19–24
6 strong breeze	whistling in telephone wires; sea spray from waves	40–50	25–31
7 near gale	large trees sway	51–61	32–38
8 gale	twigs break from trees	62–74	39–46
9 strong gale	branches break from trees	75–87	47–54
10 storm	trees uprooted; weak buildings collapse	88–101	55–63
11 violent storm	widespread damage	102–117	64–73
12 hurricane	widespread structural damage	above 118	above 74

Richter scale

The Richter scale is based on measurement of seismic waves, used to determine the magnitude of an earthquake at its epicentre. The magnitude of an earthquake differs from its intensity, measured by the Mercalli scale, which is subjective and varies from place to place for the same earthquake. The Richter scale was named after US seismologist Charles Richter (1900–1985).

The Richter scale

Magnitude	Relative amount of energy released	Examples	Year
1	1		
2	31		
3	960		
4	30,000	Carlisle, England (4.7)	1979
5	920,000	Wrexham, Wales (5.1)	1990

continued

Magnitude	Relative amount of energy released	Examples	Year
6	29,000,000	San Fernando (California) (6.5)	1971
		northern Armenia (6.8)	1988
7	890,000,000	Loma Prieta (California) (7.1)	1989
		Kobe, Japan (7.2)	1995
		Rasht, Iran (7.7)	1990
		San Francisco (CA) (7.7–7.9)	1906
8	28,000,000,000	Tangshan, China (8.0)	1976
		Gansu, China (8.6)	1920
		Lisbon, Portugal (8.7)	1755
9	850,000,000,000	Prince William Sound (Alaska) (9.2)	1964

Decibel scale

The decibel scale is used for audibility measurements, as one decibel unit (symbol dB), representing an increase of about 2.5%, is about the smallest change the human ear can detect. An increase of 10 dB is equivalent to a ten-fold increase in sound intensity.

The decibel scale

Decibels	Typical sound
0	threshold of hearing
10	rustle of leaves in gentle breeze
10	quiet whisper
20	average whisper
20–50	quiet conversation
40–45	hotel; theater (between performances)
50–65	loud conversation
65–70	traffic on busy street
65–90	train
75–80	factory (light/medium work)
90	heavy traffic
90–100	thunder
110–140	jet aircraft at takeoff
130	threshold of pain
140–190	space rocket at takeoff

Energy conversion

The main SI unit for energy is the joule (J), which is the energy consumed by using one watt of power for one second. For convenience, the joule is often supplemented by the kilowatt hour (kWh). Other energy units include the calorie, therm, and British thermal unit (Btu). The following table gives a list of conversion factors.

Energy conversion factors

1 kWh	3.6×10^6 joules
1 calorie	4.184 joules
1 Btu	1.05×10^3 joules
1 therm	4.18×10^6 joules

International paper sizes

The ISO paper size system is the most commonly used measure throughout the world. In this system, pages have a height-to-width ratio of square root of two (1:1.4142). The A series is used for publications and stationery, the B series is used for posters, and the C series is used for envelopes. Note that in the following tables, width precedes height.

International paper sizes

ISO A Series		ISO B series		ISO C series	
Name	mm	Name	mm	Name	mm
A0	841×1189	B0	1000×1414	C0	917×1297
A1	594×841	B1	707×1000	C1	648×917
A2	420×594	B2	500×707	C2	458×648
A3	297×420	B3	353×500	C3	324×458
A4	210×297	B4	250×353	C4	229×324
A5	148×210	B5	176×250	C5	162×229
A6	105×148	B6	125×176	C6	114×162
A7	74×105	B7	88×125	C7	81×114
A8	52×74	B8	62×88	C8	57×81
A9	37×52	B9	44×62	C9	40×57
A10	26×37	B10	31×44	C10	28×40

The USA and Canada are currently the only industrialized nations, where the ISO standard paper sizes are not yet widely used. In US office applications, the following paper formats are employed:

Letter	8.5 × 11 in.	216 × 279 mm
Legal	8.5 × 14 in.	216 × 356 mm
Executive	7.25 × 10.5 in.	190 × 254 mm
Tabloid	11 × 17 in.	279 × 432 mm

Web sites for further reference

Ask Dr. Math http://forum.swarthmore.edu/dr.math
A question and answer service for math students and their teachers. A searchable archive is available by level and topic, as well as summaries of Frequently Asked Questions. Probably the best single Web site for learning or teaching mathematics.

The MacTutor History of Mathematics Archive
http://www-groups.dcs.st-and.ac.uk/~history/
Web site that gives access to lists of more than 1,300 mathematicians with biographies, plus a list of 30 articles on the history of various topics in mathematics and more.

PLUS http://plus.maths.org
An Internet magazine that aims to introduce readers to the beauty and the practical applications of mathematics.

Platonic Realms
http://www.mathacademy.com/pr/index.asp
Interesting Web site featuring an encyclopedia, math quotes, mini-texts, brain teasers, and more.

Mini Dictionary of Terms

absolute value or **modulus** value or magnitude of a number irrespective of its sign. The absolute value of a number n is written $|n|$ or mod n, and is defined as the positive square root of n^2. For example, the numbers –5 and 5 have the same absolute value:

$$|5| = |-5| = 5$$

accent symbol used to express feet and inches, for example 2'6" = 2 ft 6 in, and minutes and seconds as subdivisions of an angular degree, for example 60' = 60 minutes, 30" = 30 seconds.

algebra branch of mathematics in which the general properties of numbers are studied by using symbols, usually letters, to represent variables and unknown quantities. For example, the algebraic statement:

$$(x + y)^2 = x^2 + 2xy + y^2$$

is true for all values of x and y. If $x = 7$ and $y = 3$, for instance:

$$(7 + 3)^2 = 7^2 + 2(7 \times 3) + 3^2 = 100$$

An algebraic expression that has one or more variables (denoted by letters) is a **polynomial** equation. Algebra is used in many areas of mathematics – for example, matrix algebra and Boolean algebra (the latter is used in working out the logic for computers).

alternate angles pair of angles that lie on opposite sides and at opposite ends of a transversal (a line that cuts two or more lines in the same plane). The alternate angles formed by a transversal of two parallel lines are equal.

altitude perpendicular distance from a vertex (corner) of a figure, such as a triangle, to the base (the side opposite the vertex).

angle amount of turn or rotation; it may be defined by a pair of rays (half-lines) that share a common endpoint but do not lie on the same line. Angles are measured in degrees (°) or radians (rads) – a complete turn or circle being 360° or 2 rads. Angles are classified generally by their degree measures: **acute angles** are less than 90°; **right angles** are exactly 90° (a quarter turn); **obtuse angles** are greater than 90° but less than 180°(a straight line); **reflex angles** are greater than 180° but less than 360°. Angles that add up to 180° are called **supplementary angles**.

annual percentage rate (APR) true annual rate of interest charged for a loan. Lenders usually increase the return on their money by compounding the interest payable to that loan on a monthly or even daily basis. This means that each time that interest is payable it is charged not only on the initial sum (principal) but also on the interest previously added to that principal. As a result, APR is usually approximately double the flat rate of interest, or simple interest.

area size of a surface. It is measured in square units, usually square centimetres (cm^2), square metres (m^2), or square kilometres (km^2), or square inches ($in.^2$), square yards (yd^2), or square miles (mi^2). Surface area is the area of the outer surface of a solid.

associative operation operation in which the outcome is independent of the grouping of the numbers or symbols concerned. For example, multiplication is associative, as:

$4 \times (3 \times 2) = (4 \times 3) \times 2 = 24;$

however, division is not, as:

$12 \div (4 \div 2) = 6$, but $(12 \div 4) \div 2 = 1.5$

Compare with **commutative operation**.

axis one of the reference lines by which a point on a graph may be located. The horizontal axis is usually referred to as the x-axis, and the vertical axis as the y-axis. The term is also used to refer to the imaginary line about which an object may be said to be symmetrical – for example, the diagonal of a square – or the line about which an object may revolve.

base number of different single-digit symbols used in a particular number system. In our usual (decimal) counting system of numbers (with symbols 0, 1, 2, 3, 4, 5, 6, 7, 8, 9) the base is 10. In the binary number system, which has only the symbols 1 and 0, the base is two. A base is also a number that, when raised to a particular power (that is, when multiplied by itself a particular number of times as in $10^2 =$ $10 \times 10 = 100$), has a logarithm equal to the power. For example, the logarithm of 100 to the base 10 is 2. In geometry, the term is used to denote the line or area on which a polygon or solid stands.

bearing direction of a fixed point, or the path of a moving object, from a point of observation on the earth's surface, expressed as an angle from the north. Bearings are taken by compass and are measured in degrees (°), given as three-digit numbers increasing clockwise. For instance, north is 000°, northeast is 045°, south is 180°, and southwest is 225°. True north differs slightly from magnetic north (the direction in which a compass needle points), hence northeast may be denoted as 045M or 045T, depending on whether the reference line is magnetic (M) or true (T) north. True north also differs slightly from grid north since it is impossible to show a spherical Earth on a flat map.

binomial expression consisting of two terms, such as $a + b$ or $a - b$.

calculus branch of mathematics that uses the concept of a derivative (see **differentiation**) to analyze the way in which the values of a function vary. Calculus is probably the most widely used part of mathematics. Many real-life problems are analyzed by expressing one quantity as a function of another – position of a moving object as a function of time, temperature of an object as a function of distance from a heat source, force on an object as a function of distance from the source of the force, and so on – and calculus is concerned with such functions.

cardinal number one of the series of numbers $0, 1, 2, 3, 4, \ldots$. Cardinal numbers relate to quantity, whereas ordinal numbers (first, second, third, fourth, ...) relate to order.

Cartesian coordinates components used to define the position of a point by its perpendicular distance from a set of two or more axes, or reference lines. For a two-dimensional area defined by two axes at right angles (a horizontal x-axis and a vertical y-axis), a point P that lies three units from the y-axis and four units from the x-axis has Cartesian coordinates $(3, 4)$.

chance likelihood or probability of an event taking place, expressed as a fraction or percentage. For example, the chance that a tossed coin will land heads up is 50%.

circle perfectly round shape, the path of a point that moves so as to keep a constant distance from a fixed point (the center). Each circle has a **radius** (the distance from any point on the circle to the center), a **circumference** (the boundary of the circle, part of which is called an arc), **diameters** (straight lines crossing the circle through the centre), **chords** (lines joining two points on the circumference), **tangents** (lines that touch the circumference at one point only), **sectors** (regions inside the circle between two radii), and **segments** (regions between a chord and the circumference).

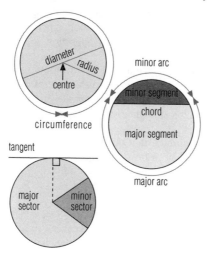

Terms used in the geometry of a circle.

circumference curved line that encloses a curved plane figure, for example a circle or an ellipse. Its length varies according to the nature of the curve, and may be ascertained by the appropriate formula. The circumference of a circle is πd or $2\pi r$, where d is the diameter of the circle, r is its radius, and π is the constant pi, approximately equal to 3.1416.

coefficient number part in front of an algebraic term, signifying multiplication. For example, in the expression $4x^2 + 2xy - x$, the coefficient of x^2 is 4 (because $4x^2$ means $4 \times x^2$), that of xy is 2, and that of $\times$ is -1 (because $-1 \times x = -x$).

In general algebraic expressions, coefficients are represented by letters that may stand for numbers; for example, in the equation:

$$ax^2 + bx + c = 0$$

$a, b,$ and c are coefficients, which can take any number.

commutative operation operation that is independent of the order of the numbers or symbols concerned. For example, addition is commutative: the result of adding $4 + 2$ is the same as that of adding $2 + 4$; subtraction is not, as $4 - 2 = 2$ but $2 - 4 = -2$. Compare **associative operation**.

compound interest interest calculated by computing the rate against the original capital plus reinvested interest each time the interest becomes due. When simple interest is calculated, only the interest on the original capital is added.

concave describes a surface that curves inwards, or away from the eye. For example, a bowl appears concave when viewed from above. In geometry, a concave polygon is one that has an interior angle greater than $180°$. Concave is the opposite of **convex**.

concentric circles two or more circles that share the same center.

cone solid or surface consisting of the set of all straight lines passing through a fixed point (the vertex) and the points of a circle or ellipse whose plane does not contain the vertex.

A circular cone of perpendicular height, with its apex above the center of the circle, is known as a **right circular cone**; it is generated by rotating an isosceles triangle or framework around its line of symmetry. A right circular cone of perpendicular height h and base of radius r has a volume $V = \frac{1}{3}\pi r^2 h$. The distance from the edge of the base of a cone to the vertex is called the **slant height**. In a right circular cone of slant height l, the curved surface area is $\pi r l$, and the area of the base is πr^2. Therefore the total surface area is:

$$A = \pi r l + \pi r^2 = \pi r(l + r)$$

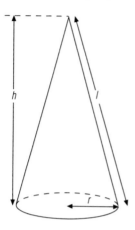

A right-circular cone.

conic section curve obtained when a conical surface is intersected by a plane. If the intersecting plane cuts both extensions of the cone, it yields a **hyperbola**; if it is parallel to the side of the cone, it produces a **parabola**. Other intersecting planes produce **circles** or **ellipses**.

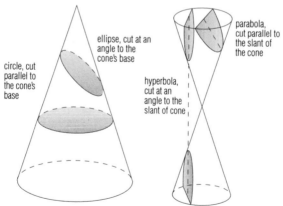

circle, cut parallel to the cone's base

ellipse, cut at an angle to the cone's base

hyperbola, cut at an angle to the slant of cone

parabola, cut parallel to the slant of the cone

The four types of curve that may be obtained by cutting a single or double Right-circular cone with a plane (two-dimensional surface).

constant fixed quantity or one that does not change its value in relation to variables. For example, in the algebraic expression $y^2 = 5x - 3$, the numbers 3 and 5 are constants.

converse reversed order of a conditional statement; the converse of the statement "if a, then b" is "if b, then a." The converse does not always hold true; for example, the converse of "if $x = 3$, then $x^2 = 9$" is "if $x^2 = 9$, then $x = 3$," which is not true, as x could also be -3.

convex describes a surface that curves outwards, or towards the eye. For example, the outer surface of a ball appears convex. In geometry, the term is used to describe any polygon possessing no interior angle greater than 180°. Convex is the opposite of **concave**.

coordinate a number that defines the position of a point relative to a point or axis (reference line).

coordinate geometry or **analytical geometry** system of geometry in which points, lines, shapes, and surfaces are represented by algebraic expressions.

cosine function of an angle in a right-angled triangle found by dividing the length of the side adjacent to the angle by the length of the hypotenuse (the longest side opposite to the right angle). It is usually shortened to **cos**.

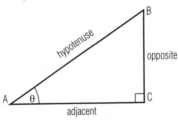

for any right-angled triangle with angle θ as shown the trigonometrical ratios are

$$\sin(\theta) = \frac{BC}{AB} = \frac{\text{opposite}}{\text{hypotenuse}}$$

$$\cos \theta = \frac{AC}{AB} = \frac{\text{adjacent}}{\text{hypotenuse}}$$

$$\tan \theta = \frac{BC}{AC} = \frac{\text{opposite}}{\text{adjacent}}$$

The relationship between the sides and angles of a triangle can be used to determine unknown length or angles, such as when working out the area of a new roof that needs to be shingled.

cube regular solid figure whose faces are all squares. It has 6 equal-area faces and 12 equal-length edges. If the length of one edge is l, the volume V of the cube is given by:

$$V = l^3$$

 and its surface area A by:

$$A = 6l^2$$

cube to multiply a number by itself and then by itself again. For example:

$$5 \text{ cubed} = 5^3 = 5 \times 5 \times 5 = 125$$

The term also refers to a number formed by cubing; for example, 1, 8, 27, and 64 are the first four cubes.

curve a line, continuously bending, without angles. The circle is the path of all points equidistant from a given point (the center). Other common geometrical curves are the **ellipse**, **parabola**, and **hyperbola**, which are also produced when a cone is cut by a plane at different angles. (See conic section.)

cylinder tubular solid figure with a circular base. In everyday use, the term applies to a **right cylinder**, the curved surface of which is at right angles to the base.

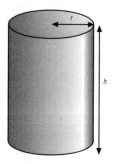

The volume and area of a cylinder are given by simple formulae relating the dimensions of the cylinder.

The volume V of a cylinder is given by the formula:

$$V = \pi r^2 h$$

where r is the radius of the base and h is the height of the cylinder. Its total surface area A has the formula:

$$A = 2\pi r(h + r)$$

where $2\pi rh$ is the curved surface area and $2\pi r^2$ is the area of both circular ends.

data (singular **datum**) facts, figures, and symbols, especially as stored in computers. The term is often used to mean raw, unprocessed facts, as distinct from information, to which a meaning or interpretation has been applied. **Continuous data** is data that can take any of an infinite number of values between whole numbers and so may not be measured completely accurately. This type of data contrasts with **discrete data**, in which the variable can only take one of a finite set of values. For example, the sizes of apples on a tree form continuous data, whereas the numbers of apples form discrete data.

decimal fraction fraction in which the denominator is any higher power of 10. Thus $^3/_{10}$, $^{51}/_{100}$, and $^{23}/_{1,000}$ are decimal fractions and are normally expressed as 0.3, 0.51, and 0.023. The use of decimals greatly simplifies addition and multiplication of fractions, though not all fractions can be expressed exactly as decimal fractions. The regular use of the decimal point appears to have been introduced about 1585, but the occasional use of decimal fractions can be traced back as far as the 12th century.

decimal point dot dividing a decimal number's whole part from its fractional part (the digits to the left of the point are unit digits). Some European countries use a comma to denote the decimal point, for example 3,5.

degree unit of measurement (symbol °) of an angle or arc. A circle or complete rotation is divided into 360°. A degree may be subdivided into 60 minutes (symbol '), and each minute may be subdivided in turn into 60 seconds (symbol "). **Temperature** is also measured in degrees, which are divided on a decimal scale.

denominator bottom number of a fraction, so called because it names the family of the fraction. The top number, or numerator, specifies how many unit fractions are to be taken.

differences the set of numbers obtained from a sequence by subtracting each element from its successor. For example, in the sequence 1, 4, 9, 16, 25 ... , the differences are 3, 5, 7, 9 ... . The patterns of differences are used to analyze sequences.

directed number number with a positive (+) or negative (−) sign attached, for example +5 or −5. On a graph, a positive sign shows a movement to the right or upwards; a negative sign indicates movement downwards or to the left.

dividend any number that is to be divided by another number. For example, in the computation $20 \div 4 = 5$, 20 is the dividend.

ellipse curve joining all points (loci) around two fixed points (foci) such that the sum of the distances from those points is always constant. The diameter passing through the foci is the major axis, and the diameter bisecting this at right angles is the minor axis. An ellipse is one of a series of curves known as **conic sections**. A slice across a cone that is not made parallel to, and does not pass through, the base will produce an ellipse.

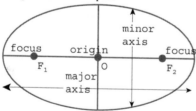

Technical terms used to describe the ellipse; for all points on the ellipse, the sum of the distances from the two foci, F1 and F2, is the same.

equation expression that represents the equality of two expressions involving constants and/or variables, and thus usually includes an equals (=) sign. For example, the equation $A = \pi r^2$ equates the area A of a circle of radius r to the product πr^2. To solve an equation means to find the value or values of the unknown quantity that satisfy the equation, for example $x + 4 = 7$ is true when x is 3. The values of the unknown that make an equation true are called its **solutions** or **roots**.

equilateral geometrical figure whose sides are all of equal length. For example, a square and a rhombus are both equilateral four-sided figures. An equilateral triangle, to which the term is most often applied, has all three sides equal and all three angles equal (at 60°).

exponent or **index** superscript number that indicates the number of times a term is multiplied by itself; for example: $x^2 = x \times x$ and $4^3 = 4 \times 4 \times 4$. Exponents obey certain rules. Terms that contain them are multiplied together by adding the exponents; for example: $x^2 \times x^5 = x^7$. Division of such terms is done by subtracting the exponents; for example: $y^5 \div y^3 = y^2$. Any number with the exponent 0 is equal to 1; for example: $x^0 = 1$ and $99^0 = 1$.

exponential descriptive of a function in which the variable quantity is an exponent (a number indicating the power to which another number or expression is raised). Exponential functions and series involve the constant e = 2.71828.... . Scottish mathematician John Napier devised natural logarithms in 1614 with e as the base.

factor number that divides into another number exactly. For example, the factors of 64 are 1, 2, 4, 8, 16, 32, and 64. In algebra, certain kinds of polynomials (expressions consisting of several or many terms) can be factorized.

factorial a positive number that is the product of all the whole numbers (integers) between 1 and the number itself. A factorial is indicated by the symbol "!". Thus:

$$6! = 1 \times 2 \times 3 \times 4 \times 5 \times 6 = 720$$

Factorial zero, 0!, is defined as 1.

formula set of symbols and numbers that expresses a fact or rule. $A = \pi r^2$ is the formula for calculating the area of a circle. Einstein's famous formula relating energy and mass is $E = mc^2$.

fractal irregular shape or surface produced by a procedure of repeated subdivision.

fraction number that indicates one or more equal parts of a whole. Usually, the number of equal parts into which the unit is divided (denominator) is written below a horizontal line, and the number of parts comprising the fraction (numerator) is written above; thus $\frac{2}{3}$ or $\frac{3}{4}$. The denominator can never be zero.

geometry branch of mathematics concerned with the properties of space, usually in terms of **plane** (two-dimensional) and **solid** (three-dimensional) figures. The subject is usually divided into **pure geometry**, which embraces roughly the plane and solid geometry, dealt with in Greek mathematician Euclid's *Stoicheia/Elements*, and **analytical** or **coordinate geometry**, in which problems are solved using algebraic methods. A third, quite distinct, type includes the non-Euclidean geometries.

gradient on a graph, the slope of a straight or curved line. The slope of a curve at any given point is represented by the slope of the tangent at that point. Slope is a measure of rate of change and can be used to represent such quantities as velocity (the gradient of a graph of distance moved against time) and acceleration (the gradient of a graph of a body's velocity against time).

group finite or infinite set of elements that can be combined in a way similar to the addition of integers. For example, the set of all integers (positive or negative whole numbers) forms a group because:

- addition is associative, that is, the sum of two or more integers is the same regardless of the order in which the integers are added

- adding two integers gives another integer

- the set includes an identity element 0, which has no effect on any integer to which it is added (for example, $0 + 3 = 3$)

- each integer has an inverse (for instance, 7 has the inverse −7), such that the sum of an integer and its inverse is 0.

group theory is the study of the properties of groups.

helix three-dimensional curve resembling a spring, corkscrew, or screw thread. It is generated by a line that encircles a cylinder or cone at a constant angle.

hyperbola curve formed by cutting a right circular cone with a plane so that the angle between the plane and the base is greater than the angle between the base and the side of the cone. All hyperbolas are bounded by two asymptotes (straight lines to which the hyperbola moves closer and closer but never reaches).

A hyperbola is a member of the family of curves known as conic sections.

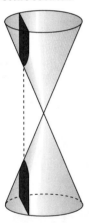

A hyperbola is produced when a cone is cut by a plane.

hypotenuse longest side of a right-angled triangle, opposite the right angle. It is of particular application in Pythagoras' theorem (the square of the hypotenuse equals the sum of the squares of the other two sides), and in trigonometry where the ratios **sine** and **cosine** are defined as the ratios opposite/hypotenuse and adjacent/hypotenuse respectively. See the illustration on page 220.

infinity mathematical quantity that is larger than any fixed assignable quantity; symbol ∞. By convention, the result of dividing any number by zero is regarded as infinity.

integer any whole number. Integers may be positive or negative; 0 is an integer, and is often considered positive. Fractions, such as $\frac{1}{2}$ and 0.35, are known as non-integral numbers ("not integers").

linear equation relationship between two variables that, when plotted using **Cartesian coordinates**, produces a straight-line graph; the equation has the general form $y = mx + c$, where m is the slope of the line represented by the equation and c is the y-intercept, or the value of y where the line crosses the y-axis in the Cartesian coordinate system. Sets of linear equations can be used to describe the behavior of buildings, bridges, trusses, and other static structures.

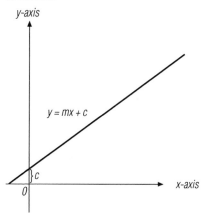

Straight-line graph of the equation $y = mx + c$.

locus traditionally the path traced out by a moving point, but now defined as the set of all points on a curve satisfying given conditions. For example, the locus of a point that moves so that it is always at the same distance from another fixed point is a circle; the locus of a point that is always at the same distance from two fixed points is a straight line that perpendicularly bisects the line joining them. The locus of points a fixed distance from a line is two parallel lines running either side.

logarithm or **log** exponent or index of a number to a specified base – usually 10. For example, the logarithm to the base 10 of 1,000 is 3 because $10^3 = 1,000$; the logarithm of 2 is 0.3010 because $2 = 10^{0.3010}$. The whole-number part of a logarithm is called the **characteristic**; the fractional part is called the **mantissa**. Before the advent of cheap electronic calculators, multiplication and division could be simplified by being replaced with the addition and subtraction of logarithms. For any two numbers x and y (where $x = b^a$ and $y = b^c$):

$$x \times y = b^a \times b^c = b^{a+c}$$

hence we would add the logarithms of x and y, and look up this answer in antilogarithm tables. Tables of logarithms and antilogarithms are available that show conversions of numbers into logarithms, and vice versa. For example, to multiply 6,560 by 980, you look up their logarithms (3.8169 and 2.9912), add them together (6.8081), then look up the antilogarithm of this to get the answer (6,428,800).

magic square square array of numbers in which the rows, columns, and diagonals add up to the same total. A simple example employing the numbers 1 to 9, with a total of 15, has a first row of 6, 7, 2, a second row of 1, 5, 9, and a third row of 8, 3, 4. See the illustration on page 189.

mean measure of the average of a number of terms or quantities. The simple **arithmetic mean** is the average value of the quantities, that is, the sum of the quantities divided by their number. The **weighted mean** takes into account the frequency of the terms that are added; it is calculated by multiplying each term by the number of times it occurs, adding the results and dividing this total by the total number of occurrences. The **geometric mean** of n quantities is the nth root of their product. In statistics, it is a measure of central tendency of a set of data.

median middle number of an ordered group of numbers. If there is no middle number (because there is an even number of terms), the median is the mean (average) of the two middle numbers. For example, the median of the group 2, 3, 7, 11, 12 is 7; that of 3, 4, 7, 9, 11, 13 is 8 (the average of 7 and 9).

modulus number that divides exactly into the difference between two given numbers. Also, the multiplication factor used to convert a logarithm of one base to a logarithm of another base. Also, another name for **absolute value**.

numerator number or symbol that appears above the line in a common fraction. For example, the numerator of 5/6 is 5. The numerator represents the fraction's **dividend** and indicates how many of the equal parts indicated by the denominator (number or symbol below the line) comprise the fraction.

ordinal number one of the series first, second, third, fourth, ... Ordinal numbers relate to order, whereas cardinal numbers $(1, 2, 3, 4, ...)$ relate to quantity, or count.

origin point where the x axis meets the y axis. The coordinates of the origin are (0,0).

parabola a curve formed by cutting a right circular cone with a plane parallel to the sloping side of the cone. A parabola is one of the family of curves known as **conic sections**. The graph of $y = x^2$ is a parabola.

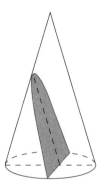

A parabola is produced when a cone is cut by a plane parallel to the sloping side of the cone.

parallel lines and parallel planes straight lines or planes that always remain a constant distance from one another no matter how far they are extended. This is a principle of Euclidean geometry. Some non-Euclidean geometries, such as elliptical and hyperbolic geometry, however, reject Euclid's parallel axiom.

parallelogram quadrilateral (four-sided plane figure) with opposite pairs of sides equal in length and parallel, and opposite angles equal. The diagonals of a parallelogram bisect each other. Its area is the product of the length of one side and the perpendicular distance between this and the opposite side. In the special case when all four sides are equal in length, the parallelogram is known as a **rhombus**, and when the internal angles are right angles, it is a rectangle or square.

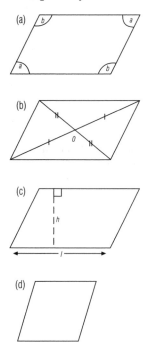

Some properties of a parallelogram: (a) opposite sides are equal; (b) diagonals bisect each other at 0; (c) area of a parallelogram is given by $l \times h$; (d) a rhombus has all sides equal.

percentage way of representing a number as a fraction of 100. Thus 45% equals $^{45}/_{100}$ and 45% of 20 is $^{45}/_{100} \times 20 = 9$.

perimeter or **boundary** line drawn around the edge of an area or shape. For example, the perimeter of a rectangle is the sum of its four sides; the perimeter of a circle is known as its **circumference**.

perpendicular at a right angle; also, a line at right angles to another or to a plane. For a pair of **skew lines** (lines in three dimensions that do not meet), there is just one common perpendicular, which is at right angles to both lines; the nearest points on the two lines are the feet of this perpendicular.

plane a flat surface. Planes are either parallel or they intersect in a straight line. Vertical planes, for example the join between two walls, intersect in a vertical line. Horizontal planes do not intersect since they are all parallel.

polygon plane (two-dimensional) figure with three or more straight-line sides. Common polygons have names that define the number of sides – for example, triangle (3), quadrilateral (4), pentagon (5), hexagon (6), heptagon (7), octagon (8), and so on. **Regular polygons** have sides of the same length and all the exterior angles are equal. These are all convex polygons, having no interior angle greater than 180°. The sum of the internal angles of a polygon having n sides is given by the formula $(2n - 4) \times 90°$; therefore, the more sides a polygon has, the larger the sum of its internal angles and, in the case of a convex polygon, the more closely it approximates to a circle.

polyhedron solid figure with four or more plane faces. The more faces there are on a polyhedron, the more closely it approximates to a sphere. There are only five types of regular polyhedron (with all faces the same size and shape), as was deduced by early Greek mathematicians; they are the tetrahedron (four equilateral triangular faces), cube (six square faces), octahedron (eight equilateral triangles), dodecahedron (12 regular pentagons), and icosahedron (20 equilateral triangles).

prime number number that can be divided only by 1 and itself, that is, having no other **factors**.

probability likelihood, or chance, that an event will occur, often expressed as odds or numerically as a fraction or decimal.

progression sequence of numbers each occurring in a specific relationship to its predecessor. An **arithmetic progression** has numbers that increase or decrease by a common sum or difference (for example, 2, 4, 6, 8); a **geometric progression** has numbers each bearing a fixed ratio to its predecessor (for example, 3, 6, 12, 24); and a **harmonic progression** has numbers whose reciprocals are in arithmetical progression, for example 1, $\frac{1}{2}$, $\frac{1}{3}$, $\frac{1}{4}$.

proportion relation of a part to the whole (usually expressed as a fraction or percentage). In mathematics, two variable quantities x and y are proportional if their ratio is always constant. This means that if x increases, y increases in a linear fashion. A graph of x against y would be a straight line passing through the origin (the point $x = 0, y = 0$).

Pythagoras' theorem theorem stating that in a right-angled triangle, the area of the square on the hypotenuse (the longest side) is equal to the sum of the areas of the squares drawn on the other two sides. If the hypotenuse is h units long and the lengths of the other sides are a and b, then: $h^2 = a^2 + b^2$.

The theorem provides a way of calculating the length of any side of a right-angled triangle if the lengths of the other two sides are known. It is also used to determine certain trigonometrical relationships such as: $\sin^2 + \cos^2 = 1$.

radian SI unit (symbol rad) of plane angles, an alternative unit to the degree. It is the angle at the center of a circle when the centre is joined to the two ends of an arc (part of the circumference) equal in length to the radius of the circle. There are 2π (approximately 6.284) radians in a full circle (360°). One radian is approximately 57°, and 1° is $\pi/180$ or approximately 0.0175 radians. Radians are commonly used to specify angles in polar coordinates.

ratio measure of the relative size of two quantities or of two measurements (in similar units), expressed as a **proportion**. For example, the ratio of vowels to consonants in the alphabet is 5:21; the ratio of 500 m to 2 km is 500:2,000, or 1:4. Ratios are normally expressed as whole numbers, so 2:3.5 would become 4:7 (the ratio remains the same provided both numbers are multiplied or divided by the same number).

reciprocal result of dividing a given quantity into 1. Thus the reciprocal of 2 is $\frac{1}{2}$; of $\frac{2}{3}$ is $\frac{3}{2}$; of x^2 is $\frac{1}{x^2}$ or x^{-2}. Reciprocals are used to replace division by multiplication, since multiplying by the reciprocal of a number is the same as dividing by that number. On a calculator, the reciprocals of all numbers except 0 are obtained by using the button marked $\frac{1}{x}$.

rectangle quadrilateral (four-sided plane figure) with opposite sides equal and parallel and with each interior angle a right angle (90°). Its area A is the product of the length l and height h; that is, $A = l \times h$. A rectangle with all four sides equal is a square. A rectangle is a special case of a parallelogram. The diagonals of a rectangle are equal and bisect each other.

rhombus equilateral (all sides equal) parallelogram. Its diagonals bisect each other at right angles, and its area is half the product of the lengths of the two diagonals. A rhombus whose internal angles are 90° is called a **square**.

right-angled triangle triangle in which one of the angles is a right angle (90°). It is the basic form of triangle for defining trigonometrical ratios (for example, **sine**, **cosine**, and **tangent**) and for which Pythagoras' theorem holds true. The longest side of a right-angled triangle is called the hypotenuse; its area is equal to half the product of the lengths of the two shorter sides. Any triangle constructed with its **hypotenuse** as the diameter of a circle, with its opposite vertex (corner) on the circumference, is a right-angled triangle. This is a fundamental theorem in geometry, first credited to the Greek mathematician Thales about 580 BC.

scale numerical relationship, expressed as a ratio, between the actual size of an object and the size of an image that represents it on a map, plan, or diagram. If an object has been enlarged, the amount of increase (scale factor) can be found by dividing a side of the enlarged object by the corresponding side of the original shape. A scale factor of less than one gives a decrease in size. An object is scaled by multiplying it by the scale factor, for example a model of a railroad may require a scale of 1 in a 100, so all measurements must be multiplied by $\frac{1}{100}$ (0.01).

set or **class** any collection of defined things (elements), provided the elements are distinct and that there is a rule to decide whether an element is a member of a set. It is usually denoted by a capital letter and indicated by braces { }. For example, L may represent the set that consists of all the letters of the alphabet. The symbol $\in$ stands for "is a member of"; thus $p \in L$ means that p belongs to the set consisting of all letters, and $4 \notin L$ means that 4 does not belong to the set consisting of all letters. There are various types of sets. A **finite set** has a limited number of members, such as the letters of the alphabet; an **infinite set** has an unlimited number of members, such as all whole numbers; an **empty** or **null set** has no members, such as the number of people who have swum across the Atlantic Ocean, written as { } or ø; a **single-element set** has only one member, such as days of the week beginning with M, written as {Monday}. **Equal sets** have the same members; for example, if W = {days of the week} and S = {Sunday, Monday, Tuesday, Wednesday, Thursday, Friday, Saturday}, it can be said that $W = S$. Sets with the same number of members are **equivalent sets**. Sets with some members in common are **intersecting sets**; for example, if R = {red playing cards} and F = {face cards}, then R and F share the members that are red face cards. Sets with no members in common are **disjoint sets**. Sets contained within others are **subsets**; for example, V = {vowels} is a subset of L = {letters of the alphabet}. Sets and their interrelationships are often illustrated by a **Venn diagram** (see the illustration on page 238).

significant digits digits in a number that, by virtue of their place value, express the magnitude of that number to a specified degree of accuracy. The final significant digit is rounded up if the following digit is greater than 5. For example, 5,463,254 to three significant digits is 5,460,000; 3.462891 to four significant digits is 3.463; 0.00347 to two significant digits is 0.0035.

sine function of an angle in a right-angled triangle which is defined as the ratio of the length of the side opposite the angle to the length of the hypotenuse (the longest side). See the illustration on page 221.

speed rate at which an object moves. The average speed v of an object may be calculated by dividing the distance s it has traveled by the time t taken to do so, and may be expressed as: $v = s / t$.

sphere perfectly round object with all points on its surface the same distance from the center. This distance is the radius of the sphere. For a sphere of radius r, the volume $V = \frac{4}{3}\pi r^3$ and the surface area $A = 4\pi r^2$.

square root a number that when squared (multiplied by itself) equals a given number. For example, the square root of 25 (written $\sqrt{25}$) is ± 5, because $5 \times 5 = 25$, and $(-5) \times (-5) = 25$. As an exponent, a square root is represented by $\frac{1}{2}$, for example, $16^{1/2} = 4$. Negative numbers (less than 0) do not have square roots that are real numbers. Their roots are represented by complex numbers, in which the square root of -1 is given the symbol i. Thus the square root of -4 is $\sqrt{(-1 \times 4)} = \sqrt{(-1)} \times \sqrt{4} = 2i$.

standard deviation measure (symbol Σ or s) of the spread of data. The deviation (difference) of each of the data items from the mean is found and their values squared. The mean value of these squares is then calculated. The standard deviation is the square root of this mean.

statistics branch of mathematics concerned with the collection and interpretation of data. For example, to determine the mean age of the children in a school, a statistically acceptable answer might be obtained by calculating an average based on the ages of a representative sample, consisting, for example, of a random tenth of the pupils from each class. Probability is the branch of statistics dealing with predictions of events.

tangent straight line that touches a curve and gives the gradient of the curve at the point of contact. At a maximum, minimum, or point of inflection, the tangent to a curve has zero gradient.

Also, in trigonometry, a function of an acute angle in a right-angled triangle, defined as the ratio of the length of the side opposite the angle to the length of the side adjacent to it; a way of expressing the **gradient** of a line.

trapezium four-sided plane figure (quadrilateral) with two of its sides parallel.

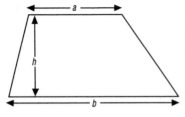

If the parallel sides have lengths a and b and the perpendicular distance between them is h (the height of the trapezium), its area A is:

$$A = \tfrac{1}{2}h(a + b)$$

An isosceles trapezium has its sloping sides equal, is symmetrical around a line drawn through the midpoints of its parallel sides, and has equal base angles.

triangle three-sided plane figure, the sum of whose interior angles is 180°. Triangles can be classified by the relative lengths of their sides. A **scalene triangle** has three sides of unequal length; an **isosceles triangle** has at least two equal sides; an **equilateral triangle** has three equal sides (and three equal angles of 60°). A **right-angled triangle** has one angle of 90°. If the length of one side of a triangle is l and the perpendicular distance from that side to the opposite corner is h (the height or altitude of the triangle), its area $A = \tfrac{1}{2}\,lh$.

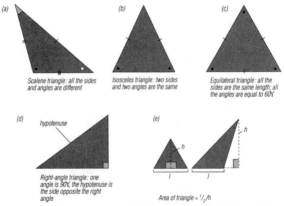

(a) scalene triangle; (b) isosceles triangle; (c) equilateral triangle; (d) right-angled triangle; (e) area of a triangle.

trigonometry branch of mathematics that solves problems relating to plane and spherical triangles. Its principles are based on the fixed proportions of sides for a particular angle in a right-angled triangle, the simplest of which are known as the sine, cosine, and tangent (so-called trigonometrical ratios). Trigonometry is of practical importance in navigation, surveying, and simple harmonic motion in physics.

variable changing quantity (one that can take various values), as opposed to a constant. For example, in the algebraic expression $y = 4x^3 + 2$, the variables are x and y, whereas 4 and 2 are constants. A variable may be dependent or independent. Thus if y is a function of x, written $y = f(x)$, such that $y = 4x^3 + 2$, the domain of the function includes all values of the **independent variable** x while the range (or co-domain) of the function is defined by the values of the **dependent variable** y.

variance square of the **standard deviation**, the measure of spread of data. Population and sample variance are denoted by Σ^2 or s^2, respectively. Variance provides a measure of the dispersion of a set of statistical results around the mean or average value.

vector quantity any physical quantity that has both magnitude and direction (such as the velocity or acceleration of an object) as distinct from scalar quantity (such as speed, density, or mass), which has magnitude but no direction. A vector is represented either geometrically by an arrow whose length corresponds to its magnitude and points in an appropriate direction, or by two or three numbers representing the magnitude of its components.

velocity speed of an object in a given direction. Velocity is a vector quantity, since its direction is important as well as its magnitude (or speed). The velocity at any instant of a particle traveling in a curved path is in the direction of the tangent to the path at the instant considered. The velocity v of an object traveling in a fixed direction may be calculated by dividing the distance s it has traveled by the time t taken to do so, and may be expressed as: $v = s / t$.

Venn diagram diagram representing a set or sets and the logical relationships between them. The sets are drawn as circles. An area of overlap between two circles (sets) contains elements that are common to both sets, and thus represents a third set. Circles that do not overlap represent sets with no elements in common (disjoint sets). The method is named after the English logician John Venn.

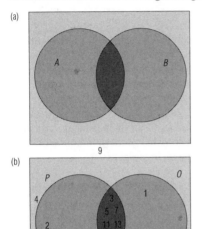

(a) is a Venn diagram of two intersecting sets and (b) a Venn diagram showing the set of whole numbers from 1 to 20 and the subsets P and O of prime and odd numbers, respectively. The intersection of P and O contains all the prime numbers that are also odd.

vertex (plural **vertices**) point shared by three or more sides of a solid figure; the point farthest from a figure's base; or the point of intersection of two sides of a plane figure or the two rays of an angle.

volume space occupied by a three-dimensional solid object. A prism (such as a cube) or a cylinder has a volume equal to the area of the base multiplied by the height. For a pyramid or cone, the volume is equal to one-third of the area of the base multiplied by the perpendicular height. The volume of a sphere is equal to $\frac{4}{3}\pi \times r^3$, where r is the radius.

Index

Note: Page references in *italic* indicate boxed examples; page references in **bold** indicate formulae